DEEP IN THOUGHT

DEEP IN THOUGHT

A Practical Guide to Teaching for Intellectual Virtues

Jason Baehr

Harvard Education Press
Cambridge, Massachusetts

Paperback ISBN 978-1-68253-670-4

Library Edition ISBN 978-1-68253-671-1

Library of Congress Cataloging-in-Publication data is on file.

Published by Harvard Education Press,
an imprint of the Harvard Education Publishing Group

Harvard Education Press
8 Story Street
Cambridge, MA 02138

Cover Design: Endpaper Studio
Cover Photo: oxygen/Moment via Getty Images.

The typefaces used in this book are Adobe Garamond Pro and Futura Standard

For the students and staff of the Intellectual
Virtues Academy of Long Beach
and
In memory of Danielle Montiel (1974–2018)

Contents

Introduction

> Many of us became teachers for reasons of the heart, animated
> by a passion for some subject and for helping people learn. But
> many of us lose heart as the years of teaching go by. How can
> we take heart in teaching once more so that we can, as good
> teachers always do, give heart to our students?
>
> —Parker Palmer, *The Courage to Teach*

If you are reading this book, there's a good chance you are a teacher. If
so, I'd like to begin by acknowledging the difficulty of the work you do.
As teachers, we are in the business of shaping hearts and minds. This is
extremely challenging work even under the best of conditions. It is even
more challenging under the conditions in which so many teachers find
themselves: feeling overburdened, exhausted, frustrated, discouraged, inad-
equately supported, underappreciated, and underpaid.

I insist on not losing sight of these challenging conditions in the pages
that follow. This book is about an educational ideal. It's about learning to
teach in light of one of the deeper and more important aims of education.
Yet, whether in the classroom or in other areas of life, pursuing ideals can
be risky business. It can inspire efforts and expectations that are unteth-
ered from reality—that ignore the actual conditions on the ground. It's no
surprise that so many idealistic pursuits are fragile and fleeting.

My aim is to approach the subject matter of this book in a way that is
sensitive to the difficulty of the work you do and the challenging conditions under which you do it. I may fail at this pursuit here and there. But I
am committed to keeping these failures to a minimum. After all, my reason for writing this book is to do what I can to benefit and support you as
a teacher. My training as a philosopher and my work in K–12 education

have given me a unique perspective on the purpose of education and how a teacher's instructional values, habits, and practices can be brought into alignment with this purpose. In my ongoing work with teachers, I've learned that many of them find this vision highly compelling. I hope you will too.

PROFESSIONAL DISCONNECTION

The consequences of the nonideal conditions just noted are several and beyond what can be cataloged here. However, I'd like to draw attention to one consequence in particular. Doing so will allow me to say a bit more about the overarching aims of the book. The consequence I'm thinking of is an abiding sense of professional disconnection or alienation. Specifically, many teachers today experience a painful discrepancy between (1) what they are expected to care about and devote themselves to on a daily basis and (2) the reasons they became teachers in the first place.

Many of us were drawn to teaching out of a sense that education is a profound human good. At some point in our educational journey, we experienced learning as joyful, exhilarating, and intrinsically worthwhile, as adding meaning and new direction to our lives. More likely than not, this experience was bound up with an experience of a particular teacher—of someone who cared passionately and intelligently about us and the subject she or he was teaching. Inspired and reoriented by this encounter, we devoted ourselves to pursuing similar experiences with students of our own.[1]

Yet far too often, the life-giving vision that compelled us to enter the profession gets swamped by a proliferation of roles and responsibilities, an overriding concern for academic achievement as measured by standardized tests, shifting policies and expectations, an absence of resources and support, inadequate compensation, and more. Such challenges can leave even the most hopeful and idealistic of teachers feeling deflated and discouraged, if not downright cynical.[2]

This state of affairs leaves many teachers wrestling with questions such as: What's the point of what I'm doing? Am I really making a difference? What can I reasonably hope to accomplish as a teacher? Is all this hard work really worth it? Isn't there a better way?

AIMS OF THE BOOK

If you occasionally find yourself wrestling with questions like these, this book is for you. It has two overarching aims. The first is to develop a rich and concrete picture of what education is *for*—of one of its ultimate aims or goals. Here and throughout the book, the focus will be on *intellectual virtues*, which are the personal qualities or character strengths of good thinkers and learners. These virtues include curiosity, open-mindedness, intellectual courage, intellectual tenacity, intellectual humility and more. My hope is that in acquainting you with the language and concepts of intellectual virtue, you'll be in a better position to articulate and practice much of what you already care about and aspire to as a teacher—and that this, in turn, will help you reconnect with your professional calling.[3]

However, the point of this book is not merely theoretical or philosophical. It is also extremely practical. Accordingly, its second overarching aim is to provide a concrete account of what it looks like to teach for intellectual virtues, that is, to show how teachers can help their students practice and grow in curiosity, open-mindedness, attentiveness, intellectual courage, and related qualities. My focus will not be a narrow set of pedagogical tricks or techniques. I won't be proffering any tidy answers or silver-bullet solutions. Instead, we will explore together a constellation of *principles, postures,* and *practices* adaptable to a variety of educational settings. Importantly, many of these principles, postures, and practices are likely to be familiar to you already; you may even be an expert in one or more of them. Such familiarity shows that teaching for intellectual virtues is not a wholly new or foreign approach. Instead, it involves engaging in practices that many of us already know to be effective, but doing so in a particular way and with a particular educational vision in mind.

In other ways, internalizing what the book has to offer may prove challenging. On the picture it develops, good teaching has as much to do with *who we are* as teachers as it does the instructional methods or practices we employ in the classroom. It bears on our fundamental beliefs, values, and attitudes about teaching and learning. Therefore, if you're going to meet the book on its own terms, there's a good chance you'll feel personally stretched and challenged by it. To my mind, this is all to the good, for such stretching can create space in our hearts and minds for a richer and more meaningful way of understanding the work we do with students every day. It's a way of helping us, as Parker Palmer envisions, "take heart in teaching once more so that we can, as good teachers always do, give heart to our students."[4]

KEY SOURCES

In prosecuting these aims, I'll be drawing on three main bodies of knowledge and experience. The first consists of research in educational theory and psychology related, directly or indirectly, to teaching for intellectual virtues. This includes research that focuses explicitly on intellectual character or intellectual virtues.[5] Because these constructs have only recently begun to capture the attention of educational theorists and psychologists, this literature is relatively small. However, there is a great deal of additional research that, in less direct but still meaningful ways, also bears on our understanding of intellectual virtues, their educational importance, and how they can be fostered in an academic context. This research includes work in the philosophy of education about the proper aims of education and the nature of intellectual and moral virtues.[6] It also includes significant bodies of research in educational theory and psychology on such topics as thinking dispositions, habits of mind, mindfulness, grit, self-control, intrinsic motivation, metacognition, active learning, growth mindset, social and emotional learning, critical thinking, and more.[7] While these topics are not identical to that of intellectual virtues, they overlap and intersect with each other in various and important ways. Thus, I'll be drawing on the research on these topics throughout the book.

The second main source I'll be relying on is my training and background as a *virtue epistemologist*. Virtue epistemology is an approach to the philosophical study of knowledge that pays special attention to the excellences, or virtues, of good thinkers and knowers.[8] Put another way, virtue epistemology focuses on the personal characteristics required for competent and motivated learning. For approximately twenty years, I've been thinking and writing about topics central to virtue epistemology. My published work in this area includes numerous journal articles, book chapters, and encyclopedia entries, as well as two books: *The Inquiring Mind: On Intellectual Virtues and Virtue Epistemology* and *Intellectual Virtues and Education: Essays in Applied Virtue Epistemology.*[9] While most of this research has been geared toward other philosophers and academic researchers, it has given me a command of the concepts central to virtue epistemology that will prove useful as we explore together what intellectual virtues are, why they're important to education, and how they can be fostered in a classroom setting.[10]

The third main source I'll be drawing on consists of extensive experience implementing a focus on intellectual character development in a K–12 setting, together with hundreds of hours of professional development work with K–12 teachers. Because this experience will inform much of the rest of the book, it bears some explanation.

From 2010 to 2013, I helped found the Intellectual Virtues Academy of Long Beach (IVA), a public charter middle school (grades 6–8) in Long Beach, California.[11] IVA is premised on the idea that a comprehensive educational program can be oriented around helping students cultivate qualities like curiosity, open-mindedness, intellectual courage, and intellectual humility. The idea is not to make intellectual virtues the focus of a separate curriculum or schoolwide program. Rather, it is about integrating opportunities to practice and develop intellectual virtues across the academic curriculum and throughout the life of the school.

IVA opened its doors in the fall of 2013. By nearly every measure, the school has met or exceeded the expectations of its founders. Enrollment is strong. The student body is diverse. Scores on state tests are well above district and state averages. And the school is in a sound and sustainable financial position.

Two additional features of the school strike me as especially indicative of its success. First, IVA is a remarkably happy place. While no school is perfect, when one sets foot on the IVA campus or in one of its classrooms, one quickly gets the impression that this is a warm, vibrant, and flourishing educational community—that the students are (mostly) glad to be there, feel cared for, and are free to be themselves. This impression is confirmed by annual surveys of students, parents, and teachers, who routinely report extraordinarily high levels of support and satisfaction. A second striking feature is that IVA has been systematically designed around the aim of giving students well-supported opportunities to practice and grow in intellectual virtues. The curriculum, core instructional practices, professional development programming, advisory program, routines, traditions, systems, and policies have been thoughtfully and painstakingly formulated in light of the school's mission and vision. This systematic approach is thanks in no small part to the school's founding and current visionary principal (Jacquie Bryant), founding program administrator (the late and beloved Danielle Montiel), founding board chairman (Eric Churchill), and an extraordinary and exceptionally hardworking group of teachers, staff, and other stakeholders.[12]

In addition to the role of cofounder and "resident philosopher," my work at IVA has involved writing significant portions of IVA's charter, serving on the board of directors, participating in the school's advisory program, assisting with grant writing, coleading training events for teachers and other stakeholders, meeting regularly with school leadership to discuss the implementation of the IVA's unique educational philosophy, and more. Together with my work in virtue epistemology, my experience at IVA has led to many opportunities to speak to and work closely with teachers from all over the world. This includes pre-K, K–12, and college and university teachers working in traditional public, charter, and private school settings. These interactions with teachers, including teachers at schools very different from IVA, have given me a good sense of what educating for intellectual virtues can look like across a diverse range of educational contexts and student populations. I will draw on this understanding throughout the book.

OVERVIEW OF THE CHAPTERS

I turn now to provide a very brief sketch of each chapter and to offer some remarks about the book's intended audience and how it might be used in different contexts.

The opening chapters revolve around two questions: What are intellectual virtues? And what is their educational significance? Chapter 1 situates intellectual virtues relative to other, more familiar educational aims (e.g., knowledge and skills, good citizenship, and career preparation). Chapter 2 focuses on the nature and structure of intellectual virtues, providing extended profiles of nine individual virtues that occupy an important role in the remainder of the book.

The next two chapters address the principles and postures central to teaching for intellectual virtues. Chapter 3 explores ten pedagogical principles that can be used to guide the thinking and practice of teachers seeking to have a favorable impact on the intellectual character of their students. Chapter 4 examines a complementary set of pedagogical postures, or attitudes, aimed at fostering a classroom environment conducive to intellectual character growth.

Chapters 5 through 9 explain and provide numerous concrete examples of the pedagogical practices involved with teaching for intellectual virtues. Chapter 5 addresses the importance of getting comfortable with, and introducing students to, the language and concepts of intellectual virtue. Chapter 6 focuses on the role of self-reflection and self-awareness in the development of intellectual virtues. Chapter 7 defends the idea that teaching for intellectual virtues goes hand in hand with teaching for deep understanding. Chapter 8 explains how to provide students with well-supported opportunities to practice the skills and abilities characteristic of intellectual virtues (e.g., asking good questions, thinking for oneself, and perspective-switching). And chapter 9 explores the practice of modeling intellectual virtues for our students.

Chapter 10 tackles the issue of assessment. While noting various pitfalls and other limitations associated with trying to assess students' intellectual character, the chapter articulates several guiding principles that can be used to govern these efforts. It also describes several specific assessment practices and tools aligned with these principles.

The final chapter, Chapter 11, reviews several steps teachers can take to begin teaching for intellectual virtues in a more deliberate and systematic way. It is aimed at helping teachers begin to align their fundamental values, concerns, and practices with the goal of helping their students make progress in a set of target virtues. It also revisits the value of doing so, which includes deep benefits for teachers and students alike.

The book concludes with two appendices. Appendix A provides a table with a brief description of, and slogan for, several key virtues. Appendix B provides several self-assessment scale items for each of these virtues.

As I hope this overview makes clear, one of the main offerings of the book is a comprehensive *framework* for thinking about and engaging in the practice of teaching. This framework is anchored in a particular vision of what teaching is *for*—of the characterological attributes that teaching at its best seeks to foster. However, the framework is not merely an educational philosophy. It also includes a suite of principles, postures, and practices that can be adapted to different educational levels and settings. In this sense, it spans both theory and practice: it addresses the why and the how of teaching for intellectual virtues. Finally, the framework is not intended to capture a wholly new or original approach to teaching. Rather, with a nod to Samuel Johnson's observation that people "more frequently require to be reminded than informed," its purpose is to motivate, deepen, and integrate many of the known elements of impactful teaching.[13]

INTENDED AUDIENCE AND USES

This book is written primarily for teachers. I give special attention to how middle school and high school teachers in particular might benefit from its core ideas and recommendations. My rationale for this focus is twofold. First, most of my hands-on work with teachers has been at the secondary (versus primary or postsecondary) level. Second, for developmental reasons, middle school and high school students are ripe for several of the ideas and practices described in the book. They are, for instance, increasingly capable of higher and more active forms of thinking. They are also beginning to carve out their own values and identities. These and other developmental factors put this group in a very good position to practice and internalize the activities and aims discussed in these pages.

That said, the overall framework of the book is readily adaptable to primary and postsecondary settings. Indeed, young children are developmentally inclined to practice such virtues as curiosity, open-mindedness, and intellectual humility in ways that many adolescent students may not be. This aptitude can make teaching for these and related virtues even more natural at lower levels. As for postsecondary students, I have been implementing the book's principles and practices in my own classes at the university level for many years. This work has resulted in many changes to my teaching. These changes have added a richness and meaningfulness to my work with students. In light of course evaluations and other feedback I have received over the years, the changes also appear to have had a favorable impact on many of my students. While the book is aimed primarily at teachers, I hope several other audiences, including educational administrators, researchers, and policy makers, may also find it of some use.

In terms of how the book might be used, I have mainly imagined its readers to be individual teachers or groups of teachers who are looking to reconnect with their passion for teaching or to reconceive of the meaning and purpose of their work with students. The book could also be used in a professional development context, where it could provide teachers and school leaders with an opportunity to wrestle with big questions in education and to reflect on, discuss, and experiment with several concrete pedagogical practices. For similar reasons, the book could also be used in teacher training programs (e.g., in educational foundations or methods courses). Regardless of how it is used, I recommend trying to read it in conversation with others. Again, some of the terms and concepts are likely to be new. Discussing this material with others can make it easier to process. It can also encourage readers to ask thoughtful questions, critically assess what they're reading, and make concrete applications of it.

While the book need not be read from beginning to end, I recommend against skipping immediately to the chapters on pedagogical practices (chapters 5 through 9), especially if the motivation for doing so is to get as quickly as possible to the "practical" parts of the book. For, as I've already suggested, teaching for intellectual virtues isn't just about how we teach; it's also about *who we are* as teachers—about our fundamental values, hopes, cares, and concerns. Chapters 1 through 4 explore these and related themes in considerable depth.

CONCLUSION

In my twenty years of experience as an educator, I've been struck, on the one hand, by how difficult it can be to teach in a way that feels connected with what I reflectively consider the most important and life-giving aims of education. I'm well aware of how easy it can be to grow complacent, even cynical. On the other hand, I've also become convinced that the language and concepts of intellectual virtue provide a rich and compelling way of understanding the purpose of education; that this purpose points in the direction of certain pedagogical principles, postures, and practices; and that the adoption of this approach can be a way of resisting the drift toward complacency or cynicism. This is the big picture we'll be exploring together in the pages that follow. I hope you'll experience the book as challenging but nourishing and that it will do something to rekindle your passion and restore your wholeness as a teacher.

CHAPTER 1

Ideals

> It is [the] business [of education] to cultivate deep-seated and
> effective habits of discriminating tested beliefs from mere
> assertions, guesses, and opinions; to develop a lively, sincere,
> and open-minded preference for conclusions that are properly
> grounded, and to ingrain into the individual's working habits
> methods of inquiry and reasoning appropriate to the various
> problems that present themselves.
>
> —John Dewey, *How We Think*

A guiding premise of this book is that our experience as teachers can benefit from thoughtful reflection on an educational ideal. Educational ideals,
as I view them, are ways of understanding or conceptualizing the purpose
of our work with students. They're an answer to the question: What's the
ultimate aim or goal of what I'm doing in the classroom?[1]

On this way of thinking about educational ideals, there needn't be only
one correct ideal. Your vision for what you're trying to accomplish in the
classroom—the ways you're trying to influence or benefit your students—
may be different from the ways I'm trying to influence my students. You
and I might subscribe to different ideals, both of which might be reasonable and worthy of pursuit.

Another notable feature of educational ideals is that they're closely tied
to the meaning and purpose we experience as teachers. If my primary goal

in the classroom is to prepare my students to score well on standardized exams, I may not get much satisfaction from, or feel much purpose in, my work. To make the point differently, ideals can be a vehicle for *hope*. If I think of myself as contributing to the long-term well-being of my students, or to the shaping of who they're becoming as people, and if I allow this goal to inform and guide the way I teach, then my experience as a teacher will be infused with a sense of meaning and purpose. This in turn will buoy me as I grapple with the more stressful and challenging aspects of my vocation.

This chapter is an opportunity to step back and reflect on the ultimate purpose of teaching. My aim is to outline and situate an educational ideal that I hope you'll find compelling and relevant. While some of the terms and concepts may be new to you, I suspect that the ideal they pick out will be at least vaguely familiar. Indeed, I hope the discussion will provide you with a conceptual framework and terminology to better understand and describe much of what you already care about and strive for as an educator.

Before proceeding, I want to reiterate the precariousness of talking about ideals in an educational context. As noted in the introduction, I recognize that most readers of this book will be teaching under conditions that are far from ideal. The danger this presents is twofold. In writing about an educational ideal, I run the risk of either (1) inspiring false or baseless hopes and expectations or (2) immediately provoking skepticism, cynicism, and exasperation. These are the two horns of a dilemma I am committed to navigating in this book.

A good educational ideal must be practical, realistic, and relevant. It must be something that we can understand and focus on, that can guide our practice, and that we can make discernible progress toward. While the ideal I'll be sketching isn't the only one that satisfies these criteria, my experience suggests that it resonates deeply with many teachers, including those working under very realistic or nonideal conditions. In ways that will become clearer later in the chapter, this ideal is also extremely timely. Therefore, as you read what follows, I hope you'll allow yourself to pause, take a step back, and consider anew the ultimate point or purpose of your work with students—even if doing so means allowing your imagination to transcend, however briefly, some of the very real challenges and constraints you face as a teacher.

WHAT'S THE POINT?

What, then, is the fundamental aim or purpose of what you do in the classroom? I have posed this question to scores of teachers at many levels and across a variety of contexts. I discuss a related question with most of my undergraduate students, namely, what's the point or purpose of the education they're receiving? The answers I receive from these groups tend to fall into one of three general categories.

Academic Ideals

The first of these categories is straightforwardly intellectual or academic. When queried about the purpose of teaching or learning, many teachers and students focus on the transmission of knowledge and intellectual skills.

That the transmission of knowledge and skills is a fundamental educational aim might seem like a truism. After all, most schools function primarily as *academic* institutions—institutions whose primary focus is to impart the knowledge and skills specific to subjects like math, science, English, and history. This impression is reinforced by the Common Core State Standards, adopted by most public schools in the United States. These standards, which cover mathematics and English/language arts and literacy, purport to describe "what a student should *know* and *be able to do* at the end of each grade."[2]

While this ideal is implied by the de facto purpose of many schools, some education theorists have given it a more explicit expression and defense. On the importance of knowledge, E. D. Hirsch has long defended cultural literacy as an educational ideal: "All human communities are founded upon specific shared information, and the basic goal of education in a human community is acculturation—the transmission to children of the specific information shared by the adults of the group or polis."[3] For Hirsch, this indispensable "core knowledge" covers language arts, visual arts, music, mathematics, history, geography, and science.[4]

Typically, a concern with imparting knowledge goes hand in hand with an interest in fostering intellectual skills. This is true in Hirsch's case. It's also true of many other education writers. Mortimer Adler, best known for his defense of a great books curriculum, also identifies intellectual skills as a fundamental educational aim: "An important end of schools is the development of intellectual skills—skills of learning by means of reading, writing, speaking, listening, calculating, problem-solving, observing, measuring, estimating . . . exercising critical judgment. These skills are the ones everyone needs in order to learn anything, in school or elsewhere."[5]

While knowledge of subjects like history, biology, and algebra isn't reducible to the possession of intellectual skills, neither is it an accident that knowledge and skills tend to be grouped together. One reason for this association is that intellectual skills aren't developed in a vacuum. Rather, they're acquired in the context of engaging with particular questions, problems, or bodies of material. Conversely, one way to tell whether people have mastered a body of knowledge is to see what use they can make of it, for instance, whether they can articulate what they have learned in the form of an argumentative essay or apply the knowledge to new questions, problems, or scenarios. Cognitive scientist Daniel Willingham makes a similar point: "The very processes that teachers care about most—critical thinking processes such as reasoning and problem solving—are intimately intertwined with factual knowledge that is stored in long-term memory (not just found in the environment) . . . [W]e must ensure that students acquire background knowledge parallel with practicing critical thinking skills."[6]

Social and Political Ideals

The fostering of academic knowledge and skills may be one of the fundamental aims of teaching. Nevertheless, in my conversations with teachers and students, and according to most education experts, this aim is not exhaustive. Indeed, many theorists and practitioners worry, as philosopher of education Hugh Sockett does, that "we are neglecting who children, students, and their teachers *are* in favor of assessable knowledge and skills."[7]

One limitation of treating knowledge and skills as an educational ideal is that they do not fully address what many people think of as education's social or political functions. For instance, especially at lower grade levels, teachers often view themselves as responsible for helping socialize their students, teaching them how to get along with others, to share, and to play fair. Several education theorists have held a similar view. Thomas Lickona, a leading expert in character education, remarks, "Schools cannot be ethical bystanders at a time when our society is in deep moral trouble. Rather, schools must do what they can to contribute to the character of the young and the moral health of the nation."[8] In an essay titled "A Tough Mind and a Tender Heart," Martin Luther King Jr. expresses a similar sentiment, asking, "What is more tragic than to see a person who has risen to the disciplined heights of tough mindedness but has at the same time sunk to the passionless depths of hard heartedness?"[9]

That the aims of teaching are not merely academic is also evident in the increasing attention paid to social and emotional learning. According to the Collaborative for Academic, Social, and Emotional Learning (CASEL), social and emotional learning is "the process through which children and adults understand and manage emotions, set and achieve positive goals, feel and show empathy for others, establish and maintain positive relationships, and make responsible decisions."[10] A driving force behind the movement for social and emotional learning in education, CASEL identifies five core competences that schools and teachers can help foster in their students: self-awareness, self-management, social awareness, relationship skills, and responsible decision-making.[11]

A closely related view, also popular among practitioners and researchers, is that teachers should prepare students to become responsible citizens. In a democratic context, this is often taken to mean that teachers should provide students with the knowledge and skills necessary for democratic participation. This includes knowledge of government institutions, policies, and laws, together with the skills required for rational deliberation, media literacy and critical thinking. Increasingly, this aim is understood in global terms, the idea being that teachers should train their students to become responsible global citizens. In 2012, United Nations Secretary General Ban Ki-Moon launched the five-year Global First Initiative, which arose from the following widespread conviction: "Education must fully assume its central role in helping people to forge more just, peaceful, tolerant and inclusive societies. It must give people the understanding, skills and values they need to cooperate in resolving the interconnected challenges of the 21st Century."[12]

While we might disagree about the relative importance of the social or political aims just noted, there is something compelling about them. They suggest that teaching isn't just about filling our students' heads with academic knowledge or equipping them with the skills of reading, writing, and arithmetic. It is also about helping them become *persons* of a certain sort, persons who are ready and willing to live good lives and make productive contributions to their communities. It isn't surprising, then, that many teachers are attracted to ideals that foreground education's social and political dimensions.

Economic and Professional Ideals

A third category of aims is economic or vocational. When I talk with my students about the purpose of a university education, the topics of gainful employment and professional accomplishment inevitably arise. They say that a central purpose of education, at least at the collegiate level, should be to prepare students to lead successful careers and to achieve economic security.

This idea has played a major role in recent debates about the value of a college education, debates that suggest, either implicitly or explicitly, that the primary criterion for measuring the value of a college education is an economic one. To illustrate, in 2014, the *New York Times* ran a story with the headline "Is College Worth It? Clearly, New Data Say." The focus of the article was "the pay gap between college graduates and everyone else." It concluded that "the decision not to attend college for fear that it's a bad deal is among the most economically irrational decisions anybody could make in 2014."[13] Five years later, the *Times* ran another story on the same topic. This time, the headline was "College May Not Be Worth It Anymore." The primary metric used to make this claim? The "economic benefit of a college degree."[14]

A similar view is evident in the familiar assertion that teachers should equip their students with so-called soft skills, noncognitive skills, or twenty-first-century skills.[15] Roughly, these skills or abilities go beyond standard academic competencies or technical know-how. According to one list, the "Top 10 Soft Skills Needed in Today's Workplace" include integrity, communication, courtesy, responsibility, social skills, positive attitude, professionalism, flexibility, teamwork, and work ethic.[16] The Partnership for 21st Century Learning identifies the "4Cs of a 21st century learner" as collaboration, critical thinking, communication, and creativity.[17] Advocates of soft skills argue that, given the increasingly collaborative and technologically dynamic nature of many occupations, schools today are failing to equip students with the full range of skills they need to succeed in the workplace. And they identify teaching for soft skills as a way of addressing this problem.

INTELLECTUAL VIRTUES AS AN EDUCATIONAL IDEAL

In the preceding sections, several academic, social, political, and economic educational ideals have been identified. While these ideals clearly have merit, the primary purpose of this chapter is to sketch an alternative ideal, one that is distinct from but also importantly connected to the ones just considered. In my conversations with teachers and students, they sometimes hint at this alternative ideal, making comments to the effect that education should foster a love of learning, help students become lifelong learners, and shape them into thinkers who can form their own opinions, ask thoughtful questions, learn from others, give a fair hearing to opposing standpoints, and speak up for what they believe in.[18]

These replies are striking. The ideals they draw attention to are, on the one hand, distinctively cognitive or intellectual. They pertain to thinking, learning, questioning, believing, and inquiring. However, these ideals cannot be reduced to knowledge of particular facts or to the possession of one or more intellectual skills. This difference is evident in the robust volitional and emotional dimension of the ideals. They're *personal* in a way that knowledge and mere skills are not. To know that someone loves learning or embraces intellectual challenges is to know something about who the individual is as a person, something admirable and attractive. In these respects, the aims in question are more closely aligned with some of the social and political aims noted earlier than they are with familiar academic aims like knowledge and skills.[19]

Intellectual Character: Virtues and Vices

This brings us to the idea of intellectual character. A central point of this chapter is that the language of intellectual character offers a concrete and compelling way of fleshing out the idea that teaching should promote a love of learning and equip students to become lifelong learners, think for themselves, ask thoughtful questions, and so on. In short, the language illuminates the idea that teaching should have an impact on students that is at once intellectual *and* personal.

Everyone has an intellectual character.[20] In general terms, your intellectual character consists of the ways you are disposed to act, think, and feel in the context of *epistemic* pursuits like learning, wondering, reasoning, observing, contemplating, and deliberating. Understood in this way, intellectual character is a neutral construct: a person's intellectual character can be good or bad, strong or weak.

If I form beliefs independently of evidence, am indifferent to whether my beliefs are true or false, have no real appetite for learning, and refuse to listen to people who disagree with me, my intellectual character will be impoverished. It will be marred by intellectual *vices*, or defects of intellectual character, including intellectual laziness, closed-mindedness, intellectual arrogance, and gullibility. Intellectual virtues, by contrast, are *excellences* of intellectual character. They're the character attributes of good thinkers and learners, such as curiosity, open-mindedness, attentiveness, and intellectual carefulness, thoroughness, autonomy, and humility.

When introducing these concepts to teachers, I almost always hear comments such as: "The language of intellectual virtues is extremely helpful for describing what I really care about as a teacher. I want so much to help my students become more curious, open-minded, courageous, and tenacious. Having this language helps me better understand and express much of what I'm already striving for as an educator." My hope is that you might have a similar response. While we will take a much closer look at the nature of intellectual virtues in chapter 2, I hope this brief introduction gives you a sense that the language of intellectual character, and of intellectual virtues in particular, offers a compelling way of "thickening" some familiar but elusive educational goals.

The Educational Significance of Intellectual Virtues

Ron Ritchhart, one of few educational theorists who have written explicitly about intellectual character, describes its educational significance in this way:

> If we truly want smarter children, we need to know what smart looks like and stop confusing it with speed and knowledge. We also need to recognize that much of the substance of schooling is fleeting. After the final test has been taken, when students have long since left our doorways and the chalkboard has been erased for the last time, what will stay with our students isn't the laundry list of names, dates, computations, and procedures we have covered. What endures are the dispositions and habits of character we have been able to nurture. What stays with us, what sticks from our education, are the patterns of behavior and thinking that have been engrained and encultured over time. These are the residuals of education. These are the foundations of intellectual character.[21]

Though he doesn't use the term *intellectual character*, John Dewey also holds that a primary aim of education consists of instilling "correct habits of reflection" and "habits of thought."[22] After identifying several ways our thinking tends to go wrong, Dewey says, "The work of teaching must not only transform natural tendencies into trained habits of thought, but must also fortify the mind against irrational tendencies current in the social environment, and help displace erroneous habits already produced."[23] Concerning these mental habits, he remarks, "The main office of education is to supply conditions that make for their cultivation. The formation of these habits is the Training of Mind."[24]

Along similar lines, in a series of recent school-based longitudinal studies, psychologist Daeun Park and colleagues were led to a "tripartite taxonomy of character," one part of which is "intellectual character," which includes character strengths such as curiosity and zest. According to the authors, their research generated strong support for thinking of intellectual character as a separate dimension of character, alongside its interpersonal and intrapersonal dimensions.[25] They conclude that "school practices and programs targeting these three dimensions of character hold promise for setting children on the path to thriving socially, academically, and intellectually."[26] Angela Duckworth, known for her groundbreaking work on grit, and a coauthor of the studies just noted, also observes that "character is plural."[27] Duckworth identifies intellectual character as one of three main dimensions of character. She emphasizes the educational importance of "strengths of mind" like curiosity and intellectual humility and remarks that "for a positive independent posture toward learning, intellectual virtue trumps the [other two dimensions of character]."[28]

The poet David Whyte tells the story of a businessman trying to persuade him to help bring poetry into American corporate culture. The man had listened to one of Whyte's talks and believed that the language of poetry was essential to naming particular experiences and realities in the corporate realm. He remarked to Whyte, "The language we have in that world is not large enough for the territory that we've already entered. And in your work, I've just heard the language that's large enough for it."[29] I propose that something similar is true in education. There are things we desire and care about as teachers—things that standard educational terms and concepts don't allow us to fully grasp or articulate. And without a language to express these values, we cannot pursue or achieve them in the most intelligent and wholehearted way possible. The language of intellectual virtues can be of service in education in much the same way that Whyte's friend thought poetry could be useful in the corporate world. It can help illuminate territory we've already entered.[30]

Maintaining a Hopeful but Realistic Perspective

Before looking in more detail at the ideal of intellectual virtues, I want to make one thing very clear: subscribing to this ideal does not require believing that it can be fully realized by individual teachers on a wide scale or within a short period of time. We can treat the intellectual character growth of our students as a worthwhile educational goal and allow this goal to inform and guide what we do in the classroom even if we know that the vast majority of our students won't leave our classes having been transformed into paragons of intellectual virtue.

Limiting our expectations in this way can be challenging. When laboring in pursuit of a goal, it helps to see immediate results. However, compare the goals or ideals of various nonprofit organizations, such as those focused on eradicating poverty, ending global warming, nuclear disarmament, or curing cancer. Do members of these organizations, or the people or agencies who support them, think they will achieve these goals on their own or within a few years or even decades? Perhaps some do, but many don't. The fact that their goals aren't immediately achievable doesn't make the aims of the organizations or the day-to-day efforts of their employees or funders somehow irrational or misguided. Rather, what's important is that the goals are worthwhile, that they can be pursued intelligently, and that some discernible progress can be made toward them.

The same is true when it comes to the ideal of helping our students grow in intellectual virtues. Again, if it were impossible to connect this ideal with our daily practices as teachers, or if we could not in any way influence the intellectual character of our students, then teaching for intellectual virtues would be a quixotic endeavor. However, I'm going to assume, at least for now, that neither of these things is true. In later chapters, I'll argue that both are false—that taking our students' progress in intellectual virtues seriously can have a substantial and revitalizing effect on our pedagogy and that we can hope to have a meaningful impact on the intellectual character of many of our students.

HOW INTELLECTUAL VIRTUES ARE RELATED TO OTHER IDEALS

One measure of an educational ideal is the extent to which it leaves room for—perhaps even encourages—the pursuit of other things we desire or care about as educators. The ideal of intellectual virtues is especially compelling in this regard. Teaching for intellectual virtues isn't merely compatible with teaching for the academic, social, political, and economic ideals discussed earlier in the chapter. It is also a way of making progress toward these goals, that is, a way of equipping our students with academic knowledge and skills, contributing to their development as neighbors and citizens, and training them for success in the workplace.

Knowledge and Skills

There is a natural and tight connection between teaching for intellectual virtues and teaching for knowledge and skills. In fact, it is difficult, if not impossible, to teach for intellectual virtues without teaching for knowledge and skills.

Intellectual virtues can be thought of as *habits of mind*, in particular, habits of good thinking and reasoning.[31] If we want to help our students develop these habits, we'll need to give them something to think and reason *about*—something to ponder, analyze, comprehend, reflect on, assess, and question. Academic subjects like history, biology, literature, algebra, and political science fit this bill perfectly. Consequently, instruction in the knowledge and skills related to these disciplines presents an excellent opportunity for us to help our students grow in intellectual virtues.[32]

As we'll consider in more detail in chapter 2, intellectual virtues also involve skills of their own. To be open-minded, for instance, one must be skilled at switching perspectives; to be intellectually courageous, one must be competent at facing down one's intellectual fears; to be intellectually autonomous, one must be capable of thinking for oneself; and to be intellectually careful, one must know how to identify and avoid intellectual pitfalls or mistakes. These skills intersect and overlap with many of the skills teachers already seek to foster in their students. They include various critical thinking abilities as well as several skills described in the Common Core State Standards and Next Generation Science Standards.[33] So, again, teaching for intellectual virtues isn't merely compatible with teaching for intellectual skills; it's part and parcel of it.

Being a Good Neighbor

Teaching for intellectual virtues can also play an important role in helping our students become good neighbors, that is, it can help with their moral or ethical development. In many situations, virtuous *thinking* is a precondition for morally responsible *behavior*.[34] Our actions often spring from our beliefs, so that if our thinking isn't careful, thorough, fair, honest, and so on, we may end up acting in ways that are irresponsible or immoral. For instance, a researcher's failure to thoroughly investigate the potential side effects of a new pharmaceutical drug might have tragic consequences once the drug hits the market. Similarly, racist behavior often arises from prejudicial thinking, which is characteristically narrow, dishonest, and unfair. The moral significance of virtuous thinking is also evident in the context of friendship. Good friends ask good questions, listen well, and want to understand one another. As a result, they regularly practice virtues like curiosity, attentiveness, open-mindedness, and intellectual humility.

In the book *Virtuous Minds*, Philip Dow makes a similar point:

> What is intellectual character? When we think of character, we usually think of moral character . . . Our intellectual character influences our lives just as moral character does, and with at least as much force. The only difference is that intellectual character is concerned not with our actions as much as it is with the thinking habits we are developing as we seek and use knowledge. Put another way, intellectual character is the force of accumulated thinking habits that shape and color every decision we make. Because our minds tend to lead our actions, in a very real sense the quality of our

intellectual character even trumps moral character in terms of its power to direct the course of our lives.[35]

If Dow is correct, the quality of a person's moral character depends significantly on the quality of his or her intellectual character. It follows that insofar as we're able to shape the intellectual character of our students, we'll be fortifying their moral or ethical character as well.

Being a Good Citizen

Teaching for intellectual virtues also helps our students become responsible citizens. One indicator of the health of a democracy is the quality of its public discourse. In many democracies today, this quality is notoriously low. Closed-mindedness, intellectual dishonesty, and intellectual arrogance are the order of the day. However, if we can train our students to think and reason in ways that are careful, fair, open, and honest, they'll be able to carry these virtues into their political interactions and conversations. In doing so, they'll be fulfilling an important civic duty and injecting some badly needed civility, intelligence, and truthfulness into our public discourse.

Another key feature of a healthy democracy is voter participation. Governance "by the people" requires that citizens exercise their right to vote and that they do so on the basis of trustworthy and credible information. However, aspects of the contemporary information landscape complicate this responsibility. In an age of twenty-four-hour cable news, a cacophony of partisan voices and perspectives, "filter bubbles," and "deep fakes," it has become increasingly difficult to know whom to trust and how to think about important political issues.

One tempting reaction to this landscape is withdrawal. As a recent news report observed, "In this volatile political moment, information, it would seem, has never been more crucial . . . But just when information is needed most, to many Americans it feels most elusive. The rise of social media; the proliferation of information online . . . and a flood of partisan news are leading to a general exhaustion with news itself . . . Many people are numb and disoriented, struggling to discern what is real in a sea of slant, fake and fact." As the article goes on to note, while some people react to this quagmire by withdrawing or suspending belief, others take a very different approach: "Many Americans have the opposite experience: They turn to sources they trust—whether on the right or left—that tell them exactly what they already believe to be true."[36] That is, instead of trying to sort through the evidential morass or giving up altogether, some people double down on their convictions, arbitrarily limiting their attention to sources and pundits who share their perspective and tickle their ears. Here, vices like closed-mindedness and dogmatism are on wide display.

Neither withdrawal nor dogmatism is good for democracy. Both cut against fundamental democratic principles. They also cede political influence to those whose political views are the result of overconfident, careless, and tribalistic thinking. In a democratic context, such thinking can lead precipitously to policies and legislation that make the world significantly less safe, just, and prosperous. Such a prospect underscores an urgent need to train our students to think and reason in the opposite way, that is, in ways characteristic of virtues like intellectual carefulness, thoroughness, honesty, open-mindedness, and fair-mindedness.[37]

Workforce Preparation

Finally, the ideal of intellectual virtues also overlaps with the aim of preparing our students for successful careers. Indeed, intellectual virtues like curiosity, open-mindedness, and intellectual humility increasingly top the list of qualities that companies today are looking for in their employees.

To illustrate, we need look no further than the hiring practices at Google. In a 2014 interview, Laszlo Bock, then senior vice president of people operations, described five qualities Google looks for in every person it hires.[38] Two of these attributes pertain immediately to intellectual character. The first is what Bock describes as "general cognitive ability, and it's not IQ. It's learning ability. It's the ability to process on the fly. It's the ability to pull together disparate bits of information."[39] A person's ability to do these things will depend in part on the extent to which the individual is disposed to ask good questions, probe for understanding, consider multiple perspectives, and embrace intellectual challenges. That is, it will depend on the extent to which the person is curious, intellectually thorough, open-minded, intellectually tenacious, and more. A second hiring attribute at Google is "intellectual humility." Bock notes that "successful bright people rarely experience failure, and so they don't learn how to learn from that failure."[40] As Bock explains, intellectual humility is the attribute of personal character that allows us to admit and learn from our intellectual mistakes and failures. These examples illustrate that training in intellectual virtues is training in good thinking, and that training in good thinking is training for a successful career.

PLATO'S CAVE ALLEGORY

I conclude this chapter with a story that illustrates several points we've been focusing on. The story comes from Plato's *Republic*, one of the most influential works in the history of Western thought. One of the best-known passages of the *Republic* is the so-called allegory of the cave.[41] In this little story, Socrates asks his interlocutor Glaucon to imagine a group of prisoners who have been held captive in an underground cave for their entire lives. Bound and shackled, the prisoners are forced to face the back wall of the cave, the entrance being some distance behind them and entirely out of their sight. Immediately behind the prisoners is a walkway, and behind the walkway is a large fire. Other inhabitants of the cave carry various artifacts across the walkway, casting shadows on the wall in front of the prisoners. Because the shadows are all they've ever known, the prisoners mistake them for ultimate reality.

One day a prisoner is freed from his chains and slowly makes his way out the cave. As he ascends, he is confused and disoriented by what he sees, and blinded by the brightness of the world outside. Eventually, he comes to the startling realization that what he and his fellow prisoners have long thought of as ultimate reality is but a pale and imperfect image of such. Eventually the man returns to the cave. Disoriented, he is met with hostility and ridicule. The prisoners dismiss him as a lunatic.

This is an allegory. At one level, it is an intriguing tale of a prisoner who finally gets to see the light of day. But it also has deeper significance. It illustrates a wide range of metaphysical, epistemological, and ethical theses central to Plato's thought. Although Plato scholars have debated about precisely which points or lessons to draw from the story, Plato himself draws a lesson that is explicitly educational. He has Socrates say to Glaucon:

> Here's what we must think about these matters. Education isn't what some people declare it to be, namely, putting knowledge into souls that lack it, like putting sight into blind eyes . . . [T]he power to learn is present in everyone's soul and the instrument with which each learns is like an eye that cannot be turned around from that which is coming into being without turning the whole soul until it is able to study that which is and the brightest thing that is, namely, the one we call the good . . . Then *education is the craft concerned with doing this very thing, this turning around, and with how the soul can most easily and effectively be made to do it.*[42]

In this passage, Plato is drawing attention to an educational ideal. According to this ideal, good teachers don't simply fill their students' heads with knowledge; nor do they merely equip them with intellectual skills that might be used well or poorly. Instead, they turn their students around, opening their hearts and minds to a bigger and broader view of reality. In the words of Parker Palmer, they guide their students toward "more truthful ways of seeing and being in the world."[43]

This is a useful way to think about the ideal of teaching for intellectual virtues. As we'll see in greater detail in the chapters that follow, when we do what we can to nurture intellectual virtues in our students, we are inviting them into a process of reorientation. We aren't simply transmitting knowledge and skills. Instead, we are seeking to have an impact on some of their fundamental values as thinkers and learners. I suggest that we continue to keep Plato's allegory in mind as we further explore what intellectual virtues are and what it looks like to help our students make progress in these qualities.

CHAPTER 2

Virtues

> One does not need to be a profound scholar to be open minded,
> nor a keen academician to engage in an assiduous pursuit of
> truth.
>
> —Martin Luther King Jr., *Strength to Love*

In his famous ethical treatise, the *Nicomachean Ethics*, the ancient Greek philosopher Aristotle sets forth a rigorous and systematic account of the "highest good" for human beings. His point in doing so is largely practical. He thinks that if we understand our highest good, we'll stand a much better chance of achieving this good: "Surely, then, knowledge of the good must be very important for our lives? And if, like archers, we have a target, are we not more likely to hit the mark?"[1]

A central thesis of this book, one that was addressed in detail in chapter 1, is that helping students make progress in intellectual virtues is a worthy educational ideal. But what exactly is intellectual character? And how should we understand the nature and structure of intellectual virtues?

These are the main questions I'll be addressing in this chapter. In keeping with Aristotle's metaphor, my goal is to help you acquire a firm understanding of what intellectual virtues are and what they look like in a classroom setting. Equipped with this knowledge, you'll be in a better position to hit the mark of nurturing intellectual virtues in your students. I'll first explore various aspects of intellectual character, intellectual virtues, and intellectual vices. I will then turn to the nature and structure of nine individual virtues, calling attention to what each one looks like in a learning context.

The couple of sections that follow are probably the most theoretical and abstract parts of this book. You may not have much interest in some of the finer points and distinctions. Nevertheless, I hope you'll do your best to stick with the discussion. While theoretical in nature, the ideas in question are of considerable practical importance. Because they will provide you with a conceptual anchor and way of understanding yourself and your students, these sections will help you implement the more practical ideas discussed in later chapters.

INTELLECTUAL VIRTUES AND VICES

Intellectual character is one dimension of *personal* character. Your personal character consists of how you are disposed to act, think, and feel across various domains or contexts.[2] It reflects who you are as a person. When faced with danger, do you lose your sense of judgment? Are you overcome with fear? Do you back down or persist? Or, in the domain of interpersonal relationships, are you inclined to listen attentively, feel sympathetically, and behave generously? Or do you often find yourself feeling distracted, having limited space for other people's needs and problems? Your answers to these questions reflect your personal character. They say something important about who you are or what you are like as a person.

Your *intellectual* character—which again is one dimension of personal character—consists of your dispositions to act, think, and feel in the context of epistemic activities and pursuits, such as learning, thinking, inquiring, observing, reasoning, wondering, and analyzing. It reflects who you are as a thinker and learner. When faced with an opportunity to learn something new, how do you tend to feel? Does the opportunity excite you? Or do you generally find yourself unmoved or uninterested? When you encounter someone who sees the world differently from you or who doesn't share your viewpoint on a particular moral or political issue, what do you typically think? Are you immediately tempted to dismiss the person as ignorant or irrational? How do you usually act in the face of intellectual challenges?

Are you quick to give up? Or do you persist? When you're presented with an argument or evidence, how do you respond? Do you automatically take it at face value? Or do you consider it carefully? Your answers to these questions say something about the substance of your intellectual character.

As noted in chapter 1, intellectual character *as such* is a neutral concept. A person's intellectual character can be good or bad, better or worse, admirable or not. Intellectual *virtues* are strengths, or excellences, of intellectual character, including curiosity, open-mindedness, intellectual humility, tenacity, and courage.[3] They dispose people to act, think, and feel well or excellently in the context of inquiring, learning, and reasoning. Intellectual *vices*, by contrast, are defects or weaknesses of intellectual character, such as intellectual apathy, laziness, arrogance, dogmatism, and cowardice. They dispose people to act, think, and feel poorly or defectively in a learning context.[4]

Before looking more closely at their structure, several brief remarks concerning intellectual virtues and vices are in order. First, intellectual virtues and vices are possessed in degrees. People are more or less—not categorically—open-minded, closed-minded, intellectually careful, careless, and so forth. These nuances can be easy to lose sight of, given our tendency to view the world, including other people, in rigid and binary terms. Second, and relatedly, the intellectual character of most people is a mixed bag, a combination of virtues and vices, each quality possessed to a greater or lesser degree.[5] Third, intellectual vices should not be confused with non-characterological qualities they might resemble. For instance, a student with attention deficit hyperactivity disorder (ADHD) shouldn't be viewed as possessing the vice of inattentiveness, even if the student exhibits some of the behavior of an inattentive learner. Unlike intellectual vices, ADHD is not rooted in the agency of the individual who has it. It is substantially if not entirely outside the person's voluntary control.[6] Fourth, while both intellectual virtues and moral virtues are attributes of character, intellectual virtues should not be confused with moral virtues. We can think of moral virtues like kindness, compassion, generosity, and respect as the character strengths of a good neighbor. And we can think of intellectual virtues like curiosity, open-mindedness, intellectual thoroughness, and intellectual tenacity as the character strengths of a good thinker or learner. While moral and intellectual virtues are closely related and may overlap in significant ways, they are not identical to each other.[7]

THE STRUCTURE OF INTELLECTUAL VIRTUES

To provide a more precise idea of what intellectual virtues are and how they manifest themselves in a learning context, I turn to a more in-depth exploration of these qualities. In the present section, I'll describe three dimensions that all intellectual virtues have in common.[8]

Skill

For each intellectual virtue, there exists a skill or competence (or cluster of skills or competences) characteristic of the virtue that sets it apart from other virtues. For example, to possess the virtue of open-mindedness, a person must be skilled or proficient at taking up and considering alternative perspectives. Perspective-switching is an important part of what's distinctive about open-mindedness; this skill separates open-mindedness from other virtues like curiosity or intellectual humility. Similarly, to have the virtue of intellectual courage, a person must be skilled at managing fears in an epistemic context. If fear always gets the best of a person, then he or she won't be intellectually courageous. Proper fear management is part of what's unique or distinctive about intellectual courage.

Motivational

While certain skills are necessary for the possession of intellectual virtues, they are not sufficient, for a person can have these skills while lacking the motivation to use them.[9] Accordingly, intellectual virtues also have a motivational dimension. To possess the virtue of open-mindedness, for instance, a person must be skilled at perspective-switching and be reliably motivated to deploy this skill. Moreover, in their most complete or admirable form, intellectual virtues involve an element of *intrinsic* motivation.[10]

At their best, intellectually virtuous people are motivated to think outside the box, take intellectual risks, ask thoughtful questions, and avoid intellectual errors because they care about things like knowledge, truth, and understanding at least partly for their own sake—not as a mere means to other ends or goals.[11]

Judgment

It can be tempting to think that if a person possesses the skill specific to a particular virtue and is highly and even intrinsically motivated to use this skill, then she will necessarily possess the virtue in question.* However, this isn't quite right. A person might be able to switch perspectives and be motivated to use this ability but have a poor sense of which perspectives she should take up, when she should do so, for how long or in what way she should consider them, and so on.[12] That is, she might lack good judgment concerning the proper use or deployment of her ability to switch perspectives. Hence, intellectual virtues also have a judgment dimension.

Aristotle's so-called doctrine of the mean is useful for further unpacking this dimension.[13] Applied to intellectual virtues, the idea is that every virtue is a mean, or midpoint, between two extremes, one a vice of excess and the other a vice of deficiency. The virtue of intellectual humility, for instance, involves owning, or taking responsibility for, intellectual limitations and mistakes *enough but not too much*. If a person were to pay too much attention to his intellectual mistakes or regularly ascribe to himself intellectual limitations he doesn't have, then he would lack the virtue of intellectual humility; instead, he would likely be intellectually servile or self-denigrating (excess). Alternatively, if a person were to think he had no intellectual limitations, or if he were extremely reluctant to admit that he had made an intellectual error, then he would be intellectually arrogant or defensive (deficiency). To possess the virtue of intellectual humility, a person must have good judgment about when, toward whom, for how long, and in what way to own his intellectual limitations and mistakes, and he

---

* This book alternates the use of gendered pronouns to be inclusive of all its readers.

must act in accordance with this judgment (midpoint or mean). A similar point holds for all the other intellectual virtues.

NINE KEY VIRTUES

In the previous section, we saw that intellectual virtues share a three-dimensional structure: each virtue has a skill dimension, a motivational dimension, and a judgment dimension. In the present section, we'll examine what is unique about several individual virtues. Specifically, I'll distinguish three main categories of virtues and offer brief profiles of three virtues in each category (for a brief description and slogan for each of these virtues, see appendix A). The result will be a thicker, more fine-grained characterization of intellectual virtues, one that will help us to begin reflecting, in the chapters that follow, on the principles, postures, and practices involved with teaching for intellectual virtues.

The particular categorization and list of virtues put forth here have emerged from my work in virtue epistemology and with teachers at the Intellectual Virtues Academy (IVA) and elsewhere.[14] While this selection is not arbitrary, and while I have found it helpful to other teachers and in my own teaching, there is nothing especially authoritative about it. There are other reasonable ways of grouping intellectual virtues and additional virtues one might wish to focus on in an educational setting.[15]

The first category consists of virtues that are especially important to *initiating the process of learning and getting this process moving in the right direction.* These virtues are curiosity, intellectual autonomy, and intellectual humility.

Curiosity

What motivates students to learn? While there may be as many answers to this question as there are students, we can move toward an answer by returning to a distinction between two types of intellectual motivation. Students are *intrinsically* motivated to learn if they are motivated to learn for its own sake. Students are *extrinsically* motivated if they are motivated to learn for the sake of something other than the learning itself, for example, to achieve a good grade, find a job, or impress their peers.

It can be tempting to think of these two forms of motivation as equally valuable in an academic context—that as long as students are motivated to learn, it doesn't matter whether their motivation is intrinsic or extrinsic. But this isn't right. For one thing, extrinsic motivation can be unreliable. It exists only insofar as extrinsic incentives for learning are on offer. However, these incentives can wax and wane. Intrinsically motivated learners, by contrast, care about and enjoy learning for its own sake. When extrinsic incentives for learning disappear, their motivation persists. Intrinsic motivation to learn is more effective and reliable than extrinsic motivation.

Psychologists Edward Deci and Richard Ryan have been studying intrinsic motivation and its relationship to self-determination for over three decades. One of their more notable findings is that intrinsic and extrinsic motivation are negatively correlated. This observation has important educational implications. It means that the more students are incentivized to learn on the basis of extrinsic rewards, the less likely they will be to develop an intrinsic interest in learning. Extrinsic incentives blind learners to the intrinsic value of learning. Moreover, as Ryan and Deci note, numerous studies have shown not only that "tangible extrinsic rewards undermine motivation for the rewarded activity" but also that "relative to extrinsic motivation, intrinsic motivation leads to better conceptual learning, greater creativity, more cognitive flexibility, and enhanced wellbeing."[16]

These observations underscore the importance of curiosity. Curious people wonder about things. They ask thoughtful and insightful questions. They aren't content with easy or pat answers. They want to know how and why things are the way they are. Moreover, curious learners desire knowledge and understanding at least partly for its own sake (not merely for the sake of something else). Therefore, curiosity involves an element of intrinsic motivation that ignites the learning process and helps sustain it once it is underway.

Often, when we think or speak about curiosity, we have in mind a purely natural intellectual appetite or inclination. Along these lines, Aristotle famously observed that "all humans by nature desire to know."[17] While human beings in general do have an innate desire to learn about the world around them, this natural appetite isn't the same thing as the virtue of curiosity. Rather, we can think of natural curiosity as the psychological soil out of which virtuous curiosity grows.[18] The emergence of the latter is not guaranteed. For natural curiosity to blossom into the virtue of curiosity, it must be nurtured, shaped, and cultivated.

What does this nurturing look like? In part it's a matter of learning to ask questions that are thoughtful and insightful. Virtuously curious thinkers ask questions that are well formulated and well timed. They also know when to stop asking questions. By contrast, someone whose curiosity is purely natural or untutored might ask questions in ways that are clumsy, haphazard, or relentless.[19]

Curiosity is sometimes referred to as the *fundamental* or *foundational* intellectual virtue.[20] For those of us who teach, this will come as no surprise. When our students are curious about what we are teaching, it is easy to get them engaged and they are quick to grasp key points, make important connections, and avoid careless mistakes.

Given the fundamental role of curiosity in learning, it can be tempting to think that if a person has the virtue of curiosity, she'll be set as a thinker or learner. Alas, this is not the case. While curiosity can facilitate the practice of other virtues, its scope is limited. It is primarily about wondering and asking questions. Other virtues are required for discovering answers to these questions.[21]

Autonomy

One such virtue is intellectual autonomy. Intellectually autonomous people think for themselves. They form their own judgments and draw their own conclusions. They aren't overly reliant on the assistance of others. Nor are they overly influenced by what other people think or say.

Sometimes learning happens passively: a teacher dispenses information, and the students absorb it. More often, however, it has an active dimension, especially the kind of rigorous or deep learning we desire for our students. This kind of learning isn't something that "happens to" a person. It must be *chosen*. It requires owning one's intellectual abilities and using these abilities in the pursuit of epistemic ends. It requires intellectual autonomy.

Intellectual autonomy is the opposite of intellectual *heteronomy*.[22] Heteronomous thinkers are those whose judgments and ways of seeing the world are dictated by other people and sources. They are incapable of thinking for themselves. What they believe or pay attention to, and the conclusions they draw, tend to vary from situation to situation. Importantly, this isn't because heteronomous thinkers are constantly encountering new evidence and trying to update their beliefs. Rather, these individuals lack a sufficient command of their cognitive powers.

Intellectual heteronomy is closely related to what Richard Paul and Linda Elder describe as "intellectual conformity." They observe: "Thinking for oneself almost certainly leads to unpopular conclusions not sanctioned by dominant groups. There are always many rewards for those who simply conform in thought and action to social pressure." As a result, many people become intellectual conformists: "They are like mirrors reflecting the belief systems and values of those who surround them. They lack the intellectual skills and incentive to think for themselves." They lack intellectual autonomy.[23]

Intellectual autonomy bears a resemblance to the kind of freedom that John Dewey attributed to a "disciplined mind." He observes that mental discipline "represents original native endowment turned, through gradual exercise, into effective power."[24] According to Dewey, when "discipline is conceived in intellectual terms (as the habitual power of effective mental attack), it is identified with freedom in its truest sense. For freedom of mind means mental power capable of independent exercise, emancipated from the leading strings of others, not mere unhindered external operation."[25] Autonomous thinkers are not wholly free of input from outside sources. They do, however, independently build on and extend their natural gifts and the support they've received from others.

With most of the written exams I give to my students, I explain that their answers must distinguish them from a (mostly) imaginary figure I refer to as the "mere regurgitator." The mere regurgitator is highly proficient at memorizing what has been said in class or has appeared on handouts or PowerPoint slides. This student can reliably repeat this information in its original form. However, mere regurgitators do not have a firm personal command or understanding of the material. They can't explain it in their own words or use their own examples. In requiring my students to distinguish themselves from the mere regurgitator, I am inviting them to practice autonomy and related virtues like thoroughness and tenacity.

Humility

Imagine a student who is virtuously curious and intellectually autonomous. He wonders and asks good questions about topics of importance. He owns his intellectual strengths and can think and reason for himself. While this student is well on his way to becoming an excellent thinker and learner, he might still be vulnerable. In particular, he might be insufficiently aware of his intellectual limitations and mistakes. Consequently, he might be disposed to bite off more than he can chew. Or he might be unaware of his need to rely on others in the learning process.

To put the point another way, a person can be curious and intellectually autonomous without being intellectually humble. While autonomy involves owning one's abilities and strengths, humility consists of owning one's *limitations, weaknesses, and mistakes.*[26] Intellectually humble learners are appropriately aware of and attentive to their intellectual limitations. They don't try to conceal these limitations; nor do they respond defensively when their limitations are brought to light. Rather, they are accepting of their limitations and take appropriate responsibility for them. They embody the following sage advice from Maria Montessori: "Everyone makes mistakes. This is one of life's realities, and to admit it is already to have taken a great step forward . . . So it is well to cultivate a friendly feeling towards error, to treat it as a companion inseparable from or lives, as something having a purpose, which it truly has."[27]

An absence of intellectual humility can take various forms. It might take the form of a student who routinely (and mistakenly) considers himself intellectually superior to his peers. It might also look like a person who is so obsessed with "impression management" that she works overtime to hide her intellectual weaknesses from others. Or it could look like a perfectionist who can't admit to himself or others when he has made a mistake. People like this are deficient in intellectual humility, at least to some extent. However, a person can also fail to possess intellectual humility on account of being excessively concerned with his intellectual limitations. As suggested earlier, if this person is always thinking about his limitations, or if he tends to think of himself as more limited than he is, this mindset may impede his capacity for intellectual growth. He may become self-denigrating, hyper-deferential, or intellectually servile. In this way, intellectual humility complements and is complemented by the virtue of intellectual autonomy. Intellectual humility mitigates a tendency that an autonomous thinker might have to go too far in trying to figure things out for herself, whereas intellectual autonomy mitigates an excessively humble tendency toward self-denigration or servility.

Research by Tenelle Porter highlights the beneficial effects of intellectual humility on various learning outcomes. Across multiple studies, Porter and her coinvestigators found that "more intellectually humble students were more motivated to learn and more likely to use effective metacognitive strategies, like quizzing themselves to check their own understanding." They also "ended the year with higher grades in math" and were rated as "more engaged in learning" by their teachers.[28]

We've seen that curiosity, autonomy, and humility are important for getting the learning process started and headed in the right direction. Curiosity supplies an intrinsic motivation to learn. Autonomy amplifies and extends this motivation. Humility helps keep it in check. The virtues in the next category function to *keep the learning process on the right track*. They include attentiveness, intellectual carefulness, and intellectual thoroughness. Like curiosity, the first virtue in this category is in some sense more fundamental than the other two.

Attentiveness

For some students, learning comes easy. Whether the ease is due to natural ability or preexisting knowledge of the subject matter, they acquire new concepts seamlessly. For many students, however, learning requires significant effort and discipline. It requires showing up when it's time to learn. This includes showing up physically, of course, but it also includes showing up mentally or psychologically. It involves being present in body and in mind. For these students, learning requires an exercise of attentiveness.

An attentive learner is one who brings her full self to the learning process. She is "personally present" as she learns. Because attentiveness is primarily an inward state, it should not be confused with the bodily posture of sitting up straight in a desk with eyes laser-focused on the teacher. Many of us have had students who adopt this posture but whose minds are elsewhere. Their true state becomes evident once they're called on to answer a question or contribute to class discussion. These students have an appearance of attentiveness but little more. On the other hand, many of us have also had students whose body language suggests that they aren't paying attention but whose subsequent and impressive contributions or performance demonstrate otherwise.

At IVA, the slogan for the virtue of attentiveness is "Look and Listen." This illustrates the point that attentive people are in possession of their senses, that they are alert, and that their minds are not distracted or elsewhere.

Attentiveness understood in this way bears a notable resemblance to what some psychologists refer to as *mindfulness*. Mindfulness researcher Shinzen Young identifies three skills central to mindfulness: sensory clarity, concentration power, and equanimity.[29] Sensory clarity and concentration power are especially relevant to attentiveness. Again, attentive learners have a firm command of their cognitive powers, including their perceptual abilities and capacity for mental focus and concentration. They also know how to maximize the potential of these powers.[30]

Similarly, psychologist Ellen Langer, whose pioneering research on mindfulness has been especially influential in education, draws a helpful distinction between mindfulness and mindlessness. She describes mindfulness as "a flexible state of mind in which we are actively engaged in the present, noticing new things and sensitive to context." When we are in a state of mindlessness, however, "we act like automatons who have been programmed to act according to the sense our behavior made in the past, rather than the present."[31] This distinction nicely captures much of what is central to the virtue of attentiveness. It also illuminates potential connections between attentiveness and related virtues like open-mindedness and intellectual autonomy.[32]

As suggested earlier in the chapter, we need to distinguish an *absence* of attentiveness from the *vice* of inattentiveness, that is, a willful or voluntary tendency to check out or be mentally absent from the learning process. An absence of attentiveness can be due to various sources or causes, some of which don't reflect negatively on the person's character. Again, where inattentiveness is a manifestation of something like ADHD, acute anxiety, or problems at home, it does not constitute a defect of intellectual character.

It should now be clear why the virtue of attentiveness is important to keeping the learning process on track. Again, this virtue keeps us present, focused, and alert. It attunes us to the demands of learning. In a striking tribute to this virtue, poet Mary Oliver writes: "This is the first, wildest, and wisest thing I know: that the soul exists, and that it is built entirely out of attentiveness."[33]

The other two virtues that help keep the learning process on track are a little less exotic or "soulful"; most teachers already value and emphasize them to some extent. Despite their familiarity, their contributions to learning must not be overlooked.

Carefulness

Intellectual carefulness is about trying to get things right. This involves, for starters, trying *not* to get things wrong. Therefore, careful learners tend to avoid the kinds of pitfalls and mistakes to which careless learners are susceptible. For example, in solving a complex equation, it might be tempting to skip a step. Or, when learning about a foreign culture, one could be led to draw premature conclusions about some of its practices. A careful student is alert to such pitfalls and is skilled at avoiding them. Thus, intellectual carefulness involves an awareness of, and a disposition to adhere to, the *rules of accuracy* specific to a given domain, especially when the possibility of violating these rules looms large. In this way, intellectual carefulness bears a resemblance to what Israel Scheffler calls "intellectual conscience," which "monitors and curbs evasions and distortions" and "combats inconsistency, unfairness to the facts, and wishful thinking."[34]

However, intellectual carefulness isn't just about avoiding mistakes. It's also about getting things just right. For example, a careful speaker does what he can to ensure that his words exactly match his intended meaning. And a careful journalist takes pains to make her description of events as complete and accurate as possible. Literally and metaphorically, careful thinkers dot their i's and cross their t's.[35]

As with other intellectual virtues, one can go too far with intellectual carefulness, in which case the virtue of carefulness may morph into the vice of intellectual scrupulosity or perfectionism. In some educational settings, perfectionism rooted in obsessive intellectual carefulness is a chronic problem. It leads to widespread procrastination and can make the experience of demonstrating one's knowledge painful and laborious.

A key difference between the virtue of carefulness and intellectual perfectionism concerns their respective motives. As noted, when possessed in their fullness, intellectual virtues flow from a desire for truth, knowledge, and understanding. Perfectionism, by contrast, tends to be motivated by fear, especially fear of failure. Accordingly, virtuously careful learners are motivated to avoid mistakes because they desire to develop or communicate a precise grasp of the relevant idea, whereas excessively careful learners avoid mistakes out of a fear of imperfection or failure.

Finally, the possibility of excessive carefulness further illustrates the point that individual virtues must be buttressed and complemented by other virtues. One virtue that complements intellectual carefulness is intellectual courage. Courageous thinkers are skilled at managing and overcoming fears in a learning context, including a fear of failure or imperfection. Intellectual humility can play a similar role by making us more accepting of our intellectual imperfections and mistakes. In the words of Fyodor Dostoevsky's Prince Mishkin, "We can't understand everything at once, we can't begin directly from perfection! In order to achieve perfection, we must first of all fail to understand a great many things! And if we understand too quickly, we may not understand very well."[36]

Thoroughness

Intellectual carefulness is also balanced by intellectual thoroughness. Intellectual thoroughness goes deep. Like curiosity, it is unsatisfied with easy or superficial answers. Thorough thinkers probe for understanding. They make connections between seemingly disparate ideas. They seek explanations for what they don't know and are capable of explaining what they do know.

As described earlier, "mere regurgitators" are deficient in intellectual autonomy: they can't think for themselves; all they can do is parrot back what they have heard from other sources. Mere regurgitators are also deficient in intellectual thoroughness. While their thinking may be accurate as far as it goes, it tends to be superficial, formulaic, and unoriginal. Mere regurgitators lack a firm grasp of the material being discussed and cannot provide cogent explanations of what they know.

I noted that intellectual thoroughness complements and balances intellectual carefulness. How exactly is this so? When talking with students or teachers about carefulness and thoroughness, I am frequently asked how the two virtues differ from one another. In response, I often distinguish between two types of answers that students regularly give on essay exams. The first type contains an accurate description of the relevant concepts, but the description is thin and merely skims the surface. When reading answers of this sort, I often find myself wondering: Does the student really *understand* what he or she is discussing? Or is this person simply restating things that were said in class? The second type of answer is the mirror opposite of the first. Here students demonstrate a firm personal grasp of the material: they explain the relevant concepts or arguments in their own words and in multiple ways, apply this knowledge to new problems and questions, and illustrate points with examples of their own. However, their answers also manifest a certain carelessness. Perhaps in haste to demonstrate their understanding, the students end up missing a critical step of an argument, neglecting a key detail, or omitting or misspelling several words.

In giving answers of the first kind, students manifest carefulness but not thoroughness. Their answers are accurate and precise, but they don't inspire confidence that the students actually understand what they are talking about. Answers of the second type manifest thoroughness but not carefulness. They indicate a genuine explanatory understanding of the material. Yet they also contain multiple careless mistakes or inaccuracies. While these mistakes aren't significant or frequent enough to call into question the student's thoroughness, they do betray a lack of carefulness.

These examples show that thoroughness and carefulness are distinct virtues. Thoroughness complements carefulness by resisting a kind of superficiality or conservativism to which careful thinkers can be drawn. In an effort to avoid making mistakes, they might say as little as possible. They might play it safe. Thoroughness, however, demands going deeper, probing for or demonstrating a genuine understanding. While going deeper can introduce the possibility of error, it remains critical to intellectual achievement and growth.

At several points, I have noted that intellectual virtues arise from a concern with *acquiring* knowledge, understanding, and related epistemic goods. While this is generally correct, it is not the whole story. As we have seen in connection with carefulness and thoroughness, intellectual virtues can also be manifested in how a person *expresses* or *communicates* knowledge. Again, a student might seek knowledge of a given topic in ways that are careful and thorough; however, when it comes to communicating this knowledge (on an exam, say), the student's explanation of the topic might be careless or superficial. Thus carefulness and thoroughness are needed both in the acquisition and the communication of epistemic goods.

So far we've examined three virtues that help initiate the learning process and get it headed in the right direction (by supplying a motivation to learn, an ability to think for oneself, and a proper awareness of one's intellectual limitations) and three virtues that help keep this process on track (by ensuring that one is mentally present and striving for accuracy and depth). The last set of virtues is a somewhat different from the first two sets. Instead of mapping onto a particular stage of inquiry, these virtues are important for overcoming familiar obstacles that arise during the learning process.

Open-Mindedness

One such obstacle is narrow-minded, rigid, or inside-the-box thinking. This kind of thinking can come about in different ways. It might arise in response to a subject matter that is especially difficult, complex, or foreign to ordinary ways of thinking, as in a high-level math or science course. Or the person in question might be stubborn and reluctant to admit that other ways of thinking are more reliable than her own. Or perhaps a perspective the person is ignoring threatens to undermine one of her cherished beliefs.

Open-minded people are willing and able to bracket their usual ways of thinking about something to give a fair and honest hearing to an alternative point of view. Their thinking is supple, not inflexible. They aren't uptight or fearful about expanding their horizons. On the contrary, open-minded thinkers welcome opportunities to do so. As noted earlier, one of the skills central to open-mindedness is perspective-switching. Open-minded learners can move competently and with relative ease from one way of thinking about an issue to another. Their thinking doesn't get stuck in ruts.[37]

In discussions of open-mindedness, we sometimes encounter statements like "Don't be so open-minded that your brains fall out." Understood as arguments against open-mindedness, these criticisms fall flat. However, they do illustrate the need to distinguish between the virtue of open-mindedness, on the one hand, and intellectual weakness or wishy-washiness, on the other. Open-minded people don't switch perspectives for its own sake or because they are unconcerned with truth. On the contrary, they believe that switching perspectives will help them develop a more accurate and informed view of the world, a view that is neither arrogant nor prejudiced.[38]

Contrary to what some critics of open-mindedness seem to think, a person can have a firm conviction about something while still being open-minded about it. As long as the person is open to being mistaken and willing to consider new evidence as it arises, she can be confident and open-minded at the same time. As William Hare, a philosopher of education who has written extensively about open-mindedness, observes, "A willingness to reconsider one's principles should genuine difficulties arise . . . does not diminish the seriousness with which our present principles are now regarded, nor does it mean that contrary principles are regarded as equally acceptable."[39]

The compatibility of open-mindedness with firm conviction underscores an important connection between open-mindedness and another key virtue, namely, intellectual humility. Intellectual humility puts us in touch with our cognitive limitations, including the limitations of our personal, political, and cultural perspectives. It acquaints us with our fallibility as believers. In this way, it often leads to or facilitates applications of open-mindedness.[40]

In his book *Virtuous Minds*, Philip Dow recounts a story about Abraham Lincoln that illustrates the interplay of open-mindedness and intellectual humility. At a critical point during the Civil War, Edwin Stanton, Lincoln's secretary of war and a frequent critic of the president, refused to carry out a direct order from the president. Instead of reacting angrily or defensively to Stanton's insubordination, Lincoln is said to have replied, "If Stanton said I was a . . . fool then I must be one. For he is nearly always right, and generally says what he means. I will step over and see him."[41] As the story goes, Lincoln met with Stanton, listened to his misgivings, agreed with them, and withdrew the order. In this situation, Lincoln's intellectual humility empowered him to recognize the limitations of his own thinking and knowledge. This in turn led him to give an open-minded hearing to an opposing but more accurate point of view.

Courage

As suggested at various points, fear is another formidable obstacle to learning. Fear is ubiquitous in many classrooms: fear of struggling, fear of failure, fear of speaking up, fear of having one's ignorance or lack of ability exposed, fear of looking foolish in front of one's peers, and so on.

The consequences of fear in a learning environment can be severe. Fear keeps students on the sidelines, disengaged. It makes for an untold number of missed opportunities, which compound over time, exponentially widening ignorance and solidifying inability. It also fuels passivity, the death knell of deep learning. Fear can be a formidable impediment to intellectual growth and maturity.

Dewey makes a similar point in connection with his notion of reflective thinking. He says that reflective thinking is "always more or less troublesome because it involves overcoming the inertia that inclines one to accept suggestions at their face value; it involves willingness to endure a condition of mental unrest and disturbance." According to Dewey, this often involves suspending judgment rather than jumping to a conclusion, which "is likely to be somewhat painful."[42] The terrain of reflective thinking can be a painful and fearful one.

The ubiquity of fear in the context of thinking and learning points to the pervasive importance of intellectual courage. This virtue does not entail an absence of fear; it does not imply fearlessness. Rather, intellectual courage involves an ability to manage and regulate fear, to prevent fear from driving one's intellectual activity. Thus, while an intellectually courageous student might feel fearful about speaking up in class or volunteering to do a problem on the board, the student will not allow this fear to dictate behavior. Judging that there is a better chance of learning something new if fear is kept in check, the student will proceed to take an intellectual risk.

Note also that an absence of intellectually virtuous activity does not entail the existence of an intellectual vice. Many students who struggle with anxiety, for instance, are paralyzed by fear in a classroom setting. Although this fear may impede their intellectual growth, these students are not intellectual cowards. Given the source and nature of their fear, their reluctance to act courageously does not reflect poorly on who they are as persons. It does not reveal anything negative about their intellectual character.

Intellectual courage is one of several virtues whose operation is enhanced by the possession of a *growth mindset*. Learners with a growth mindset believe that intellectual progress and improvement are possible—that their current abilities are not fixed or immutable. Consequently, they can experience intellectual challenges and even failures as an opportunity to learn, improve, and grow. When they struggle or fail, they think about what went wrong and how they can improve next time. Carol Dweck, who pioneered research on this topic, explains that learners with a growth mindset "value effort; they realize that even geniuses have to work hard to develop their abilities and make their contributions." They are also "more likely to respond to initial obstacles by remaining involved, trying new strategies, and using all the resources at their disposal for learning."[43]

A growth mindset is critical to the practice of intellectual courage. We need intellectual courage when fear threatens to interfere with our efforts to learn or to believe what is true. It supplies the inner strength necessary for facing our fears so that we may continue to learn and grow. If, when confronted with a fearful or risky learning opportunity, we fixate on how the occasion might expose our ignorance or inability, then we will struggle to practice intellectual courage. However, if we are convinced that intellectual challenges and even failure can be an opportunity to improve and develop as thinkers and learners, then when it comes to these risky or fearful situations, our mindset will help lower the perceived stakes and bolster our confidence. It will put intellectual courage within our reach.

Tenacity

A third familiar obstacle to deep learning is a desire or temptation to quit when the going gets tough. Deep and meaningful learning is demanding. Although some information can be passively absorbed or received, this is rarely the case with deep understanding or cognitive mastery. These epistemic goods must be pursued and fought for.

Our readiness for this fight depends not necessarily on whether we feel tempted to give up but rather on how firm a grip this temptation has on us or our behavior. If, when the going gets tough, we are quick to surrender or to revise our cognitive aspirations downward, this reaction will hamper our intellectual maturity, especially if we do so repeatedly or over significant periods of time. To achieve epistemic goods like deep understanding, we must keep our eyes on the prize, resisting the temptation to quit.

In other words, we must practice intellectual tenacity. Tenacious learners embrace intellectual challenges and struggles. They don't back down when the going gets tough. They fight through the difficulty. And they emerge smarter and tougher.

Intellectual tenacity is not mindless. When tenacious learners fail, they don't simply try again, using the same strategy as before. Students who repeatedly retake an exam or rewrite a paper but do little to adjust their approach from one attempt to another aren't manifesting the virtue of tenacity. The persistence of tenacious learners is intelligent. When they find themselves struggling, or when they experience failure, they reflect on these challenges and recalibrate their efforts accordingly. In rare cases, tenacious learners may even give up or cease what they are doing. As grit expert Angela Duckworth notes, "It isn't hard to think of situations in which giving up is the best course of action. You may recall times you stuck with an idea, sport, job, or romantic partner longer than you should have." She adds, "In my own experience, giving up on piano when it became clear I had neither interest in it nor obvious talent was a great decision."[44] Thus when tenacious learners struggle, they tend to ask themselves questions like: Why am I struggling? Had I prepared differently, would I be struggling in the same way? How important is the activity I'm struggling with? What does my experience of struggle have to teach me? How might I approach this activity differently next time?

As suggested earlier, intellectual tenacity bears a notable resemblance to Duckworth's notion of grit, which she defines as "passion and perseverance for long-term goals."[45] Perhaps unsurprisingly, grit has been shown to have powerful educational benefits. For instance, in an influential series of studies by Duckworth and coinvestigators, grittier learners were found to achieve higher levels of education compared with their less gritty peers. They also earned higher GPAs, despite scoring lower on the SAT.[46]

When applied to a learning context, the two primary ingredients of grit—perseverance and passion—map nicely onto two key elements of intellectual tenacity, understood as an intellectual virtue. Again, tenacious learners persevere in the face of obstacles; they're quick to keep trying and slow to give up. Moreover, they persevere at least partly out of an intrinsic interest in or passion for what they're learning. They aren't motivated strictly by grades or status or any other extrinsic reward. One difference between grit and intellectual tenacity is that grit, by definition, is geared toward long-term goals. This extended focus needn't be true of intellectual tenacity, which can be deployed in the service of short- or long-term goals.

Again, a lack of grit or intellectual tenacity doesn't always imply the presence of intellectual laziness or other vices. Research has shown that many students lack grit for reasons that have little or nothing to do with their intellectual character.[47] For similar reasons, it is unhelpful (or worse) for teachers to try to encourage their students in the direction of grit by telling them to "be gritty" or to "be tenacious." Again, for many students, grit and tenacity aren't the kind of thing that can be willed on demand.[48]

Intellectual tenacity bears an important resemblance to intellectual courage in three ways. First, tenacity and courage both involve a kind of persistence or movement forward in the face of resistance. With tenacity, the resistance consists of a desire or an inclination to give up. With courage, it consists of fear or a perception of danger.[49] Second, both virtues are enhanced by a growth mindset. Similar to courageous learners, when tenacious thinkers encounter a topic or concept that is difficult or demanding, they don't immediately deem themselves incompetent and throw in the towel. Rather, believing in their ability to learn from challenging experiences and to use this knowledge for their own intellectual growth, they persist in their efforts to understand. As Duckworth observes, every student is bound to experience challenges and setbacks: "With a fixed mindset, you're likely to interpret these setbacks as evidence that, after all, you don't 'have the right stuff'—you're not good enough. With a growth mindset, you believe you can learn and do better."[50] Third, both tenacity and courage can be critical to the practice of almost any other intellectual virtue. Depending on the situation, the practice of any virtue can be challenging or risky so that it demands an exercise of tenacity or courage.[51]

CONCLUSION

A great deal of ground has been covered in this chapter. We've considered the nature of intellectual virtues and vices, looked closely at the structure of intellectual virtues, and examined the profiles of nine individual virtues.

Hopefully, you will allow the language and concepts of intellectual virtue to sink in and begin to inform how you perceive and experience the landscape of teaching. In keeping with Aristotle's point, I hope this chapter will also help you clarify your target as a teacher. In particular, I hope it gives you a livelier and more concrete sense of what it might look like for your students to mature as thinkers and learners.

CHAPTER 3

Principles

> Let it not be implied that educators know all of the answers
> to the problems which arise in the field. But it can safely be
> asserted that they are aware of certain essential perspectives and
> appreciations which successful teachers must possess in order
> to instill them in youth.
>
> —G. D. McGrath, "The Status and Importance of
> Principles of Education in Teacher Education"

Most of us want more for our students than we feel equipped to provide. We are trained to impart skills and knowledge. While doing so is an indispensable part of good teaching, we remain uncomfortably aware that education at its best does much more than transmit knowledge and skills—that it is profoundly reorienting and revitalizing. Most of us sincerely desire that our students would experience this "something more" that education has to offer. Yet we often lack a good grasp of what this intangible something is, let alone how to make it a reality.

This book is aimed at addressing this challenge. Part of the challenge is imaginative: it's a matter of finding the thoughts and words that will allow us to give expression to the deeper and more personal dimensions of teaching and learning. The introduction and chapters 1 and 2 were aimed at addressing this part of the challenge. I've argued that the language and concepts of intellectual virtue capture a significant part of what many of us have in mind when, in a reflective moment, we imagine having the kind of impact on our students that our own best teachers had on us. The idea, again, is that we desire to nurture in our students the deep personal qualities of good thinkers and learners—qualities like curiosity, open-mindedness, intellectual courage, and intellectual humility.

With this vision in place, a further question presents itself: How do we teach for these qualities? What steps can we take to align who we are and what we do with this worthwhile educational goal? Most of the remainder of the book is devoted to answering this question.

It can be tempting to think that a response to the question should begin with a description of pedagogical practices. Although we will explore several such practices in chapters 5 through 9, such a discussion would be premature at this point. That's because, as we saw in the introduction, teaching for intellectual virtues isn't strictly a matter of what we do in the classroom; it's also a matter of what we *believe* and how we are *oriented*. These additional factors include the pedagogical principles we subscribe to and the postures or attitudes we adopt toward ourselves and our students. In this chapter, we will examine ten principles central to teaching for intellectual virtues. In the chapter that follows, we will turn to several pedagogical postures that reflect and embody these principles.

WHY PRINCIPLES?

Why should we reflect on principles in this context? First, the principles we'll be exploring describe several general features of teaching for intellectual virtues. For this reason, they are a helpful segue to the more specific and concrete features explored in later chapters. Second, our actions generally are governed by the principles we accept, even if we're unaware of having accepted them. Therefore, if we're committed to having an impact on the intellectual character of our students, we need to accept and internalize pedagogical principles that will facilitate rather than impede this aim.

Third, teaching for intellectual virtues is not an exact science. There's no rulebook or decision procedure for determining what we should do or say in every situation. Consequently, when teaching for intellectual virtues, we need to have principles to turn to and reflect on for guidance.

Like the ideal sketched in chapter 1, the ten principles discussed in the following sections may initially strike you as attractive in theory but unrealistic in practice. Here again I invite you to keep your skepticism at bay, at least for now. Faithful adherence to these principles is not an all-or-nothing affair. It can be achieved more or less, and in ways that honor your particular context and limitations, even if these are far from ideal.

1. Process Versus Product

Teaching for intellectual virtues is a goal-oriented endeavor. It's about accompanying and supporting our students on their journey to becoming thinkers and learners whose mental lives are characterized by qualities like curiosity, open-mindedness, humility, and courage.

Some goals can be achieved through a variety of pathways. The goal of helping our students grow in intellectual virtues does not enjoy this level of flexibility. On the contrary, the precise way this goal is pursued determines whether it will be attained. To return to Plato's cave allegory, in teaching for intellectual virtues, we aim to facilitate in our students a kind of personal reorientation, a reconfiguring of some of their fundamental beliefs, attitudes, and feelings about thinking and learning. This is an extremely delicate and complex process that must be handled with great thoughtfulness, intelligence, and care.

It is also a process that takes time. Despite what we might wish or naively hope for, character formation doesn't happen in a day or week or month. Sometimes it takes years. Those of us who are seeking to nurture the intellectual character of our students must adopt the long view. We must be prepared to engage in thoughtful and patient planting, watering, fertilizing, and tending.

2. Active Versus Passive

The kind of learning that facilitates deep understanding and genuine cognitive mastery is active rather than passive. It involves the agency or volitional capacity of the learner.[1] This is no less true of the kind of learning that arises from, and demands, an exercise of intellectual virtues. Therefore, when teaching for intellectual virtues, we must ensure that our students are actively engaged with the subject matter.

Student engagement is especially important when it comes to helping our students develop the skills characteristic of intellectual virtues. As we saw in chapter 2, part of possessing an intellectual virtue is having one or more skills specific to that virtue. To be open-minded, one must be skilled at switching perspectives; to possess intellectual carefulness, one must be competent at noticing and avoiding potential errors; to be intellectually autonomous, one must be able to reason and form beliefs for oneself. And so on.

How are these skills acquired? Minimally, they must be practiced. Again, as Aristotle notes in connection with ethical virtues, "We become builders by building, and lyre-players by playing the lyre. So too we become just by doing just actions, temperate by temperate actions, and courageous by courageous actions."[2] Accordingly, if we're committed to helping our students cultivate the skills characteristic of intellectual virtues, we'll need to provide them with frequent and well-supported opportunities to practice these skills (see chapter 8). If we do so, their approach to learning will be deeply and consistently active.

Bertrand Russell observed, "Wherever it is possible, let the student be active rather than passive. This is one of the secrets of making education a happiness rather than a torment."[3] Similarly, Maria Montessori highlighted imagination's ability to push cognition past perception: "The work of the mind in this quest must necessarily be *active*."[4] The idea that students should be actively engaged in the learning process isn't novel. Yet it cuts against the way that many educators, especially those of us who teach older students, have been trained to teach. For many of us, our default pedagogical mode is lecturing. While lecturing does not necessarily prohibit active intellectual engagement, this mode of teaching can make it easier for our students to occupy a merely passive role.[5]

To get a sense of whether our students are actively engaged by our teaching, we might ask ourselves questions like the following: (1) When I think about an average (not an especially good or bad) class period, what percentage of the time are most of my students actively thinking, wondering, reasoning, observing, discussing, or otherwise actively engaged? What percentage of the time are they just sitting back and (hopefully) listening? (2) When have I seen my students practice virtues like curiosity, autonomy, open-mindedness, tenacity, or courage? What was the effect of this practice on the students in question or on the class as a whole? How did my own actions as a teacher contribute to this activity? (3) What's the greatest obstacle I face to teaching in ways that might elicit active engagement from my students?

3. Depth Versus Breadth

If we seek to have a favorable impact on the intellectual character of our students, there is no escaping a concern with depth—depth of learning, depth of thought, depth of understanding. The idea that teaching for intellectual virtues would go hand in hand with teaching for deep understanding is probably no surprise. But what exactly is the connection? Why should my interest in helping my students grow in intellectual virtues also lead me to help them develop a deep understanding of the material we're exploring?[6]

The answer goes back to a point made in chapter 2 about the motivational basis of intellectual virtues. Recall that these qualities aim at a deep understanding of worthwhile subjects or topics. Intellectually virtuous people care about, desire, and are motivated to pursue a deep understanding of these subjects. Put another way, such people think outside the box, admit their mistakes, pay close attention, and embrace intellectual struggle because they want to understand and master what they are learning. It would be more than a little odd, then, if we were to teach for intellectual virtues without teaching for deep understanding.

Moreover, because some virtues are particularly concerned with depth, teaching for these virtues demands placing a premium on deep and rigorous intellectual engagement. Intellectual thoroughness, for instance, is precisely a matter of probing for deep understanding by doing things like making connections, seeking or offering explanations, and applying one's knowledge to new contexts and problems. Therefore, if I seek to nurture intellectual thoroughness in my students, I'll need to provide them with frequent opportunities to engage in these activities, which will demand a concern with deep learning and understanding.

In chapter 7, we will look more closely at what's involved with teaching for deep understanding.[7] But note that the value of depth can conflict with the value of breadth. While we can and should seek to teach for both breadth *and* depth, the reality is that our time with students is limited, and occasionally we'll need to prioritize helping them develop a deep understanding of an issue over covering a wider range of topics. This is not an exceptionless rule. And we can apply it only as circumstances permit. But without a consistent emphasis on deep learning, our students won't have an opportunity to engage in the kind of intellectual activity that contributes to intellectual character development.

4. Messy Versus Tidy

It can be tempting to think of qualities like clarity, organization, and efficiency as the hallmarks of effective instruction. To be sure, these qualities have their place. Compared with instruction that is unclear, disorganized, or unproductive, they are valuable pedagogical attributes. Yet an outsized or imbalanced concern with these attributes can be the enemy of deep learning and active intellectual engagement. Consequently, an overemphasis on clarity, organization, and efficiency can also be antithetical to teaching for intellectual virtues.

Teaching for intellectual virtues requires creating space for and rolling with unexpected learning opportunities: momentary insights, spontaneous questions, and unanticipated challenges. It also involves providing our students with opportunities to wonder and puzzle—even to be confused or to struggle to make sense of what they're learning. Therefore, it requires a certain amount of messiness. Unpredictability, spontaneity, paradox, and ambiguity come with the territory.

An approach to teaching that places an overriding emphasis on clarity, organization, and efficiency is at odds with these activities and experiences. It leaves little room for things to go wrong or for unexpected questions or challenges to arise. It resists ambiguity and paradox. As a result, it also runs the risk of relegating students to a largely passive and thoughtless role, a role in which they need only sit back and absorb neatly packaged content. As Ron Ritchhart observes, "When something is labeled, decided, listed, or given in an absolute fashion, one's mind often takes it in without questioning. In contrast, when even a small amount of ambiguity is introduced, allowing for the possibility of interpretation and change based on context and conditions, the mind is more likely to remain open."[8] Curiosity researcher Susan Engel makes a similar point: "Instead of presenting children with material that has been made as straightforward and digested as possible, teachers should make sure their students encounter objects, texts, environments, and ideas that will draw them in and pique their curiosity."[9]

The messiness involved with teaching for intellectual virtues shouldn't be confused with, or be used to justify, disorganization or laziness. Teaching for intellectual virtues isn't easier or less demanding than a tidier approach. On the contrary, it requires that we as teachers be alert, perceptive, adaptable, and flexible. It also requires intentionally engineering opportunities for our students to think freely, ask challenging questions, and wrestle with ambiguity.

5. Relational Versus Transactional

It can also be tempting to think of our work with students in transactional terms: my job, as the teacher, is to impart knowledge and skills to my students; their job, as students, is to demonstrate that they have mastered said knowledge and skills. When they do their job, they get credit for taking my course; when I do my job, I get a paycheck.

This is a pretty dismal and uninspiring way of thinking about teaching. For my part, I never would have become a teacher had this been my view of the craft. Among other things, the paychecks simply aren't large enough.

According to a less dismal picture, education is fundamentally relational rather than transactional. It occurs, in its best and fullest forms, in the context of respectful and caring relationships, including those between teachers and their students. To use Parker Palmer's insightful phrase, deep and impactful learning occurs when we "know as we are known," that is, when we have the privilege of learning with and from someone who sees and cares for us.[10]

Some educators are likely to bristle at this picture. They'll contend that it mistakenly casts them in the role of friend, parent, or therapist. And this role, they'll object, is at odds with the idea that education is an *academic* enterprise, one that is aimed primarily at equipping students with knowledge and intellectual skills. Alternatively, these educators may claim, with somewhat greater plausibility, that a relational approach places too great a burden on teachers, most of whom are already overworked and underpaid. Given everything else that teachers today are saddled with, isn't it too much to ask them also to forge caring and trusting relationships with their students?

The suggestion that education is primarily an academic venture and therefore not a fundamentally relational one is a false dichotomy.[11] As a rule, we learn better and more willingly from people we like, know, and respect. In trusting relationships, we're far more likely to come out from under our shells, to show up with a fullness of heart and mind. We're also more likely to admit what we don't know and to consider perspectives very different from our own.[12] Therefore, the foundation of a trusting and supportive relationship can facilitate the practice of virtues like attentiveness, intellectual humility, intellectual courage, and open-mindedness, all of which are conducive to deeper learning and intellectual growth.[13]

This point about the relational dimension of teaching does little, however, to allay the concern that teachers today simply don't have the time, let alone the energy, to develop close connections with their students. These limitations are real and need to be respected. When it comes to the relational aspects of teaching, we can only do what we can do. Nevertheless, as with most other aspects of teaching for intellectual virtues, establishing a caring and trusting relationship with our students is not an all-or-nothing achievement. If I teach several classes with forty or fifty students in each class, there's little chance that I'll be able to cultivate a meaningful relationship with most of them. But this reality needn't prevent me from making a connection with some of my students, and it certainly needn't prevent me from intentionally cultivating a classroom ethos marked by mutual respect, care, and concern.

Furthermore, showing appropriate care and concern for our students doesn't need to be something that happens over and above our teaching of academic content. In their comprehensive study of American high schools, Jal Mehta and Sarah Fine found that teachers who were most effective at fostering deep learning "cared about their students *through* their disciplines or subjects. In other words, in contrast to the role of parents, as teachers they expressed love for their students by showing them the corner of the world that inspired them."[14] Thus we might do well to consider these questions: Within the practical limits I face as a teacher, what can I do to make my classroom feel less transactional and more relational? How can I help my students feel seen and cared for by me and by one another?

6. Bottom-Up Versus Top-Down

There is no one-size-fits-all way of teaching for intellectual virtues. There are several reasons for this. One is that, at its best, teaching for intellectual virtues involves significant student buy-in. Such buy-in is more likely to occur when students see value in deep and active intellectual engagement and when they desire to become more curious, open-minded, and intellectually courageous. But securing this kind of commitment is no small task. It requires that our efforts as teachers be sensitive to and informed by who our students are—by their particular identities, developmental capacities, and interests. Because these things are likely to vary significantly from one group of students to another, teaching for intellectual virtues must be approached in an organic or bottom-up way.[15]

As we'll see in chapter 5, when we set out to teach for intellectual virtues, it is useful to begin by selecting a list of target virtues that we plan to introduce and focus on with our students. If we adopt a bottom-up approach to this selection process, we will allow the distinctive identities and characteristics of our students to inform which virtues we decide to emphasize, how we describe these virtues, the examples we use, and what we expect in terms of the students' practice of, and growth in, these virtues.

To illustrate, suppose the cultural background of my students favors deference to authority. When thinking about which virtues to focus on with them, I'll want to be careful about prioritizing a virtue like intellectual autonomy, which involves thinking for oneself and forming one's own opinions. Minimally, I'll want to make clear to my students that intellectual autonomy doesn't require thinking for oneself about *everything*—that this virtue is quite compatible with and even complements virtues like intellectual humility. I'll also want to allow their cultural backgrounds to guide my understanding of how they might practice this virtue or how much progress I expect them to demonstrate over a short period. Alternatively, if several of my students come from racial or socioeconomic groups that traditionally have been marginalized, I may want to think twice about making intellectual humility one of the main virtues I focus on with them. This isn't to say that intellectual humility has no value for these students. However, all things considered, I may do better to focus on helping them cultivate virtues like intellectual courage, autonomy, or tenacity.[16]

Our efforts also need to reflect the developmental stages and capacities of our students.[17] In particular, developmental considerations should influence our understanding of how our students might practice our target virtues. For instance, suppose I'm a middle school teacher and open-mindedness is one of my target virtues. It will be important for me to know and remain mindful of the fact that the brain development of younger adolescents—especially adolescent boys—is such that the kind of perspective-switching characteristic of open-mindedness may not come naturally to them.[18] Therefore, the way open-mindedness is likely to appear in my students, or the kind of progress they're likely to make in this virtue, may be very different compared with students who are considerably younger or older.

In addition to facts about their identities or developmental abilities, it is also appropriate to allow our students' own interests and desires to inform how we teach for intellectual virtues. Which virtues do they want to focus on? How would they propose to define these virtues? Can they formulate a slogan or identify a real-life exemplar for each virtue? Taking seriously our students' answers to these questions is a way of empowering them as learners.[19] It gives them a voice in the process. While this kind of empowerment is worth doing for its own sake, it can also enhance our students' commitment to intellectual character growth.[20]

7. Collaborative Versus Competitive

Competitive classroom environments are not uncommon. For some students, competition appears to work quite well, in the sense that the students are more likely to engage in certain learning activities if they regard these activities as an opportunity to win. However, in the context of teaching for intellectual virtues, competition tends to do more harm than good.

The prospect of winning—be it winning an actual game or achieving higher marks or status than one's peers—is a classic example of extrinsic motivation. When students engage in learning activities for the sake of winning, they are not interested in learning for its own sake. Moreover, as we saw in the previous chapter, extrinsic motivation tends to crowd out and diminishes intrinsic motivation. This is problematic, given the many intellectual benefits of intrinsic motivation, which include "better conceptual learning, greater creativity, more cognitive flexibility, and enhanced wellbeing."[21]

Competitive classroom environments pose other problems as well. In some students, competition breeds an attitude of self-protection. When learning feels competitive, these students tend to keep to themselves, avoid taking intellectual risks, and conceal their ignorance and weaknesses from others. They adopt a stance of invulnerability. In competitive environments, students are also more likely to limit the success of their peers. They are more likely to withhold their knowledge or abilities from others and to interpret each other's contributions in a less-than-charitable light. Even worse, a preoccupation with winning may motivate some students to silence the voices of others and to interact with them in ways that are intellectually arrogant, closed-minded, or hostile.

For these and other reasons, a heavily competitive classroom environment is opposed to teaching for intellectual virtues. As we saw in chapter 2, intellectual virtues are rooted in a love of learning (intrinsic motivation), and their development requires a willingness to freely wonder (curiosity), take intellectual risks (courage), admit ignorance and ask for help (humility), and give thoughtful consideration to opposing viewpoints (open-mindedness). The competitive impulses just described can undermine and discourage precisely this kind of intellectual engagement.

By contrast, in collaborative classroom environments, success and achievement aren't viewed as a zero-sum game. Students work together to advance their own and each other's learning and intellectual growth. They are neither passive nor isolated. Rather, they are thoughtfully engaged, contributing to and sharpening each other's knowledge and skills. Collaborative environments are also marked by an air of generosity and supportiveness. As a consequence, students feel more comfortable being honest about what they don't know and where they need help. Unlike competitive environments, collaborative settings also provide the kind of space and safety in which intrinsic motivation can flourish. In all the ways they differ from competitive environments, collaborative environments are fertile soil for the cultivation of intellectual virtues.

8. Holistic Versus Atomistic

I have noted at various points in the book that intellectual virtues are personal in that they reflect some of our deeper cares and concerns as thinkers and learners. I have also noted that they are multidimensional. Again, to possess an intellectual virtue, we must possess the skills specific to this virtue, be motivated to use these skills, and have good judgment about when and how to use them.

This somewhat complex picture underscores the fact that cultivating intellectual virtues, whether in ourselves or others, is not a simple or quick process. When it comes to nurturing these qualities in our students, there is no silver-bullet strategy—no magical intervention that certifies growth in curiosity, open-mindedness, or any other virtue. Rather, teaching for intellectual virtues is a decidedly holistic undertaking. It involves the implementation of a range of pedagogical practices that complement and reinforce each other (chapters 5 through 9). It also involves the adoption of various pedagogical principles and postures (chapter 4).

This plurality of practices may strike you as overwhelming. Perhaps you're attracted to the idea of helping your students grow in intellectual virtues, but fear that doing so might require a major overhaul of your current approach to teaching. As we will see later, your fear may or may not be justified. However, should we really expect a personally deep and formative approach to teaching to be simple, easy, or undemanding?

Many educators today are rightly skeptical of the latest pedagogical technique or intervention touted as a panacea for education's inumerable woes. Teaching for intellectual virtues isn't about tricks or techniques. Personally, this is part of what attracts me to the approach. I'm encouraged by the fact that teaching for intellectual virtues can't be boiled down to a pithy slogan or mastered in a six-week (let alone a three-day) professional development seminar. Indeed, I suspect that when we are honest with ourselves, most teachers know that any approach to teaching aimed at facilitating deep learning and personal growth must be complex and demanding.

Having, perhaps, exacerbated your concern about the feasibility of teaching for intellectual virtues, I will now say a few things to try to mitigate this concern. First, for the most part, teaching for intellectual virtues is not something we do over and above teaching for academic knowledge and skills. Rather, as we'll explore in later chapters, it is primarily a *way* of teaching knowledge and skills. Second, as we'll see in chapters 5 through 9, many of the practices involved with teaching for intellectual virtues hang together and complement each other. Implementing them feels more like implementing a single comprehensive approach to teaching than it does like a jumble of disparate practices. Third, given that you're taking the time to read this book, your existing beliefs and practices may already be in line with teaching for intellectual virtues, in which case an overhaul would be unnecessary. Finally, any required adjustments to your teaching need not be implemented instantly or all at once. Instead, they can be experimented with and adopted incrementally and over an extended period of time.

9. Growth Versus Fixed Mindset

Practicing intellectual virtues can be costly. Tenacity requires embracing—rather than avoiding—intellectual struggle, courage involves persisting in a belief or an inquiry despite an apparent threat, and humility demands an admission of ignorance. These and other virtues leave us vulnerable to experiences of embarrassment or failure. Sometimes it's easier just to give up, play it safe, or conceal our intellectual limitations.

This aspect of intellectual virtues underscores the importance of a growth mindset. Relative to a learning context, a growth mindset is the belief that the basis of successful learning or intellectual achievement is substantially under our voluntary control.[22] To illustrate, suppose a student finds herself struggling to understand how to correctly divide fractions. In response to this struggle, she might conclude either (1) that she has not yet mastered this operation but that, with appropriate consideration and effort, she'll be able to figure it out or (2) that she wasn't born a "math person" and therefore is doomed to incompetence.

The first response is indicative of a growth mindset because the student sees her capacity for success as substantially under her control, as something she can cultivate, develop, and improve on. The second response expresses a *fixed mindset*, which consists of the belief that success in a given domain is a matter of certain natural and immutable gifts or talents that people either possess or lack. From the standpoint of a fixed mindset, improvement or growth is not a realistic possibility.

Carol Dweck describes the importance of a growth mindset this way: "When students view intelligence as fixed, they tend to value looking smart above all else. They may sacrifice important opportunities to learn—even those that are important to their future academic success—if those opportunities require them to risk performing poorly or admitting deficiencies.

Students with a growth mindset, on the other hand, view challenging work as an opportunity to learn and grow."[23]

Having a growth mindset doesn't require thinking that improvement and success are entirely under our control. Each of us is born with certain natural abilities and limitations, and these inevitably play some role in our achievements, struggles, and failures. A growth mindset does, however, involve believing that through intelligent and persistent effort, we can improve—building up our abilities and strengthening our prospects for success.

In a study of more than eighteen hundred primary and secondary students, Yukun Zhao and colleagues examined the effect of a growth mindset on several learning outcomes. They discovered that students with a growth mindset were "less prone to the external manipulation of others, and gain a better sense of self through motivating themselves by values, meaning, self-identity, and passion." These students were also "more likely to persevere in the face of challenges and less likely to give up pursuing an interest in the face of a variety of temptations."[24]

How do these findings relate to the presumed costliness of practicing virtues like tenacity, courage, and humility? As we saw in chapter 2, if I have a growth mindset, I'll be more likely to view the kind of struggle and risk that go hand in hand with these virtues not as a final judgment about who I am or what I can do but rather as an occasion for learning, recalibrating, and positioning myself for future growth. If I fail at an intellectual task, I might think to myself: "Things didn't go as I wanted them to this time around. I'm disappointed about that. But I also believe that improvement is possible—that success is not wholly beyond my reach. What, then, can I learn from this experience? How can I adjust my thinking or actions so that I stand a better chance of succeeding the next time around?"[25]

These observations have important implications when it comes to teaching for intellectual virtues. First, they illustrate the point that as teachers, we must have a growth mindset concerning our students' intellectual potential. As John Hattie notes, the most effective teachers believe that "achievement is changeable and enhanceable and is never immutable or fixed."[26] Similarly, if we think of intellectual virtues as fixed qualities—qualities that students are either born with or not—there will be little point in adopting postures or practices aimed at helping them make progress in these virtues. Second, these reflections illustrate how important it is for students also to have a growth mindset about their own potential for cultivating qualities like intellectual courage, humility, and tenacity. If they don't believe they can become better thinkers and learners, they'll be much less likely to engage in the kinds of activities that nurture intellectual virtues.

10. Realistic Versus Naive

Writer and blogger Maria Popova remarks, "Critical thinking without hope is cynicism. Hope without critical thinking is naïveté."[27] As the discussion of a growth mindset suggests, teaching for intellectual virtues is a fundamentally hopeful enterprise. It involves aspiring to a rich personal ideal. While aspiring to this ideal is part of the attraction of teaching for intellectual virtues, it can also be a liability. If, for instance, we expect to instantly or radically transform the intellectual character of all of our students, we're bound to be disappointed. Therefore, as Popova's remark suggests, the hope and idealism at the heart of teaching for intellectual virtues must be informed and tempered by critical thinking, which includes a certain kind of realism.

What does this realism look like? To begin with, it involves not being naive or overly optimistic about the immediate impact we're likely to have on our students. Not all of our students will be ready to accept our invitation to deeper intellectual participation, to making the ascent out of Plato's cave. That is to be expected, and it needn't be a source of deep disappointment or frustration. We should also keep in mind that intellectual character growth occurs along different dimensions and that growth along one dimension doesn't guarantee growth along the others. For instance, some students might grow in their ability to think outside the box (open-mindedness) or to manage their intellectual fears (intellectual courage) yet still have only a shaky grasp of when they ought to deploy these skills or a limited desire to do so. In cases like this, we needn't regard ourselves as having failed to influence the intellectual character of these students. Instead, we should remind ourselves that intellectual character development is a delicate and complex process and that sometimes the best we can do is contribute to this process incrementally.[28]

In view of these points, we should also think seriously and concretely about the short-term character-based goals we have for our students, that is, the kind of growth we're hoping to see in the limited time we have with them. Our thinking here should be influenced by the nature of intellectual virtues and intellectual character growth. It should also be influenced by the kind of developmental considerations noted earlier and by factors like the amount of freedom we have over our instructional practices and the kind of support we enjoy from colleagues and administrators. Sensitivity to these matters will help ensure that our character-based goals remain grounded in reality.

CONCLUSION

We've considered ten principles that can be used to guide and inform our efforts at teaching for intellectual virtues. At the heart of each principle is a pair of contrasting elements: (1) process versus product, (2) active versus passive, (3) depth versus breadth, (4) messy versus tidy, (5) relational versus transactional, (6) bottom-up versus top-down, (7) collaborative versus competitive, (8) holistic versus atomistic, (9) growth versus fixed mindset, and (10) realistic versus naive. The principles explored here are a mere starting point. To have a meaningful impact on the intellectual character of our students, we must also allow these principles to inform, among other things, the way we relate to and are oriented toward ourselves and our students. We turn in the next chapter to explore this idea at greater length.

CHAPTER 4

Postures

> Each time I walk into a classroom, I can choose the place within myself from which my teaching will come, just as I can choose the place within my students toward which my teaching will be aimed.
>
> —Parker Palmer, *The Courage to Teach*

In the previous chapter, we examined ten pedagogical principles that together provide an overview of what it looks like to teach for intellectual virtues. In the chapters following this one, we will turn our attention to several complementary practices. These chapters will add considerable flesh and specificity to the principles discussed in chapter 3.

Before turning to the topic of practices, however, we need to spend some time reflecting on a middle ground between pedagogical principles and practices. We can begin to locate this middle ground by recognizing that, as teachers, we can believe many of the right things about teaching, and employ several good pedagogical methods, yet fail to be *with* or *for* our students in ways that reflect and reinforce our pedagogical beliefs and practices. We might be distracted, aloof, bored, or uncaring. Despite having sound principles and methods, we will enjoy limited effectiveness in the classroom at best.

As Parker Palmer notes above, every time we enter the classroom, we are in a position to choose the place within ourselves from which we will encounter and address our students. From which "inner place" do you teach? How do you choose to carry or orient yourself in the classroom? Which self do you bring to your students?

Our answers to these questions are no less important to teaching for intellectual virtues than they are for our pedagogical principles or the methods we employ. I'll use the term *postures* to describe the attitudes or stances we adopt in the classroom, including attitudes toward ourselves and our students. I'll argue that adopting certain postures and avoiding others plays a critical role in our efforts to help shape the intellectual character of our students.

DIFFERENCE BETWEEN POSTURES AND VIRTUES

There is a striking similarity between the postures I'll be discussing and intellectual virtues. How are these things related? Are they one and the same? If not, how do they differ?

To begin, because the essential ingredients of some postures overlap with the essential ingredients of some intellectual virtues, we can sometimes use a single word to pick out either a posture or a virtue. To illustrate, one important pedagogical posture is humility. This posture requires being aware of and willing to admit our limitations as teachers. I can choose to adopt this posture on various occasions. However, this posture may not be sufficient for possessing the actual virtue of humility. The virtue requires that I sufficiently internalize a willingness to admit my limitations—that I develop a thoughtful and well-motivated habit of doing so.[1]

While postures and virtues are similar, there are also some notable differences between the two. First, as the humility example suggests, postures tend to be under our immediate voluntary control. Again, I can choose to strike a posture of humility or openness toward my students or toward their intellectual activity and contributions. I cannot, however, simply choose to possess a virtue. Virtues cannot be acquired on demand. Rather, they are settled psychological dispositions that are integrated into the fabric of our character, and they take time to develop.[2]

Second, the specific postures I'll be discussing have a significant moral or ethical dimension that is not an essential or defining feature of intellectual virtues. As I'll explain later, although teaching for intellectual virtues is aimed at affecting the intellectual character of our students, it demands a holistic orientation toward our students, an attention to their overall well-being, or at least to a very broad range of their needs and capacities. The postures we'll be exploring here are a vehicle for this kind of attention or orientation. As such, they have a broader application compared with intellectual virtues.[3]

This is not to suggest that intellectual virtues are entirely void of ethical content. Indeed, many of them have significant ethical dimensions. Open-mindedness, for instance, bears on how we treat the beliefs and ideas of other people. Moreover, as noted in chapter 1, the quality of our intellectual character can affect the moral quality of our actions. And the moral status of our actions depends in part on the quality of the intellectual activity from which they arise.[4]

Nor do I, in focusing on the importance of pedagogical postures, mean to suggest that we as teachers can be indifferent about whether we possess or practice intellectual virtues. Far from it. Indeed, chapter 9 is devoted entirely to the importance of authentically modeling intellectual virtues for our students, and we can only model these virtues if we possess them at least to some extent. Nevertheless, I have chosen to focus on postures rather than virtues in this chapter because postures are easier to adopt and because of the distinctively moral or ethical role they play in bridging the gap between principles and practices.

CONTROL

I'll begin in negative territory, that is, by reflecting on a posture that is deeply opposed to teaching for intellectual virtues. This is the posture of control. I take this as my starting point for two reasons. First, I suspect this posture is fairly widespread among teachers. Second, some of the postures we'll be exploring later in the chapter can be understood as antidotes to this posture.

A posture of control is marked by a strong felt need to engineer and maintain a tight grip on exactly what is taught and learned in the classroom. When I'm teaching from this posture, I know exactly what I want to say and how I want to say it. I have a very clear picture of the way I'd like my students to behave and what I intend for them to take away from my lesson. I have the relevant content formulated in extremely careful and precise detail. When things don't go as planned, when I take longer than expected to explain a particular point, or when my students have unanticipated questions or need unexpected assistance, I am quick to get frustrated or feel irritated. I immediately begin worrying about how to get my lesson back on track so that I can get caught up before the end of the period, unit, or term.

This approach to teaching is not wholly bad or misguided. As noted in the previous chapter, clarity, organization, and efficiency can be quite useful from a pedagogical standpoint. However, if we wish to take seriously the intellectual character formation of our students, these cannot be our overriding priorities.

It has taken me some time to appreciate the limitations of, and my own susceptibility to, a pedagogical posture of control (indeed, I am still coming to terms with these things). In my training as a philosopher, I was taught to be as clear, precise, and organized in my thinking as possible. Applied to teaching, this approach led me to try to spell things out for my students in the clearest, most straightforward, and comprehensible way possible. Over time, however, and thanks to the guidance of some thoughtful fellow educators, I began to see how, in spelling everything out for my students, I was robbing them of important educational opportunities, including opportunities to wonder, puzzle about, and wrestle with important ideas. Although I have always been committed to encouraging my students to become actively involved in the learning process (e.g., by regularly asking thoughtful questions), the way I was formulating and communicating the material often left them with little room to do anything but sit back and passively absorb the tidy morsels of content I had prepared for their consumption.

In looking back on my outsized preoccupation with clarity and precision, I can now see that it was driven largely by a concern for control. I had a clear picture of exactly what I wanted to say and what I wanted my students to do and learn. While there may be worse pedagogical vices, the result was that my students had relatively few opportunities to practice and cultivate virtues like curiosity, intellectual autonomy, and intellectual courage. On this point, Lola Hill marks a useful distinction between "controlling teachers" and "autonomy-supportive" teachers: "Controlling teachers essentially aim to control learners' goals and behaviors toward teacher-prescribed ends; autonomy-supportive teachers, on the other hand, aim to strengthen all learners' sense of individual agency, helping them to set and pursue their own agendas."[5]

Why Are We Controlling?

Why are we led to teach from a posture of control? What underlies or motivates this stance? Answers to this question are likely to vary from one teacher to the next. I will describe four of what I suspect are among the more prevalent motivations.

First, we sometimes adopt a posture of control in an effort to stave off a chaotic classroom environment. If I fear that giving my students a greater voice or role in what we're learning will immediately draw us into seemingly irrelevant territory, elicit problematic student comments, or open the door to sheer pandemonium, then I'll be motivated to maintain a tight grip on what's being taught and how. While this attitude is understandable, I believe that sometimes we are too eager to make catastrophic forecasts. Indeed, the need for control can itself cause us to exaggerate the potential fallout of loosening our hold on exactly what or how our students learn.

Second, we sometimes desire control out of a concern with impression management, that is, the need to be liked by our students or to avoid letting them see us sweat. This temptation is especially acute for inexperienced teachers, who tend to feel less confident in their abilities and are fearful of appearing incompetent to their students. On the one hand, it's easy to sympathize with the teacher who, in a genuinely chaotic or hostile classroom environment, adopts a controlling posture to avoid being overwhelmed or overrun. Yet here again, our fears about how students will perceive or react to our vulnerability may be significantly exaggerated and as much an expression of our desire for control as they are an adequate justification of it. Moreover, by worrying less about the impression we make, we are modeling qualities that our students are likely to find inviting and compelling. Admitting that we struggle, make mistakes, and don't have it all figured out can have a humanizing effect on how our students experience us. This kind of humility and courage can be contagious.

A third and potentially related motivation is perfectionism. The teaching profession seems to attract its share of perfectionists, people who possess high personal standards and judge themselves harshly when they fall short of these standards. Perfectionism and control go hand in hand, with control being a way for perfectionists to ensure the satisfaction of their high standards. Perfectionist teachers need to have everything just so. They have trouble leaving anything to chance, and they become seriously disappointed and irritated when things don't go as expected.

Fourth, a posture of control can also be rooted in a kind of professional laziness. Though it can be challenging to secure on the front end, once a sense of control has been established, it can make for smooth pedagogical sailing. The rules are clear, the standards are high, and the students are compliant. This path-of-least-resistance approach to teaching frees us from having to deal with unpredictable outcomes, a welcome prospect for teachers interested in putting forth as little effort as possible.

Consequences of Control

We've considered four possible concerns or motivations that might underlie a pedagogical posture of control: averting chaos, impression management, perfectionism, and laziness. Before turning to some antidotes to this posture, it will be useful to examine some of the consequences of control in a little more detail.

To begin with, teaching from a posture of control limits our opportunities to forge meaningful connections with our students. As we've explored in previous chapters, and as most teachers know from experience, the kind of gentle but vital turning, or reorientation, that we desire for our students is more likely to occur if they feel seen and cared for by us. However, if we're preoccupied with trying to follow—or getting our students to follow—a demanding script, or if we're fearful of revealing any of our vulnerabilities, no such connection is likely to be forged. Our students are unlikely to feel known or cared for. Similarly, if laziness compels us to overemphasize order and predictability, there's a good chance that our motives will be transparent to our students and that they'll be unwilling to engage wholeheartedly with us.

A controlling pedagogical posture also precludes genuine conversation. As Socrates famously taught and illustrated, knowledge and understanding emerge from a *dialectical* process, that is, from a free and honest exchange between two or more truth-seekers. The basic idea is straightforward: if you want to reconsider some of my basic intellectual values or habits, your odds of success will depend on how you approach me. You can (1) simply tell me what to think and how to be or (2) engage me in genuine and respectful conversation on the matter. When we as teachers are preoccupied with control, we leave little room for the second kind of exchange. Instead, we inadvertently treat our students as a means to dubious ends, such as maintaining a favorable image, perpetuating our perfectionism, or avoiding the messy and demanding work of transformative teaching.

A posture of control also works against another characteristic of good conversations and meaningful learning, namely, spontaneity. In many cases, we learn best when we can ask questions, go back and forth with an interlocutor, or test our thoughts and conjectures. These activities are an opportunity to practice virtues like curiosity, open-mindedness, intellectual courage, and intellectual tenacity. They also involve an element of spontaneity: we don't always know in advance what will puzzle us, how a conversation will unfold, or what hypotheses or speculations might come to mind. A controlling pedagogical posture leaves little room for this kind of spontaneity. It thrives on predictability and structure and consequently suppresses opportunities for deeper learning.

A posture of control is at odds with other vital intellectual activities as well. One of these is imagination. As a rule, human imagination operates freely. When we set out to imagine something, we don't know where our thinking will end up. There is an open-endedness and unpredictability to imaginative thinking. It cannot be controlled or coerced. Yet few would deny that imaginative thinking is important for intellectual growth. A similar point applies to our capacities for wonder and intellectual exploration. While clearly important to deep learning, these capacities cannot be manufactured or manipulated. They demand a certain latitude. They require us to take a step back and allow our students' intellectual interests and questions to lead the way. As Alfred North Whitehead notes, "The only avenue towards wisdom is by freedom in the presence of knowledge."[6]

While a posture of control may have some short-term benefits, these benefits are outweighed by the propensity of control to suppress relationships, genuine conversation, spontaneity, imagination, wonder, and intellectual exploration. Unsurprisingly, then, this posture is deeply at odds with teaching for intellectual virtues.

PRESENCE

Which pedagogical postures complement or facilitate teaching for intellectual virtues? In the remainder of this chapter, I will discuss three such postures.

The first is what I will refer to as a posture of presence. This posture is about showing up with one's students—not just physically, of course, but mentally and emotionally as well. Presence is about being with them in mind and heart. To be present in this sense is to be *here*, not elsewhere, and to be here *now*, in the present moment.

As humans, we have a remarkable mental ability to transcend our location in space and time. We can, at will, transport our minds to remote physical locations or to distant moments in the past or future. Adopting a posture of presence involves using the same cognitive powers—powers like reason and imagination—not to transcend our present situatedness, but to inhabit it in a deeper way. It's about being fully alive to exactly where we are, at precisely this moment in time.

You've likely heard the saying "Wherever you go, there you are." On the face of it, this sounds silly and trivial. But it's a truth that is surprisingly easy to lose sight of, especially when one is teaching. Teaching is a formidable juggling act. It requires constant multitasking under conditions that are always changing. This continuous shifting can make it especially easy for us to become preoccupied while teaching. It is no small challenge to teach from "where we are."

Challenging as it is, a posture of presence is vital to the approach to teaching explored in this book. As the saying goes, "Life is what happens to you when you're busy making other plans." A similar principle applies to teaching. When I'm distracted by events outside the classroom or when I'm focused primarily on the content I "need" to get through in the next thirty minutes, I'm not fully present with my students. As a consequence, I'm bound to miss opportunities to listen closely to what they're saying, to notice and draw out their latent questions and insights, or to perceive when I've said something that might be confusing or off-putting. Opportunities to encourage deeper learning and engagement will pass me by.

On the positive side, when I am fully present with my students, they tend to take notice. They see that I'm serious about what I'm teaching—that I'm not simply "dialing it in." Just as importantly, they see that I'm here, available, and committed to helping them learn. In this way, my own presence can serve as an invitation for them to be present as well.[7] In a poem titled "What to Remember When Waking," David Whyte writes:

> To be human
> is to become visible
> while carrying
> what is hidden
> as a gift to others.[8]

As teachers, we carry the hidden gifts of learning and understanding. If we can become more present and visible, we will be well positioned to extend these gifts to our students, and they will be more open to receiving them.[9]

The posture of presence involves a kind of authentic self-disclosure. This might lead some teachers to wonder whether it blurs the line between the personal and the professional, or whether it could lead to oversharing or other inappropriate ways of being or communicating with our students. This worry is mostly unfounded. The posture of presence is primarily a way of relating to *oneself*. To be present in the relevant sense, I must locate myself in my body, here and now. I must attend to what I am thinking and feeling, to where my heart and mind reside at precisely this moment. I must allow myself to become fully present to myself. When I do this, fear, anxiety, or other uncomfortable thoughts or emotions may bubble up. If they do, I'll need to exercise wise and mature judgment concerning how, if at all, to give expression to these states. However, nothing about the posture of presence itself necessitates or even encourages inappropriate or otherwise unprofessional forms of expression. Nor do the potential costs of adopting this posture, such as they are, outweigh its considerable benefits.

The idea that we should, in the interest of professionalism, avoid being fully present to ourselves or to our students suggests that teaching and learning are an impersonal and transactional affair wherein the role of the teacher is to dispense information and the role of the student is to absorb it. On this picture, the personal qualities and dispositions of teachers matter very little. A core argument of this book, however, is that teaching and learning are not impersonal or transactional—that at their best they are deeply interpersonal and characterological.

We must figure out for ourselves what exactly it looks like for us to show up and be present with our students. We must also seek to identify practices or exercises that will help us facilitate being present. In the remainder of this section, I briefly discuss two exercises I have found helpful in this regard.

In the hour or so before I begin teaching, and sometimes even as I'm walking to class, I often take a moment to pause and ask myself, In the class period to come, or for my course as a whole, what do I desire most for my students? How do I want our time together to affect them? Typically, my answer is something like, I want to have a favorable impact on my students' *relationship* to learning. I want them to appreciate its value, to increase their appetite for knowledge and understanding, and to enjoy thinking, wondering, contemplating, and reasoning. Surprisingly, this simple exercise tends to have a significant impact on my overall frame of mind. In calling forth some of my deepest aims and hopes for my students, I feel more grounded. I enter the classroom feeling calmer and less rushed—less concerned about what "needs" to get done or the material we "must" get through. It becomes clear to me that if I want to influence my students in the desired way, I must be present with them.

A second example is related to the first. In several freshman-level courses I have taught over the years, I have formulated a course mission statement intended to serve as a reminder of the fundamental purpose of the course. One example is as follows: "We are a community of inquirers tasked with philosophical learning and reflection. My primary aim as your instructor is not to impart to you a body of knowledge. It is rather to nurture your relationship to learning by providing you with well-supported opportunities to practice the virtues of good thinking." At least once a week, I read slowly and thoughtfully through the statement at the beginning of class, often pausing to elaborate on one aspect of it or another. This exercise has a calming, centering effect on my students and on me. It reminds us that what we are up to isn't merely the transmission of knowledge and skills. A greater, more meaningful good is at stake, a good that is distinctively personal. Recognizing this fact has the further effect of opening up space for us to bring our full selves to what we're doing and learning together.

HUMILITY

Another posture important to teaching for intellectual virtues is humility. This posture does not strive or grasp. It does not thirst after or thrive on control. It isn't obsessed with outcomes or results. In the broadest sense, humility is about acceptance. It's about being aware of and okay with who I am and where I am.[10]

How might I as a teacher come to adopt this posture? Depending on the day, I might undertake an honest mental inventory of the specific limitations or deficiencies I'm faced with at that moment: for example, that I'm not as prepared as I was hoping to be, that I feel distracted or anxious, that several of my students seem uninterested in what we're learning, that we're not nearly where I had hoped we'd be at this point in the unit or semester, and so on. Just naming these limitations and deficiencies, and acknowledging them for what they are, can bring me back down to earth, back to the "humus," or ground beneath my feet.

Adopting a posture of humility often requires a healthy dose of self-compassion. For some of us, reflecting on our powerlessness or what we've failed to do or accomplish can elicit feelings of frustration, stress, anxiety, and even shame. These emotions can keep us from planting our feet on solid ground, which is the only place from which we can truly meet and be present with our students. We must, then, learn to be gentle, merciful, and forgiving of our own limitations, weaknesses, and mistakes. These things are part of our reality. They are not an illusion. Here, as in other areas of life, little good comes of ignoring or denying the truth.

This observation about self-compassion points to a connection between humility and presence. Our circumstances and very selves will always be limited and flawed. To be fully present, to bring our whole selves into the classroom, we must be honest with ourselves about these limitations and flaws. Therefore, we cannot adopt a posture of presence if we have not already, at least to some extent, adopted a posture of humility. Humility also plays an important role in *sustaining* a posture of presence. A therapist friend of mine regularly talks about the importance of "staying down," by which he means something like staying close to the ground, resisting the temptation to think too highly of oneself or to seize control of people or circumstances over which one has little or no authority or power. This is no small thing. Humility mitigates and negates the sense of distorted pride that compels us to resist our limitations and to strive for control. In doing so, it allows us to be rooted in the here and now. It helps keep us present.

Thus far, we've been focusing largely on the intrapersonal effects of humility. However, this posture is also important from an interpersonal or relational point of view. In particular, humility has important implications for how we are oriented toward and relate to our students. On the one hand, there is a real sense in which we as teachers are the experts in the room. There's no point in denying that we have knowledge, experience, and skills that our students lack—indeed, that's part of why we're qualified to do what we do. Yet this difference or distance between our students and us can easily cause us to lose sight of the limitations of our knowledge and skills. It can make us overlook the fact that, our relative expertise notwithstanding, we have a great deal to learn from our students, even about the very things we are experts in. Precisely because they haven't received the training we've received, and don't share all our assumptions and conceptualizations, students are often in a good position to notice things, make connections, and ask questions that would not occur to us. If we adopt a posture of humility, we'll be in a better position to recognize these abilities and to teach in ways that elicit student-generated questions and insights.

A posture of humility also has important bearing on those moments when we bump up against the limitations of our own knowledge and abilities. For example, although I've been teaching courses at the college level for more than twenty years, it's still quite common for me to feel like there are things related to what I'm teaching that I should know but don't. Sometimes these gaps appear unexpectedly and while I'm in the act of teaching: a student asks a difficult question I hadn't thought of, or I find myself stuck trying to solve a challenging logic proof or to articulate a difficult philosophical point. In these moments, I have a choice: Do I deflect my students' attention and bluff my way through a response? Or do I admit my ignorance and allow myself to struggle in their midst?

It can be tempting to think of the former as the safer and more prudent route. What good does it do my students for them to see the limits of my knowledge or to watch me struggle? Won't it make them less confident in my qualifications and therefore less likely to trust other things I have to say? Might it lead them to begin challenging my authority? Won't this show of vulnerability leave us all in a worse position, educationally and otherwise?

Perhaps in some cases it may, but in many other cases, it will not. In my own experience and in that of the many teachers I have worked with, students tend to find it extremely refreshing, even reassuring, when their teachers are willing to admit their ignorance or acknowledge their mistakes.[11] To be sure, there is significant vulnerability in doing so. As we noted above, such openness can have a humanizing effect on how students experience us. At the Intellectual Virtues Academy (IVA), when students describe how their school is different from other schools they've attended, a common response concerns how much the school values intellectual struggle and risk-taking, and how consistently they are encouraged to learn from rather than to fear or feel bad about their mistakes. Students also frequently point to their teachers as exemplars of these attitudes, that is, as people who are willing to admit their own intellectual limitations and to struggle along-side their students.

OPENNESS AND RECEPTIVITY

As important as humility and presence are, when it comes to teaching for intellectual virtues, they are not the only postures that matter. While they can have a powerful effect on our interactions with students, humility and presence each consist of a certain kind of *self*-orientation or self-awareness. However, when teaching for intellectual virtues, we must also be oriented toward our *students* in a particular way. Hence the value of a posture of openness and receptivity.[12]

What does this posture involve? To begin with, it requires turning toward our students and extending the scope of our attention and concern to include them and their well-being. It is about establishing within ourselves an openness or capacity for their needs and contributions, for whatever they might think or say or do. It involves attending to them gently, patiently, and wholeheartedly.

In the early days of IVA, the slogan "Love and Rigor" emerged as a succinct description of the kind of orientation that teachers and other stakeholders were seeking to adopt toward the students at the school. It was a given that we wanted to push and challenge the thinking of the students (rigor). However, we recognized that we could succeed at this only if we adopted a more holistic and deeply caring and open posture toward them (love).

Sound challenging? There's no question that it is. Thus, I must reiterate that the territory we're exploring represents a kind of pedagogical ideal. An open and receptive posture isn't the sort of thing teachers can have toward all their students all the time. Students can be challenging in ways that can make adopting such a posture quite difficult. However, none of these challenges means that we can't or shouldn't attempt to adopt an open and receptive posture toward our students. As with many other aspects of teaching for intellectual virtues, doing so is not an all-or-nothing affair. I might be quite satisfied, on a given occasion, if I manage to be *more* open and receptive toward my students than I would have been had I not even tried, even if my actual level of openness and receptivity, considered by itself, leaves something to be desired. There's a good chance my students will notice and appreciate this effort as well.

Also, to be clear, adopting an open and receptive posture toward one's students doesn't always or necessarily involve liking them or having fond feelings for them. Nor does it require interpreting their words or actions uncritically or being entirely free of feelings of frustration, impatience, or annoyance. Instead, openness is about locating my ground and opening up a space within myself, in my heart and mind, for who my students are and for what they have (or don't have) to offer in the present moment. Similar to how a posture of humility involves accepting where I am and how I am limited, a posture of openness and receptivity involves being open to and accepting of my students and their limitations.

This posture is important to cultivating a classroom environment in which students are willing to take intellectual risks (courage), embrace struggle (tenacity), and admit when they need help (humility). As John Hattie has noted, effective teachers develop positive relationships with their students to "allow students to feel okay about making mistakes and not knowing, and to establish a climate in which we welcome errors as opportunities."[13] A posture of openness and receptivity is an important way of fostering such a climate.

How can we go about adopting this posture? If I'm stressed or rushed or on the verge of losing my patience with my students, what can I do to locate a capacity within myself for who my students are or for what they might bring to the learning process? There's no simple answer to this question, no single lever to pull or trick to perform. However, it may be helpful to note some connections between this posture and some of the other postures we've been considering.

While there's no mental shortcut to a posture of openness and receptivity, I'll be unlikely to adopt this posture if I haven't already adopted a posture of presence. That is, I cannot open up a space within myself to receive and carry the needs and contributions of my students if I'm not already present to myself, if my mind is elsewhere, or if I'm ignoring my own emotions. Moreover, we've seen that in many instances, we can be present with our students only if we are also willing to be humble, that is, only if we are willing to admit our limitations and imperfections. Put another way, the path to openness and receptivity often overlaps and originates with the paths of humility and presence. Instead of attempting, by sheer force of will, to muster an open and receptive posture toward my students, I might do better to focus first on acknowledging my limitations and becoming more present to myself and to my students.

Gregory Boyle, founder of Homeboy Industries in Los Angeles, regularly makes the point that before we can respond in an open or capacious way to the needs of others, we must first be honest with ourselves about our own needs and wounds. In *Barking to the Choir*, he tells the story of a "homie" named Sergio, whose body was scarred by the physical abuse he had suffered as a child. Years later, after a remarkable journey of personal growth, Sergio explains to an audience, "But now I welcome my wounds. I run my fingers over my scars. My wounds are my friends." After all, he continues, "how can I help others to heal if I don't welcome my own wounds?"[14] Few of us bear wounds like Sergio's. Yet unless we can learn to accept our own limitations, flaws, and wounds, all of us will in some sense remain strangers to ourselves. And if we are strangers to ourselves, we will always struggle to be open and receptive to our students.

CONCLUSION

David Whyte defines *ground* as "a place to step onto, a place on which to stand and a place from which to step."[15] Drawing together some of our reflections on presence, humility, openness, and receptivity, we might say that to be present is to stand with full awareness on the ground beneath our feet. Doing so, we have seen, often takes considerable humility. But once we are there, with our feet firmly planted, we will be well positioned to step from this ground into an open and receptive posture toward our students.

These postures can play a powerful role in the formation of our students' intellectual character. According to a significant body of empirical research, positive relational experiences and attachments can contribute to the possession of several skills and qualities central to intellectual virtues like as curiosity, autonomy, humility, integrity, tenacity, and perseverance.[16] As one author puts it, "A major theme that emerges from a survey of the virtue development research is that interpersonal relationships are important to developing character strengths over the lifespan."[17] The postures described in this chapter are a way of forging caring and respectful connections with our students. When we reliably adopt these postures in the classroom, our students know that we are present, attentive to, and concerned with their well-being. As Steve Porter explains, they are then more likely to have "a desire to explore and take appropriate risks, a tendency to trust others as sources of important information, an ability to regulate their emotions in stressful situations, a realistic optimism about the future, and other emotional and attitudinal tendencies that are conducive to inculcating intellectual virtues."[18]

Taken together, the postures discussed in this chapter can be a gentle but powerful invitation to deeper learning and intellectual character growth. This invitation complements and is reinforced by a host of pedagogical practices discussed in chapters 5 through 9.

CHAPTER 5

Language

The beginning of wisdom is to call things by their right names.

—Chinese proverb

At this point in the book, we move from a focus on the principles and postures that support teaching for intellectual virtues to a concern with pedagogical practices. As we make this shift, we cannot lose sight of the ground covered in the previous chapters. In chapter 1, we examined intellectual virtues as a rich and attractive educational ideal, one worthy of our attention and commitment as teachers. To sharpen our focus on this ideal, chapter 2 explored the core ingredients and features of intellectual virtues. In chapter 3, our attention shifted to a collection of principles that can be used to guide our efforts to teach for intellectual virtues. And in chapter 4, we explored several pedagogical postures or attitudes that complement and reinforce these efforts. The practices we will explore in chapters 5 through 9 must not be viewed or implemented in isolation from this content. These practices are most effective when implemented by teachers who understand the nature and value of intellectual virtues and who have adopted the principles and postures already discussed.

In this chapter, we will examine the practice of incorporating the language of intellectual virtues into our teaching and related pedagogical activities like goal setting, lesson planning, and assessment. However, this topic must be approached with some caution, for some ways of using the language of the virtues are ineffective or worse. I begin, then, with four caveats.

CAVEATS

First, I will nowhere suggest that using the language of intellectual virtues is *sufficient* for helping our students grow in intellectual virtues. If it were, then teaching for intellectual virtues would be a breeze. Were we to tell our students about intellectual virtues and make regular use of the language of the virtues, our students' growth in these qualities would be certain. Alas, the dynamics of intellectual character growth aren't so simple. Instead, intellectual virtues are the result of a variety of factors. Accordingly, using the language of intellectual virtues is but one tool among many, the combination of which can have a favorable impact on the intellectual character of our students. Tim Van Gelder draws a similar connection between introducing students to the language and theory of critical thinking and helping them grow as critical thinkers: "A bit of theory is like the yeast that makes bread rise. You only need a small amount relative to the other ingredients . . . [but] if you have nothing but yeast, you have no loaf at all."[1]

Second, the language of the virtues is not strictly necessary for helping our students grow in intellectual virtues. Great teaching has always nurtured qualities like curiosity, attentiveness, intellectual humility, and intellectual autonomy. This is true regardless of whether the teachers in question knew anything about intellectual virtues. While this much is right, it doesn't follow that the language of intellectual virtues is useless. Again, my aim in this chapter is to demonstrate how using this language can play an important role in helping us shape the intellectual character of our students.

Third, students will benefit from being introduced to the language of intellectual virtues only if this language is not overused or used inauthentically. Many students—especially those in middle school and high school— have a keen eye and zero tolerance for clumsy adult attempts to tell them what's worth caring about. If I go on and on about intellectual virtues and their value, such talk may very well backfire. Similarly, if my use of the language reveals a flimsy grasp of what I'm talking about or suggests that I don't really believe in what I'm saying, my words will be impotent. Discretion regarding when and how we use this language is essential.

The danger of overusing the language of the virtues is something we've tried to be sensitive to at the Intellectual Virtues Academy (the name of the school notwithstanding). On the one hand, we've wanted to foreground the unique mission and vision of the school, underscoring its resolute commitment to helping students experience meaningful growth in intellectual virtues. Nevertheless, it isn't uncommon for students who have been at the school for a couple of years to roll their eyes when the topic of the virtues comes up. In cases like this, what should teachers do? Should we cease using the language of the virtues altogether? In my estimation, doing so would be a costly overreaction. At IVA and elsewhere, this language is a powerful culture-building force. Therefore, instead of dropping the language completely, we as teachers must learn, as the teachers at IVA have learned, to differentiate our use of it, in terms of both the specific words we use and how often we use them. In the event of "virtue fatigue," we must do our best to be appropriately thoughtful and sparing in how we talk about the virtues.[2]

This leads to a fourth and final caveat, namely, that the language of the virtues should never be used to criticize or disparage our students. Suppose that after introducing my students to this language and helping them appreciate the educational ideal it picks out, I proceed to castigate some of them for lacking intellectual carefulness or for being narrow-minded or intellectually lazy. Whatever interest or enthusiasm these students might have had for intellectual virtues is likely to dissipate. Of course, the language of intellectual virtues can be used to highlight how students can improve or have fallen short. Indeed, we'll consider some examples of what this might look like here and in chapter 10. But when we use this language, we must do so thoughtfully and sensitively, taking care to preserve the sense that intellectual character growth is an ideal worthy of ongoing aspiration rather than a standard that is forever shoring up our faults and limitations.

WHY USE VIRTUES LANGUAGE?

Given these caveats, we should examine in a little more detail the value of introducing our students to the language and concepts of intellectual virtue. What would be lost if we were to refrain from doing so? In this section, I'll briefly discuss three reasons why introducing our students to the language of intellectual virtues is a worthwhile practice.[3]

Calling Attention to Educational Aims

Introducing students to the language of the virtues can help draw their attention to what we hope they will take away from our classes and from their education as a whole. As seen in previous chapters, most of us who teach want more for our students than the mere acquisition of knowledge and intellectual skills. As important as these things are, we also want to have an impact on *who our students are* as thinkers and learners. We want to nurture their love of learning and help them become lifelong learners and critical thinkers. As we saw in chapter 1, the language of the virtues provides a way of unpacking and "thickening" these laudable but elusive educational aims. On this point, recall Aristotle's remark about the "highest good" for human beings: "Surely, then, knowledge of the good must be very important for our lives? And if, like archers, we have a target, are we not more likely to hit the mark?"[4] Similarly, if we equip our students with the language and concepts of intellectual virtue, they'll be in a better position to perceive and pursue the goal of intellectual character growth.

Meaning and Purpose

Intellectual character growth is not simply one educational goal among many. It is a particularly rich, personal, and attractive goal. There's something appealing about people who ask good questions (curiosity), think outside the box (open-mindedness), admit their mistakes (humility), but also demonstrate strength of conviction (courage) and persist in the face of intellectual challenges (tenacity). Even young children can appreciate this point, which is illustrated nicely in a remark by Judith Shapiro, former president of Barnard College: "You want the inside of your head to be an interesting place to spend the rest of your life."[5] By making appropriate and intelligent use of the language of the virtues, we can increase the perceived importance of what we are asking our students to learn and do, thereby adding additional meaning and purpose to their educational experience.[6]

A group of researchers recently found that children are willing to try harder to complete an intellectual task when they can observe adults struggling with and eventually completing the same task.[7] They try even harder when the adults they are observing use positive language to describe their own experience of struggle (e.g., "Trying hard is important!"). Commenting on this study, Angela Duckworth notes, "We should not only practice what we preach, but also preach what we practice . . . If you're actively trying to appreciate political perspectives that conflict with your own, talk about the value of intellectual humility. Actions may speak louder than words, but actions and words *together* send the clearest message of all."[8]

A Shared Language

An additional reason for making consistent use of the language of the virtues concerns the power of a shared evaluative vocabulary. It is well known that a culture is defined in part by its language. A common language binds people together, shaping their collective identity. The language of intellectual virtues can play a similar role. In philosophical parlance, intellectual-virtue terms and concepts are *thick*, meaning they are concrete and pick out qualities that are attractive and compelling. Put another way, these terms and concepts are both informative and action-guiding.[9] For this reason, the language of intellectual virtues can contribute to a sense of unity or common purpose among the learners in a classroom. It can help them feel like they are part of a shared and worthwhile endeavor, namely, developing the character strengths required for good thinking and learning. According to Character.org's 11 Principles Framework for character education, "a school committed to its students' character development uses a common language to teach, model, and integrate their core values into all aspects of school life."[10] Similarly, the intelligent and ongoing use of the language of intellectual virtues can contribute to a sense of intellectual community or to what Ron Ritchhart calls a "culture of thinking."[11]

We began this section by asking what, if anything, would be lost if we were to refrain from introducing our students to the language and concepts of intellectual virtue. We've seen that, in fact, the loss could be considerable. Psychologist Deanna Kuhn makes a similar point about teaching for thinking skills, noting that "practice does not make perfect in the absence of understanding." She explains that the "best approach" to teaching skillful thinking "may be to work from both ends at once—from a bottom-up anchoring in regular practice of what is being preached so that skills are exercised, strengthened, and consolidated as well as from a top-down fostering of understanding and intellectual values that play a major role in whether these skills will be used."[12]

WAYS OF INCORPORATING THE LANGUAGE OF THE VIRTUES

So far in this chapter, we've been reflecting on why it is worthwhile to incorporate the language of intellectual virtues into our instructional practices. But what exactly would this look like? What are some specific ways we can go about intelligently, authentically, and positively drawing on these linguistic and conceptual resources?

Before answering this question directly, I will briefly describe what I mean by the language of intellectual virtues. When speaking of this language, I am not referring merely to words like *intellectual character* and *intellectual virtue* or even to the names of specific virtues like *curiosity* or *intellectual autonomy*. I am also referring to more fine-grained descriptions of the mental moves expressive of these qualities. These fine-grained descriptions include "admitting our intellectual limitations and mistakes" (humility), "considering an issue from multiple perspectives" (open-mindedness), "thinking for oneself" (autonomy), "embracing intellectual struggle" (tenacity), and so on.[13]

The richness and complexity of the language of the virtues is important to keep in mind, especially when it comes to not overusing this language. Intellectual virtues can be described at different levels, from general to specific. When using this language, we should draw on its complexity and variety to keep the language fresh and meaningful for our students and ourselves.

Direct Instruction

We've seen the value in acquainting our students with the language of intellectual virtues. To maximize this value, we can help them understand what intellectual virtues are; what virtues like curiosity, open-mindedness, and intellectual courage involve or look like in practice; and how these virtues are related to each other. In other words, it can be useful to engage in some direct instruction on the topic of intellectual virtues.[14]

How we do this will vary significantly from one situation to another, depending on the developmental capacities of our students, their particular backgrounds, the amount of time or freedom we have to devote to instruction of this sort, and similar factors. Accordingly, several of my suggestions for direct instruction can be adapted to a variety of levels and circumstances.

I will begin at one end of the spectrum, describing an entire "mini unit" I've used in many of my own classes. I recognize that most teachers are unlikely to be in a position to do something this involved. But, again, my hope is that you might see fit to pick and choose from the activities I describe and to adapt them in ways that are feasible and relevant to your immediate instructional context. After describing my own approach, I will then turn to some additional, less demanding ways of introducing students to similar ideas and content.

For a number of years, I've begun most of my undergraduate courses with a brief unit on intellectual virtues and their relationship to learning and living well. I begin these courses by asking the students an open-ended question: "What's the ultimate point or purpose of education?" As they share their responses, I write them on the wipe board. Their answers tend to be extremely varied. Some highlight values like career preparation and financial stability. Others point to less tangible factors, such as "expanding our minds," "preparing us to be good citizens," or "teaching us how to learn." We take our time with these replies, probing their meaning and looking for connections between them. Eventually, I circle a subset of answers that point in the general direction of intellectual character. I explain that my hope for the course isn't merely that they will learn about philosophical ideas and arguments or even that they will hone their philosophical thinking and writings skills. I make clear that I also want to provide them with frequent opportunities to practice and make some progress in the virtues of good thinking, which I then connect back to some of the replies I've just circled.

After this initial conversation, I unpack what I mean by the "virtues of good thinking," offering brief and simple definitions of intellectual character and intellectual virtues, distinguishing intellectual virtues from moral virtues (e.g., kindness and compassion), other cognitive excellences (e.g., natural intellectual ability), and intellectual vices (e.g., intellectual arrogance, laziness, and closed-mindedness). I also introduce them to the nine virtues discussed in chapter 2. For each virtue I provide a concise definition, a pithy slogan, and a concrete example (see appendix A). For instance, I define intellectual tenacity as "a willingness to persist in the face of intellectual challenges," the gist of which is captured by the slogan "Embrace struggle!" I then use a selection from Frederick Douglass's autobiography to illustrate personal persistence in a quest for knowledge in the face of numerous and formidable obstacles.[15]

As part of this introductory unit, I also engage my students in a brief self-reflection exercise during which they take an inventory of their intellectual character strengths and limitations (for more on this exercise, see chapter 10). We also spend some time reflecting on the results, discussing what they found interesting or surprising.

With few exceptions, this overview of intellectual virtues seems to engage the interest of my students at a fairly deep level. In light of their comments in class and feedback on teaching evaluations, the overview seems to provide them with language and concepts to describe things they consider important to their education but don't always know how to articulate. It also seems to be a compelling way of framing or motivating the courses in question. As indicated earlier, the discussion gives students the sense that there's a deeper and more personal point to what they are being asked to learn and do.

When I began using this mini unit, I found it to be a helpful introduction to intellectual virtues, but I struggled to keep its content in view as the semester progressed. Therefore, I have subsequently made efforts to extend the unit. First, I incorporate short reading assignments on intellectual virtues throughout the semester. Here I have tended to rely on Philip Dow's *Virtuous Minds* or Nathan King's *The Excellent Mind*, both of which provide an illuminating and accessible introduction to intellectual virtues.[16] While these selections usually have little to do with the primary academic content of the course, I explain to my students that we are taking time to read and discuss the material so that we can better understand and remain mindful of one of the primary aims of the course (i.e., practicing and growing in intellectual virtues). Second, I assign two brief self-reflection papers that require my students to relate the material from the reading selections to their own experience and character as thinkers and learners.[17] These additional assignments demand some extra work from the students and take up a small amount of class time. However, I have found that they generally enjoy doing this work and that it is well worth whatever instructional minutes it consumes.

This overview of how we can introduce our students to intellectual virtues may feel overwhelming and way beyond what you feel capable of or interested in doing. This concern needn't be a problem. Again, the activities just described may be adopted piecemeal and tailored to fit your own needs or constraints. To better illustrate the feasibility of introducing your students to intellectual virtues, I will also describe a more modest approach.

On the first day or during the first week of classes, you might explain to your students what your hopes are for them in the upcoming year or semester. You might include in this explanation the hope that they will regularly practice and pursue growth in the virtues of good thinking and learning. Drawing on material from this book or other sources, you might offer a brief explanation of what intellectual virtues are and identify a few virtues you would like to focus on with them (or you might let them identify two or three target virtues). As indicated earlier in this chapter, I recommend giving your students simple definitions or descriptions of these virtues and sharing some concrete examples of each one. You could also engage your students in a meaningful discussion about what these virtues are like, why they're valuable, what seems challenging or problematic about them, how they are related to each other, and so on.

You might also consider other ways of keeping these virtues and their educational significance before the minds of your students as the semester or year progresses. For instance, I often give my students a very simple bookmark (photocopied on a half sheet of colored 8½ × 11-inch paper) that lists several virtues and provides a brief definition and slogan for each one. Alternatively, you might organize a weekly or monthly discussion of a real-life example of one of the virtues you've decided to focus on. If your students are younger, you might devote part of a wall or bulletin board to creative representations or expressions of some key virtues. For instance, at IVA, one veteran math teacher puts students' "conjectures" about mathematical concepts on colorful cards and posts them on the walls in her classroom. These cards are a tangible expression of virtues like autonomy and courage.

While worthwhile, efforts like these need to be kept in perspective. As we've seen, simply telling students about intellectual virtues is not sufficient for helping them make progress in them. It is, at most, one strategy or tool among many. Therefore, we must avoid the trap of thinking that we are successfully teaching for intellectual virtues simply because we have introduced our students to the language and concepts of these virtues. As mentioned, if we talk too much about intellectual virtues or inundate our students with reminders or representations of the virtues, our efforts may backfire, particularly if this type of instruction is our primary method of teaching for intellectual virtues. Again, we must be thoughtful, creative, and somewhat sparing in how we incorporate the language of the virtues. Our aim should not be to impose an intellectual virtues framework on the thinking of our students. Rather, we should invite them into the practice of these virtues and equip them with some linguistic and conceptual tools and resources that will make this invitation clear and compelling.

Objectives and Outcomes

I turn now to discuss several additional and complementary ways of integrating a focus on intellectual character into our instructional routines and activities. Instead of using a separate unit or content module, we can also find ways of incorporating the language of intellectual virtues into some existing elements of our courses.

Teachers are often expected to articulate learning outcomes or objectives in their course syllabi or lesson plans. These objectives provide a concrete specification of what teachers want their students to have achieved or be competent at once the course or lesson is complete. They also provide a good opportunity to integrate the language of intellectual virtues.

I divide the objectives of my own courses into three categories: (1) knowledge, (2) skills, and (3) intellectual virtues. The idea is that by the time students leave my courses, they will know certain things, will have sharpened some of their intellectual skills, and will have been exposed to and practiced several intellectual virtues. On the latter point, my aim, more specifically, is that students will develop a firm grasp of what intellectual virtues are and why they are important, acquire a concrete understanding of some of their own intellectual character strengths and limitations, and consistently and deliberately practice a range of intellectual virtues. I include this material in my syllabus and review it with my students at the beginning of the semester. Doing so helps signal that I'm serious about the development of their intellectual character. It also helps keep me accountable to this commitment.

The character-based objectives just mentioned are quite realistic and measurable. In ways that will be become even clearer later in this chapter and in the chapters that follow, I take several specific actions aimed at fostering these objectives and assessing how well my students have achieved them. These assessments are important, for as we saw in chapter 3, we can be tempted to be overly idealistic or ambitious in the characterological aims we have for our students. Such would be the case, for instance, if one of these aims were described as follows: "Over the course of the semester, every student will experience substantial growth in a wide range of intellectual virtues." Although some of my students will probably experience significant growth in intellectual virtues, it would be naive for me to think that all of them will or that most of them will grow substantially in a wide range of virtues. Nor, in any case, can growth of this sort be measured with a high degree of accuracy. We will return to this and related issues in chapter 10.

A related exercise, also discussed in the previous chapter, consists of incorporating the language of the virtues into a course mission statement. Again, a mission statement I've used in several freshman-level courses is, "We are a community of inquirers tasked with philosophical learning and reflection. My primary aim as your instructor is not to impart to you a body of knowledge. It is rather to nurture your relationship to learning by providing you with well-supported opportunities to practice the virtues of good thinking." Similarly, a friend of mine who taught third grade had his students recite the following Scholar's Pledge each morning alongside the Pledge of Allegiance: "Be intellectually aggressive. Be intellectually humble. Be respectful of all people and things. Sit like a scholar. Be an intellectual leader." Rehearsing statements like these in a consistent and thoughtful way can help us and our students remain attentive to the aim of intellectual character growth.

Calling Attention to Opportunities for Practice

Another way of incorporating the language of intellectual virtues into our teaching involves calling attention to opportunities to practice these virtues. We can do so in the prompts we give our students for assignments or exercises. Or we can call attention to these opportunities in a more spontaneous and strictly verbal way. I'll begin with a brief example of some virtue-based prompts.

When designing an assignment or exercise, I often pause to ask myself: Which virtues will this assignment encourage my students to practice?

Sometimes the answer is "none" or "not many," in which case I usually retool the assignment. Once I've done this, it is an easy further step simply to note, in the prompt itself, which virtues my students are being asked to practice and at what point. For instance, in the guidelines for an argumentative essay, I might say something like: "This assignment requires you to think for yourself (autonomy) and to explain the material you are discussing accurately and deeply (carefulness and thoroughness)." Elsewhere in the prompt, I might say: "After developing your argument, you must anticipate a minimum of two to three thoughtful objections that could be raised against it (humility, open-mindedness, and curiosity). You must then proceed to formulate in-depth and plausible rebuttals to these objections (autonomy, tenacity)."

Prompts like these are a quick and easy way of incorporating the language of the virtues into your instructional materials. If I have already introduced my students to the nature and value of intellectual virtues, and if they have come to appreciate the value of these qualities, small efforts like this can serve to remind them of what's at stake. These prompts can draw students' attention to the fact that what they are being called on to do is tightly connected with their own growth as thinkers and learners.

More frequently, I call attention to these opportunities verbally and during instruction. For instance, when exploring a philosophical idea or argument with my students, I sometimes ask them to formulate the best arguments they can in support of a viewpoint with which they personally disagree. To frame this exercise, I point out that it is an opportunity for them to practice—and therefore to grow in—virtues like open-mindedness and intellectual humility. Similarly, I have found that intellectual courage is the virtue my students are most interested in cultivating. When explaining why, they often cite their reluctance to speak up in class even when they're confident they have something worthwhile to say. Accordingly, when I have posed a thoughtful question that my students greet with silence, I sometimes pause and say, gently and with a touch of humor, something like: "I suspect that several of you have some very good and relevant responses in mind but are feeling a little fearful about sharing them with the rest of the class. While I won't force you to respond, I'd like to point out that this is an opportunity for you to practice intellectual courage. And since we develop intellectual courage by practicing it, it's also an opportunity for you to become a little more intellectually courageous, which is something that I know many of you care about." Usually, by the time I'm done with my spiel, two or three hands are in the air.

The suggestion here is simple enough: we need to be mindful of the opportunities we are giving our students to practice intellectual virtues and call attention to these opportunities as they arise. Again, if our students have already been introduced to the nature and value of intellectual virtues, this practice can enhance their motivation to engage in intellectually virtuous conduct. It can also improve their own ability to identify when and where to practice intellectual virtues. Ron Ritchhart makes a similar point about a rich and varied "language of thinking." He says that such language provides "new labels and categories [that] foster new perceptions and new responses . . . They help sensitize us to thinking occasions and the particular types of thinking called for in those occasions."[18]

Noticing and Naming

In thoughtful and learning-oriented classroom environments, intellectual virtues are on wide display. Students are asking insightful questions, probing for deeper understanding, admitting what's unclear or confusing, taking intellectual risks, and persevering in the face of obstacles. Noticing and naming these manifestations of intellectual virtue is an additional way of incorporating the language of the virtues into our instructional practices.

Several years ago, a student of mine confidently dismissed a particular philosophical position that I had introduced and had invited the class to comment on. The student couldn't see why anyone would take the position seriously. Across the room, another student raised his hand. When I asked him to share what he was thinking, he offered a gentle but cogent rationale in support of the position that had just been dismissed. Hearing this student's perspective, the first student paused, thought for a moment, and said, "Huh, I guess you're right." She showed no sign of defensiveness. Nor did she make a big deal out of the fact that her initial impression had been refuted. Instead, she simply considered the matter from a different point of view and proceeded to change her mind. Watching these events unfold, I seized the opportunity to apply an intellectual virtues lens to what had just occurred. I pointed out to the class that the first student's conduct was a perfect example of open-mindedness (a virtue we had talked about earlier in the course). The student smiled, and several of her classmates nodded their heads.

In *Making Thinking Visible*, Ritchhart and coauthors note that a good education should equip students with "habits of mind and thinking dispositions that will serve [them] as learners both in our classrooms and in the future." They say that, to nurture these habits, we "must help students to recognize the key features and contexts for the use of various types of thinking." This in turn requires us to "draw on our understanding of what thinking is and the types of thinking we need to foster so that we can *name, notice, and highlight* thinking when it occurs in the class."[19] The same applies to our use of the more personal and fine-grained language of intellectual virtues.

Formal Feedback

In chapter 8, we will explore the importance of creating frequent opportunities for students to practice intellectual virtues, including opportunities to ask thoughtful questions (curiosity), consider alternative perspectives (open-mindedness), demonstrate deep understanding (thoroughness), and take intellectual risks (courage). Building these opportunities into the assignments, exams, and projects we give our students is an additional way of incorporating the language of the virtues into our courses. For example, if one of the requirements of a project is to consider and respond to potential challenges or problems with one's core proposal, then students should be able to score well on the project only if they have practiced virtues like open-mindedness, humility, and autonomy. Thus, in our assessment of their performance, it should be entirely natural to use the language of intellectual virtues to highlight what they have done well and some of the ways in which they might improve.

Such feedback can take the form of written comments or a rubric that incorporates the language of the virtues. We will explore some of these issues in greater detail in chapter 10, which is devoted to the topic of assessment. In the meantime, I'll briefly note some possible rubric items that correspond to specific virtues:

Thoroughness: "Demonstrates a firm personal understanding of the material. Includes detailed explanations of key concepts."
Carefulness: "Is free of careless mistakes and errors. Demonstrates precision."
Autonomy: "Shows an ability to formulate original ideas and to engage in independent thinking."
Curiosity: "Raises thoughtful and insightful questions."
Open-mindedness: "Considers multiple and diverse perspectives."

While these rubric items may skew in the direction of secondary or postsecondary students, similar items can be formulated to assess the intellectual activity of younger students.

CONCLUSION

In this chapter, we've considered the merits of introducing our students to the language of intellectual virtues. We've also examined several ways of doing this. Clearly, these ways are not mutually exclusive. Indeed, they are likely to have the greatest impact when used together. To begin applying some of these ideas, you might spend some time reflecting on questions like the following: Do you see value in introducing your students to the language of the virtues? If so, what is it? Of the practices discussed in this chapter, which one strikes you as the most relevant or feasible? Can you think of any additional ways of integrating the language of intellectual virtues into your teaching?

CHAPTER 6

Reflection

> The less somebody knows & understands himself the less great
> he is, however great may be his talent.
>
> —Ludwig Wittgenstein, *Culture and Value*

Socrates famously declared that "the unexamined life is not worth living."[1]
A related classical Greek maxim exhorts: "Know thyself."[2] From ancient
times to the present, many people have placed a premium on self-awareness, self-knowledge, and self-reflection. Why? What's so important about
knowing ourselves?

We can begin to answer this question by reflecting on the state of *not*
knowing ourselves, that is, on self-ignorance. Think of the vain and narcissistic public figure whose need for adulation is painfully obvious to everyone but himself. Or of the overambitious and stressed-out college student
who, oblivious to her limitations, has badly overcommitted to too many
tasks and roles. Or the person who has spent his entire life trying to live
up to the expectations of others and has since become a stranger even to
himself, scarcely aware of having any of his own beliefs and desires. These
are not attractive ways of living or being. They are not conducive to human
health or happiness. There must, then, be some value in self-reflection and
the kind of self-knowledge it can elicit. At a minimum, self-reflection can
help us avoid the bog of self-ignorance.

This chapter focuses on the role of self-reflection in the development of intellectual virtues. More precisely, I want to consider how engaging our students in self-reflection can contribute to their intellectual character growth. I'll argue that certain types of self-reflection can help our students form mental models of themselves as thinkers and learners and that these models can in turn help them practice and cultivate a wide range of intellectual virtues.

THE LIMITS OF SELF-REFLECTION

Before looking at the value of self-reflection, we must acknowledge some of its limitations. Clearly, it is possible to be excessively self-reflective. For instance, for those who obsessively or scrupulously question their own motives, self-reflection is a liability rather than a strength. More importantly, our ability to know ourselves is considerably more complicated and limited than we might imagine. It is tempting to think of introspection as an expansive window that opens onto the landscape of our own minds. But this isn't how introspection works. Our access to our own thoughts and feelings isn't nearly that straightforward. Our biases, blind spots, and other cognitive limitations interfere, not just with our knowledge of other people or events in the world, but also with our knowledge of ourselves.[3] Especially when it comes to accessing our deeper or more implicit beliefs and desires, introspection is more like a cloudy porthole than an open window.

Our expectations regarding our students' growth in self-knowledge must reflect these limitations. We shouldn't expect our students to be able to accurately identify their deeper intellectual motives or to have immediate access to the whole truth about their intellectual character strengths and limitations. And we should encourage them to balance what they appear to learn about themselves on the basis of self-reflection with what they hear or learn from other sources.

THE VALUE OF SELF-REFLECTION

Although it is limited, our capacity for self-reflection is not wholly or categorically unreliable. Many of our own thoughts, feelings, beliefs, and desires are readily accessible via introspection.[4] What role, then, might self-reflection play in the cultivation of intellectual virtues?

When operating reliably, self-reflection is a means to self-knowledge, including knowledge of ourselves as thinkers and learners. Through self-reflection, I can learn a good deal about what sparks my curiosity, my typical reactions to intellectual challenges, or the common sources of my fear or anxiety in a learning situation. Put another way, self-reflection can help me develop a *mental model* of who I am, what I care about, and how I tend to operate as a learner. While such a model will not be infallible and will always be incomplete, it can provide me with at least a rough understanding of the geography of my own mind.

But how can a mental model of this sort contribute to a person's intellectual character growth? I will discuss three ways in which developing an informed and accurate understanding of ourselves as learners can put us in a better position to cultivate intellectual virtues.[5]

Removing Obstacles

First, developing such a model can help us identify and weed out beliefs and desires that inhibit our cultivation of intellectual virtues. I'll begin with a discussion of beliefs. What we believe about ourselves as learners can have an important bearing on our intellectual conduct and the intellectual character it fosters. For instance, if I believe statements like "I'm stupid," "I can't learn," or "I'm not a math person," I'll be less likely to embrace intellectual struggle or to take intellectual risks in certain contexts. I'll forgo opportunities to practice and grow in virtues like tenacity and courage. Similarly, if I believe (mistakenly) that I am intellectually superior to all my peers or that I can always figure things out on my own, without any support or assistance from others, then I will miss opportunities to grow in virtues like intellectual humility, trust, and open-mindedness.

These distorted perceptions of ourselves constitute what some psychologists refer to as an "internal working model" of the self. As Steve Porter notes, when our internal working models are flawed, they can inhibit growth in intellectual virtues: "On one understanding of what constitutes psychological readiness for virtue formation, a fundamental element that often stands in the way of a person's acquiring virtue is an internalized representation of one's self that is psychologically incompatible with the formation of virtue."[6] Examples of such representations, according to Porter, include statements such as "Anything less than perfection means I am worthless," "If I am wrong about something, then I am the stupidest kid in the class," and "I am always right because I am the smartest kid in the class."[7]

Internalized representations incompatible with intellectual-virtue formation aren't limited to representations or beliefs about the self. They can also be rooted in beliefs about the nature of learning or intellectual achievement. For instance, if I have a fixed mindset about what it is to be smart or intelligent, I will see intelligence as a natural gift that a person is either born with or without. Such a belief excludes the possibility that through an appropriate course of effort and practice, I can increase my level of intelligence.[8] It follows that at least two types of beliefs can get in the way of our cultivation of intellectual virtues: beliefs about ourselves and beliefs about the process of learning or intellectual growth.

Importantly, for at least some of the beliefs we've been considering, we can have them and not know it. I may spend so much time and effort trying to cover up or compensate for my low view of myself as a learner that I fail to realize or come to terms with the fact that I view myself in this way. Or I might be oblivious to my implicit belief that my competence in one area entitles me to make pronouncements in areas in which I lack expertise. To use a term from philosopher Nathan Ballantyne, I might fail to recognize that I am an "epistemic trespasser."[9] Nor is it difficult to imagine that I might have a fixed mindset about intelligence yet fail to realize it.

These potential pitfalls underscore the importance of self-reflection and developing an accurate mental model of ourselves as learners. Through an appropriate course of self-reflection, beliefs like the ones just noted can be brought to light and challenged. In this way, we can enhance our self-understanding and remove obstacles to our growth in intellectual virtues.

A similar point can be made about some of our intellectual desires. If I have a very low desire to learn or no real interest in what I'm learning,

I might become intellectually lazy or careless. Or if my desire to learn is fairly strong but weaker than one or more of my competing desires (e.g., a desire to play video games), then a similar result might occur. Intellectual desires can also be downright vicious, for example, a desire to vanquish my intellectual opponents or to always be viewed as the smartest person in the room. These are a few ways in which our desires can inhibit our progress in virtues like curiosity, carefulness, perseverance, and humility.

For some of the desires just noted, we might wonder whether it's possible to possess the desire and not know it (e.g., a desire to play video games). But for other desires, this lack of awareness doesn't seem unlikely at all. If I'm a hardworking and conscientious student, it might take significant effort for me to realize that I'm not really interested in what I'm learning. Likewise for my need to be right or my desire to appear smarter than my peers. Again, in cases like this, a well-designed course of self-reflection can help bring to light desires that are inhibiting our intellectual character growth. And a recognition of these desires can be an opportunity to loosen their grip on our motivational structure.

A Foundation for Humility and Autonomy

A second and partly overlapping point is that developing an accurate mental model of ourselves as learners can create a solid foundation for two virtues in particular: intellectual humility and intellectual autonomy. Intellectual humility, we've seen, is about owning our intellectual weaknesses and limitations. Intellectual autonomy, which is about thinking for ourselves and drawing our own conclusions, requires owning our intellectual strengths and abilities. Thus, we can possess these virtues only if we have a reasonably good grasp of what our intellectual limitations and abilities are.

This is precisely the kind of knowledge that self-reflection can help make possible. To illustrate, suppose I am regularly given well-designed opportunities to reflect on my life as a learner. This might include opportunities to reflect on questions like the following: Which intellectual accomplishments am I most proud of? Where do I tend to struggle? What am I fearful of as a learner? How do I respond to intellectual struggle or fear? While this kind of reflection won't provide me with an entirely accurate or exhaustive grasp of my intellectual limitations and abilities, it can open my eyes to some important features of my mental geography. In doing so, it can lay the foundation for growth in humility and autonomy.

Virtuous Judgment

Having an accurate mental model of ourselves as thinkers and learners is also critical to developing intellectually virtuous judgment. In chapter 2, we saw that to possess an intellectual virtue, a person must manifest good judgment about when, to what extent, and toward whom or what to deploy the skills or competences specific to that virtue. For instance, to be virtuously open-minded, we must exercise good judgment about which views to be receptive to, how seriously to take these views, when to curtail our openness, and so on.

We also saw, however, that the dictates of good judgment can vary from one person to another. For example, if I know myself to be gullible, then I might need to be cautious about listening in an open-minded way to a view that strikes me as barely credible. Conversely, if I am generally resistant to considering alternative perspectives, then if an opposing viewpoint strikes me as even remotely plausible, this sense might be an indication that I should give the viewpoint an open-minded hearing. Similarly, if I know that I am a fearful learner and that my fears tend to be unwarranted, then the fact that an intellectual activity strikes me as fearful or costly may not be a reason for me to avoid that activity. On the other hand, if I rarely experience fear in a learning context, I might do well to conclude that this is not the time or place for an exercise of intellectual courage.

A similar point is made in the literature on *metacognition*, or thinking about thinking. According to a National Academy of Sciences report, metacognition "can help students learn to take control of their own learning by defining learning goals and monitoring their progress in achieving them."[10] Educational psychologist Paul Pintrich divides metacognition into three types of knowledge: strategic knowledge, task knowledge, and self-knowledge.[11] The kind of knowledge described in the previous paragraph overlaps significantly with task knowledge and self-knowledge. Pintrich defines task knowledge as "knowledge of cognitive tasks as well as when and why to use these different strategies" and self-knowledge as "knowledge of the self . . . in relation both to cognitive and motivational components of performance."[12] Again, to learn and inquire in intellectually virtuous ways, we must know which virtue-specific skills to deploy, when, for how long, and so on. Moreover, to make these determinations, we must know certain things about ourselves: our strengths and limitations as learners, what motivates us, what we fear, and so on. In other words, we must possess a fair amount of task knowledge and self-knowledge, as Pintrich describes them.[13]

In short, we can't know how to negotiate the landscape of thinking and learning if we don't know ourselves, that is, if we don't have an informed and accurate understanding of who we are as thinkers and learners. As Shari Tishman and coauthors note: "The good thinker in virtually any field is intellectually self-watchful, self-guiding, and self-assessing."[14] To the extent that it can facilitate self-understanding, self-reflection plays an important role in the cultivation of intellectual virtues.

CREATING OPPORTUNITIES FOR SELF-REFLECTION

We've seen that self-knowledge is an important part of growing in intellectual virtues and that well-designed opportunities to engage in self-reflection can be a means to self-knowledge. What does this suggest about teaching for intellectual virtues? More to the point, how can we provide our students with opportunities to develop an informed and accurate understanding of themselves as learners?

In response to this question, I'll describe several ways of encouraging self-reflection. Some of these approaches are relatively simple and informal, while others are more complex and structured. Again, my suggestion isn't that the activities and exercises in question are capable of providing students with infallible or exhaustive knowledge of how their minds work. Rather, the kind of self-awareness and self-knowledge they are designed to facilitate is considerably more modest and achievable, at least for many students. Also, as with the other practices described in this book, it will be up to you to determine which of the activities might be appropriate for you and your students or whether you might want to adapt one or more of them to better suit your needs and interests.[15]

Modeling

One indirect way of encouraging our students to engage in self-reflection is to model the kind of self-awareness or self-knowledge that results from such reflection. As we noted at the outset of the chapter, self-awareness and self-knowledge are attractive personal qualities: we tend to admire people who know themselves, and we are critical of people who lack self-awareness. Given the attractiveness of self-aware people, if we can regularly model self-knowledge and self-awareness, our students may take notice and begin to reflect on how their own minds work.

What might this look like in practice? One example is modeling an understanding of and comfort with our intellectual limitations. Suppose I'm teaching a concept I find somewhat confusing. I might acknowledge this limitation to my students by saying something like: "I tend to have a difficult time with this material. It doesn't come naturally to me. I'm still trying to develop a mastery of it." Or suppose I'm explaining a viewpoint or perspective that I think has some serious flaws. I might say to my students: "I need to watch myself here. I don't find this view very plausible. If I'm not careful, I may describe it unfairly or inaccurately, which I don't want to do." In making observations like these, I am modeling a kind of self-awareness expressive of intellectual humility.

We can also model self-awareness by thinking aloud about our intellectual desires and passions. When discussing a topic I'm especially curious about with my students, I might explain to them *why* I find the topic so interesting. Suppose, for example, that the object of study is a favorite poem of mine. I might say something like: "One of the things I love about this poem is how simple and direct it is. I find that when poems are highly abstract or metaphorical, they tend not to move me. I have an easier time receiving what a poem has to offer when it provides a simple and concrete image or idea to focus on. That's just how my mind works." In making a remark like this, I am demonstrating to my students an understanding of my own mind, including what I find interesting or fascinating.

The broader point of these examples is as follows. When teaching, we often have a choice about whether to focus strictly on the topic or content we're discussing or to occasionally step back and offer our students a glimpse of our internal reaction to it. While the latter kind of digression clearly shouldn't dominate our teaching, it can be a way of inspiring students to pursue a similar awareness of their own mental lives. As Parker Palmer notes, "In every class I teach, my ability to connect with my students, and to connect with the subject, depends less on the methods I use than on the degree to which I know and trust my selfhood—and am willing to make it available and vulnerable in the service of learning."[16]

To gauge how well you already model this kind of self-awareness, you might consider asking yourself how you think your students would answer questions like the following: Does my teacher possess a good understanding of his or her intellectual character strengths and weaknesses? Does my teacher ever reflect on how his or her mind works? Does this person seem to lack self-awareness about these things? Or is it difficult to tell one way or another?

Spontaneous Encouragement

Another informal way of encouraging students to reflect on their identities as thinkers and learners involves being on the lookout for situations in which a bit of self-reflection might be fruitful. Suppose, for instance, that my students and I are discussing a controversial issue and that one of them makes a comment that does a particularly good job of capturing both sides of the issue. In response, I might say to the student: "I want to quickly draw attention to the comment you just made. This is a really difficult and delicate issue. Because we tend to have strong opinions about it, it can be very difficult to see and appreciate both sides. But your comment did just that. You did a really good job of capturing the tension and complexity of the issue." Or imagine a scenario in which a student points out a very subtle but important connection between something we're discussing now and something we covered earlier in the semester or year. Here I might say: "Wow, what a great insight. I'd never thought about that. You demonstrated an ability to perceive important connections between what seem like very different and disconnected ideas." In each of these cases, I am directing my students' attention to positive features of their intellectual conduct or character. In doing so, I'm providing them with an opportunity to better understand and appreciate the geography of their own minds.

The exact form these opportunities might take is somewhat context-sensitive. In the examples just noted, it probably wouldn't make sense for me to pause and encourage the students to engage in additional, more focused self-reflection. Suppose, however, that the comments were made outside of regular classroom instruction (e.g., during a one-on-one interaction in class or during office hours). In that case, I might do even more to encourage the students to reflect on their mental moves. I might ask, "Is this something you find yourself doing in a lot of your classes? Or in other areas of life? Is this something you're known for among your friends or family? How do you think you developed this ability?" Again, such questions might serve as a gentle encouragement to the students to begin thinking in more specific ways about who they are or what they are like as learners.

These less public settings can also present opportunities to encourage students to reflect on some of their intellectual limitations or weaknesses. Imagine that a struggling student comes to me after class or during office hours and announces, "I'm just stupid. I can't learn this material. I don't know what to do." Instead of moving immediately to reassure or to contradict the student's self-assessment, I might say something like, "It sounds like you're feeling pretty frustrated and impatient with yourself. Is that so?" Assuming it is, I might continue: "Have you experienced this kind of frustration in previous courses? If so, what happened? Did you fail to make any progress?" Provided that the student's pessimistic predictions haven't always come to fruition, I might say, "It looks as though, when you're frustrated, you sometimes make negative predictions about your ability to learn or understand—predictions that often turn out to be mistaken. All of us have plenty of room for intellectual growth. It sounds like one area for you to work on might be recognizing your tendency to get frustrated with yourself and taking some steps to prevent this tendency from dominating your thinking."

Alternatively, suppose a student has a difficult time listening to or taking seriously the opinions of other students. On hearing something he doesn't agree with or thinks is mistaken, the student ceases to listen and shoots up his hand, eager to criticize. Although I would likely avoid drawing attention to this student's behavior during class, I could ask to speak with him afterward. I might say something like, "I'd like to draw your attention to some ways I've seen you interacting with some of your peers. You clearly have a lot of your own ideas and feel passionately about them. This is very good. However, it also seems like, once you figure out what you think, you sometimes stop listening to what other people have to say. While you may not realize it, these behaviors can come across as insensitive or disrespectful, even if you don't intend them to. They also cut you off from other ways of thinking that could deepen your understanding of the issues." Context permitting, I might probe a little further: "Are you aware of this tendency? Is it something you find yourself doing in other situations? What benefits do you receive from responding in this way? Does it have any costs?" Again, the idea would be to encourage the student to attend to and reflect on these mental habits and their consequences.[17]

Obviously, conversations of this sort need to be handled with great care. Moreover, I recognize that they may leave some of us feeling more like therapists than classroom teachers. Nevertheless, I don't think this is a reason to avoid having the conversations. On the contrary, I think there is something to the comparison between therapy and teaching.

In teaching for intellectual virtues, our aim is to touch students at a deeply personal level. To return to Plato's cave allegory, it is about "turning students around" so that they can develop "more truthful ways of seeing and being in the world."[18] Understood in this way, teaching does bear a resemblance to therapy. Therapists help their clients develop an awareness of beliefs, desires, and feelings that may unconsciously but adversely be affecting their behavior and overall well-being. They facilitate self-understanding, which in turn is conducive to psychological health. As one author notes, "There is a tradition in [education] that pays attention to the counselling and therapeutic process . . . as a site for insights about change, learning and facilitating learning." According to this view, the teacher is "neither a mere conduit for information (though that is important) nor a therapist." The teacher does, however, give special attention to the "emotional dimension" of teaching.[19] Similarly, the kinds of interactions that I have sketched are aimed at helping students develop an awareness of some of the beliefs, desires, and feelings that affect their lives as thinkers. These interactions are about helping students develop a mental model of how their minds work.

Self-Reflection Exercises

We've considered some fairly indirect ways of encouraging students to develop a better understanding of themselves as learners. However, we can also provide more direct and structured opportunities for self-reflection. In the remainder of the chapter, I will consider two opportunities of this sort: self-reflection exercises and a self-reflection project. These activities have a somewhat narrower scope than the ones discussed in the previous section. They are aimed, in particular, at helping students develop a better understanding of their intellectual character strengths and limitations.[20]

One fairly straightforward way of facilitating this kind of understanding involves the use of self-assessments. Because the constructs of intellectual character and intellectual virtues have only recently begun to capture the attention of empirical researchers, there aren't fully validated self-assessments for all the virtues discussed in this book. However, high-quality assessments do exist online and elsewhere for at least a few intellectual virtues, including curiosity, intellectual humility, and open-mindedness.[21]

These assessments generally consist of roughly ten to twenty-five items or statements, such as "I like finding out why people behave the way they do" or "I welcome different ways of thinking about important topics." Respondents register their level of agreement or disagreement with each statement using a Likert-type scale (e.g., 1 = "Strongly disagree," 2 = "Disagree," 3 = "Neither agree nor disagree," 4 = "Agree," 5 = "Strongly" agree). Scoring instructions provide guidance on how to convert responses to individual survey items into an overall evaluation.

Many of these scales are designed for adults. Consequently, they may not, at least in their existing form, be suitable for use with younger students.[22] However, we can administer these assessments with older students and invite them to reflect on the results by answering questions such as these: What (if anything) did you find surprising about the results of the survey? Which beliefs or attitudes did they challenge? Which beliefs or attitudes did they reinforce? Can you think of specific examples of how the qualities pointed to by the results have been manifested in your life as a thinker or learner?

Where existing self-report measures are inapplicable, either because they are geared toward an older audience or because they don't target the virtues you're most interested in, you might consider developing a self-assessment exercise of your own. If you aren't an experienced psychometrician, the assessment you come up with may not meet the standards of validity and reliability that govern social science research. While this drawback is important to bear in mind and should keep you and your students from reading too much into the results, even psychometrically imperfect self-report measures can help students begin paying closer attention their intellectual habits.

At the Intellectual Virtues Academy (IVA), we've come up with short (eight-item) scales for each of the school's nine virtues (see appendix B). These assessments are used in various capacities at the school, from semi-annual character surveys to informal self-reflection exercises. While most of the scale items haven't been comprehensively evaluated by empirical researchers, they have the advantage of closely matching the way that IVA staff, students, and other stakeholders conceptualize and understand the virtues in question.[23] Overall, we've found the assessments to be an effective way of helping students get acquainted with the language of the virtues and begin applying it to how they think and talk about their own intellectual character strengths and limitations.

In my own courses at the college level, I use a related self-reflection tool. On one side of an 8½ × 11-inch sheet of paper, I include thirty-six scale items corresponding to IVA's nine virtues (four items per virtue).[24] After the students assign themselves a score of 1 to 5 on all thirty-six items, they turn the paper over and tally and graph their scores for each virtue. After they spend some time reflecting on the results, we discuss their responses to the following questions: (1) According to the assessment, what are your greatest intellectual character strengths? Which virtues do you most need to work on? (2) Do you think these results are mostly accurate? Do any of the results surprise you? Why or why not? (3) Up to this point of your life, how have you benefited from your intellectual character strengths? Support your answer with examples. (4) How have you been affected by your intellectual character limitations? Again, support your answer with examples.

I've used this tool in many courses, and it always generates lively reflection and discussion. Students enjoy the opportunity to reflect on their mental habits, for example, on how these habits might have come about, what they look like in practice, and how they affect the students' lives inside and outside the classroom. The activity works especially well as part of an introduction to intellectual virtues. Again, it provides students with an opportunity to apply what they've learned about intellectual virtues to their understanding of themselves as learners.

This leads to an important point about *identity*, which for our purposes refers to how a person conceives of himself or herself and what the individual stands for or cares about.[25] One way to think about the goal of the self-refection exercises we've been considering is in terms of their potential impact on the identity of our students. Again, intellectual virtues are admirable and attractive personal attributes. Therefore, if given an opportunity to learn about intellectual virtues, and to reflect on their own intellectual character strengths and limitations, our students may begin to incorporate virtue concepts into how they conceptualize what they stand for and the kind of persons they want to be. This can be a way of helping them own and internalize a commitment to intellectual character growth.[26]

Self-Reflection Project

I will conclude the chapter by describing an even more ambitious approach to helping students develop an understanding of their own intellectual character. In many of the introductory courses I teach, I assign a multipart self-reflection project that incorporates several of the steps or exercises described in this chapter. While this project may not be feasible for, or applicable to, you or your students, perhaps it will spark your imagination as you seek to identify more suitable ways of encouraging your students to engage in self-reflection. (Elements of this project will be familiar from chapter 5, but the project presented here is more complex and layered than the combination of readings and self-reflection papers discussed there.)

The project consists of the following activities and assignments: (1) reading a short and accessible book on intellectual virtues, (2) composing a journal entry for each chapter, and (3) writing two self-reflection papers that incorporate material from the chapters and journal entries.[27] I will briefly explain each of these elements and how they fit together.

I ask students to read approximately one chapter of the selected text per week; most of the chapters explore a particular virtue. I devote a small amount of class time to a discussion of each chapter. Typically, I ask students to do a Sentence-Phrase-Word thinking routine to prepare for these discussions (see chapter 8 for more on this thinking routine and others). For each of the chapters, students also write journal entries of no fewer than 250 words. These entries address questions like: What stood out to you most in this chapter? Why? What does the chapter suggest about your own intellectual character strengths and limitations? Did you learn something about yourself or feel challenged by reading it? What are some specific things you might continue to do or do differently as a result of what you've read?

In the first self-reflection paper, students begin by summarizing what they've learned about their intellectual character from their reading and journaling. I ask them to include examples of what their intellectual character strengths and limitations look like in practice and the impact of these qualities on their lives as thinkers or learners. I also invite them to reflect on the possible origins of these attributes (i.e., on the experiences, relationships, or other factors that might have led to their development). Next, students identify several concrete steps or practices aimed at deepening some of their intellectual character strengths and mitigating some of their intellectual character limitations. They also commit to engaging in one or more of these practices.

The second self-reflection paper follows up on and extends the first. Students begin by reflecting on what they've learned from their recent reading and journaling, paying special attention to how their intellectual character strengths and limitations tend to manifest themselves, where they might have come from, and so on. Next, the students discuss their experience with the concrete steps they committed to taking in the first paper. Did they follow through with these steps? If so, what, specifically, were some of the results? If they didn't follow through, why not? In particular, what beliefs, attitudes, or feelings might have gotten in the way? Finally, they identify the two or three intellectual virtues they most want to develop or exemplify, explain some potential obstacles to their growth in these virtues, and describe some additional concrete steps or practices aimed at overcoming these obstacles.

Although the project is fairly demanding and clearly geared toward advanced secondary or postsecondary students, my students tend to enjoy and learn a good deal from the project. This impression is based on many conversations with students over the years and on semester course evaluations in which students regularly identify the project as the most beneficial part of the course. Once again, the project aims to provide students with an extended opportunity to reflect on and build a mental model of their intellectual character strengths and limitations, a model that will equip them to better practice and cultivate intellectual virtues.[28]

CHAPTER 7

Understanding

> Between "understanding" because another person seeks to
> impress upon us the explanation of a thing by speech, and
> "understanding" the thing of ourselves, there is an immeasur-
> able distance.
>
> —Maria Montessori, *Spontaneous Activity in Education*

What is understanding? According to one way of thinking about it, to
understand something is to comprehend its linguistic meaning. For example, as my teenage son darts out the door, he clearly *understands* my statement that he must immediately move his car if he wants to avoid getting a
ticket from the street sweeper. According to a different view, understanding is a considerably richer and more complex state of mind. I might, for
instance, know several facts about the Battle of the Bulge: that it was fought
in Belgium under snowy conditions, involved a surprise attack by the Ger-
mans, resulted in a large number of American casualties, and so on. While
knowing and comprehending several facts about the battle, I might not
understand it. I might fail to grasp why the Allies were surprised by the
attack, the role the weather played in how the battle unfolded, or the battle's broader significance within the whole of the World War II.

This chapter is about teaching for understanding in this second, more
complex and demanding sense.[1] It is, we might say, about teaching for
deep understanding. This is the kind of understanding that philosophers of

education Paul Hirst and Richard S. Peters presumably had in mind when they observed that "whatever else an educated person is, he is one who has some understanding of something."[2] Many of us presumably care a good deal about teaching for understanding. At least in principle, we oppose methods of instruction that favor mere memorization or the rote application of principles and formulas. Instead, we want our students to achieve cognitive mastery. We want them to acquire a broad explanatory grasp of the material, make connections between the things they're learning and what they already know, and apply what they're learning to new questions and problems.

UNDERSTANDING AND INTELLECTUAL VIRTUES

What is the connection, then, between teaching for understanding and teaching for intellectual virtues?[3] This is an important question given that understanding is not itself an intellectual virtue. Understanding is a type of knowledge or a way of knowing; it is not an attribute of character on par with intellectual humility, autonomy, courage, or tenacity. While intellectual virtues are helpful for acquiring understanding, intellectual virtues and understanding are different kinds of things.[4] So, again, why should a book on teaching for intellectual virtues include a chapter on teaching for understanding?

Why Focus on Understanding?

To answer this question, we need to look more closely at how intellectual virtues and understanding are related to each other. As we saw in chapter 2, intellectual virtues point beyond themselves. Exemplars of intellectual virtue aren't preoccupied with being or becoming intellectually virtuous. That's not the primary thing they think about or strive for. Instead, their focus lies elsewhere: on exploring new ideas and perspectives, wrestling with challenging questions, and acquiring new knowledge. Intellectually virtuous thinkers tend to care about and enjoy these exploratory, challenging activities.[5]

To keep matters simple, let's imagine that intellectual virtues aim, specifically, at knowledge. This idea can be unpacked in a few ways. First, consider how odd it would be for an exemplar of intellectual virtues to be passionately curious about trivial or sordid subject matters—for example, about the number of blades of grass on one's front lawn or the latest Hollywood sex scandal. This doesn't compute. That's because caring about knowledge of this sort isn't personally admirable or praiseworthy, while exemplars of intellectual virtue *are* admirable and praiseworthy. What these considerations suggest is that intellectual virtues aim at knowledge of "worthy" or "important" subject matters.

What counts as a worthy or important subject matter? This is a tough question, one that philosophers have shed quite a bit of ink attempting to answer. Some think the answer depends entirely on the subject matter itself. Others think it depends at least in part on the abilities, interests, or backgrounds of the knower or knowers in question.[6] Fortunately, we need not settle this issue here. Our concern in this book is with *academic* teaching and learning, that is, with teaching and learning about familiar subjects like history, biology, geometry, and poetry. While some people might doubt that knowledge of this sort is worthy or important, I assume that most teachers don't feel this way. Put another way, for most readers of this book, it makes good sense to think of academic knowledge as among the worthy or important kinds of knowledge that an intellectually virtuous person might value or pursue.

Second, as I've noted in other chapters, intellectually virtuous people tend to care about important knowledge at least partly for its own sake. They don't treat knowledge as a mere means to an end. Instead, they regard it as having at least some intrinsic value. This attitude is entirely consistent with the possibility—indeed the fact—that even exemplars of intellectual virtue also value knowledge instrumentally, that is, on account of its usefulness for achieving various nonepistemic goals. To illustrate, an intellectually virtuous virologist might have an interest in understanding a particular mechanism in white blood cells partly because she's fascinated by cellular biology but also because she cares about finding a cure for an infectious disease.[7]

Third, the kind of knowledge that interests intellectually virtuous people generally has a certain structure. Imagine someone who knows many isolated facts about the Civil War or the history of science, say, but who has a very limited grasp of how these facts fit together or their broader historical significance. Surely there is something lackluster about this person's knowledge; it lacks a certain depth and complexity, both of which are valuable from an intellectual or educational point of view. As a result, the pursuit of knowledge like this—knowledge of isolated or decontextualized facts—is not especially virtuous. This example suggests that intellectually virtuous people care about and are motivated to pursue not just any kind of knowledge, but complex understanding in particular.

When I have a complex understanding of something (be it an event, a theory, a poem, a mathematical concept, or a person), I have a firm grasp of its various aspects and of how these aspects are related to each other and to the thing as a whole. Typically, I can explain what I understand to others. I can also apply my knowledge to new situations, problems, and questions and make reliable predictions on the basis of this knowledge. As Douglas Newton explains, understanding "confers flexibility in thought and action" and "imparts feelings of competence and confidence," enabling us to "think for ourselves, make reasoned choices, [and] evaluate ideas."[8] Similarly, Tina Blythe describes understanding as an ability to "carry out a variety of actions or 'performances' that show one's grasp of a topic and at the same time advance it. It is being able to take knowledge and use it in new ways."[9]

We are now in a position to appreciate the relationship between intellectual virtues and understanding. In short, intellectual virtues *aim* at understanding. Understanding is the kind or variety of knowledge that intellectually virtuous people prize and pursue. More precisely, they prize and pursue (at least partly for its own sake) deep understanding of important or worthy subject matters.

Implications for Teaching

The picture just sketched of understanding and intellectual virtues is rather abstract and idealistic. What does it suggest about *teaching* for intellectual virtues? At a minimum, it suggests that if I am interested in helping my students grow in intellectual virtues, I should do what I can to help them develop a concern for understanding. And what better way to do this than to help them pursue and achieve a firm understanding of the subject matter we are exploring together? In short, teaching for intellectual virtues demands teaching for understanding.[10]

This point also holds in the other direction. Not only does teaching for intellectual virtues require teaching for understanding, but teaching for understanding requires teaching for intellectual virtues. To see why, note that when it comes to acquiring certain forms or items of knowledge, there is little for us to do but sit back and absorb this knowledge. Although this is a form of learning, it assigns the learner a merely passive role. Genuine understanding, by contrast, is not received; it is *achieved*. Describing the view of Maria Montessori on this point, Patrick Frierson comments, "To really understand something, to understand it *for oneself*, one must be *active*."[11]

In the typical case, genuine understanding takes sustained and rigorous effort. It involves probing for and making connections, asking the right questions, entertaining relevant possibilities, and considering problems from multiple perspectives. Intellectual virtues are attributes of character that enable us to perform these activities and to perform them well. Virtues like intellectual thoroughness, curiosity, and open-mindedness play a critical role in the acquisition of understanding. Therefore, when teaching for understanding, we must also help our students practice and cultivate intellectual virtues.

TEACHING FOR UNDERSTANDING

Given the connection between teaching for intellectual virtues and teaching for deep understanding, let's now consider some implications of this connection for what we teach and how we teach it, that is, for curriculum and instruction. I will describe five features of understanding-based curriculum and instruction. While doing so, I recognize that some of us have more control than others do over the curriculum we use and the instructional practices we select. Although latitude in these matters can be a significant benefit, I will focus here on values and practices that can be implemented to a greater or lesser extent and within relatively fixed parameters.

Depth Before Breadth

Like teaching for intellectual virtues, teaching for understanding involves favoring depth over breadth. Depth of knowledge is important for two reasons, one having to do with the content of what is being learned, and the other having to do with how this content is engaged or processed.[12]

As described earlier, understanding is closely related to the goal of cognitive mastery. To understand something is to have an illuminating and firm grasp of it. It involves perceiving how or why the object of understanding is the way it is and how it is related to other things one knows about. For most topics and issues, acquiring this kind of mastery takes time. It isn't fostered by a series of simple definitions, a list of bullet points, or a tidy PowerPoint presentation.

For this reason, teaching for understanding often requires limiting the scope or quantity of the material covered in a given class period, unit, or course. This narrowed scope is not a trivial cost. Breadth of knowledge is a good thing: it's good to know a lot about a lot. Nevertheless, given the limited time we have with our students, if we're committed to going deep with them—to probing, analyzing, and reflecting—then some kind of trade-off with breadth is inevitable. To be sure, there are ways of minimizing this trade-off, for example, by performing a systematic review of how we allocate our instructional minutes and eliminating unnecessary practices and activities.[13] But in the end, there will always be tension between depth and breadth of coverage. Where facilitating understanding is the goal, depth must be prioritized.

An emphasis on depth extends not just to content but also to the kind of intellectual engagement we elicit from our students. A course of mine might be very well designed in that it doesn't attempt to cover too much ground and includes readings and other curricular materials that reflect the depth and nuances of the subject matter. However, if I neglect to encourage rigorous thinking on the part of my students—if I don't provide them with well-supported opportunities to probe the subject matter, to ask thought-ful questions, to seek and provide explanations, and to raise and respond to potential objections—then I won't be teaching for understanding in a seri-ous way. Therefore, a further aspect of teaching for understanding consists of fostering a level of critical engagement commensurate with the depth and complexity of the subject matter in question.

Later in the chapter, we will consider some examples of how to fos-ter rigorous engagement in a clasroom setting. Presently, we'll examine one additional implication of teaching for understanding. As any seasoned teacher knows, many of the most fruitful moments of going deep with our students on a particular point or idea occur spontaneously—they're occa-sioned by unexpected comments or insights from students or by their con-fusion about something we've said or tried to explain. If we are attempting to cover too much material or haven't left space for deep engagement with the subject matter, we'll be ill equipped to make the most of these moments. This failure to engage can be costly. Our students' insights have the power to help us and their peers see things in a different light. And their expres-sions of confusion or frustration can compel us (or their peers) to explain things differently or from a different point of view. In either case, the aim of understanding is well served.

Explanation

Perhaps the most salient difference between someone who genuinely under-stands a topic and someone who merely knows a lot about it is a capacity for explanation. Understanding and the ability to explain go hand in hand. This connection should not be too surprising given the nature of understand-ing. If I have a genuine understanding of a concept, I'll have a firm grasp of how its various parts fit together and how it is related to other concepts. I'll also be able to apply the concept to new contexts and questions. If I can do these things, I should also be able to explain the concept to others. Conversely, if I think I understand a concept but find myself struggling to explain it to myself or to someone else, there's a good chance I don't actu-ally understand it. As David Perkins observes, we can "gauge a person's understanding at a given time [by asking] the person to do something that puts understanding to work—explaining, solving a problem, building an argument, constructing a product."[14]

The connection between understanding and explanation has important implications for how we go about teaching for understanding. First, to the extent that we have control over which texts or other curricular materials we use, we'll want to select materials that place a premium on explanation, that is, that give considerable attention to the how and why of the subject matter. A history curriculum that focuses mainly on dates, basic facts, and key events will neglect the deeper causes and significance of the events as well as how the events are related to each other and to other events across history. Such a curriculum leaves a lot to be desired. Contrast this with a curriculum that raises probing and thought-provoking questions about historical events, considers these events from a broad range of perspectives, rigorously explores their underlying causes, and situates them within a broader historical context.[15] While this approach might be more demanding of students and teachers, it is more likely to facilitate a complex understanding of the subject matter.

The value of an explanation-rich curriculum might seem obvious in a subject like history but less obvious in an area like mathematics. However, it is now much more common for math curricula to emphasize outcomes such as conceptual understanding and the ability to explain mathematical ideas and reasoning. This shift in focus is due partly to the influence of the new Common Core State Standards in mathematics, the preamble to which says:

> One hallmark of mathematical understanding is the ability to justify, in a way appropriate to the student's mathematical maturity, why a particular mathematical statement is true or where a mathematical rule comes from. There is a world of difference between a student who can summon a mnemonic device to expand a product such as $(a + b)(x + y)$ and a student who can explain where the mnemonic comes from. The student who can explain the rule understands the mathematics, and may have a better chance to succeed at a less familiar task such as expanding $(a + b + c)(x + y)$.[16]

Michigan State University's Connected Mathematics Project is an example of a mathematics curriculum that adheres well to these insights. Its aim is "to help students and teachers develop mathematical knowledge, understanding, and skill along with an awareness of and appreciation for the rich connections among mathematical strands and between mathematics and other disciplines."[17] Achieving this goal is inseparable from seeking and providing explanations of mathematic concepts.

Our own words and actions as teachers must also reflect the importance of explanatory understanding. When planning to teach a body of material, we must pay close attention to the how and why of this material and build our observations into our lessons and classroom-based discussions and exercises. We need to be ready and willing to go deeper, to allow ourselves to take a step back and wonder, and to seek out and make connections among the topics or concepts we're exploring. This sort of intellectual exploration can be challenging: old habits die hard, and we are often pressed for time. However, with appropriate forethought and discipline, it can be an effective way of giving the activity of explanation, and the value of understanding, a central place in our teaching.

A focus on explanation can also be worked into the assignments and assessments we give our students. As I've mentioned elsewhere in the book, I regularly talk with my undergraduate students about distinguishing themselves—in their papers, exams, projects, and so forth—from the "mere regurgitator," a person who simply regurgitates or repeats ideas exactly as they were presented in class, from a book, or elsewhere. Mere regurgitation does not demonstrate genuine understanding. A student who memorizes the notes from class and simply "copies and pastes" the relevant material into an exam or another assignment might have a very poor grasp of the topic. One of the best ways to distinguish oneself from the mere regurgitator is to explain the idea or concept that one is discussing—to say something about what the concept means, why it's true, how it's connected to other concepts, or what it looks like in practice.

In my courses, we sometimes study succinct, premise-by-premise formulations of philosophical arguments. On exams, I ask students to demonstrate an understanding of these arguments. Some students do little more than reproduce the arguments exactly as they were presented in class and leave it at that. In doing so, they fail to make clear that they actually understand the material they've rehearsed. Other students, by contrast, begin by restating the premises of an argument but then go on to explain what these premises mean and why they have some degree of plausibility; or they illustrate the premises using their own examples. When students take the latter approach, it's much clearer to me, as the person evaluating their work, whether they have a firm personal grasp of the material they are discussing.

In keeping with this picture, when I assess a student's grasp of a concept or chunk of material, I ask myself the following sorts of questions: Does the student really understand what he or she is talking about? Or does the student's grasp of the subject matter appear to be superficial or flimsy? Could a "mere regurgitator" have produced this answer? Despite the simplicity of attending to these questions, I find this practice quite powerful. It keeps me attuned to the difference between cursory knowledge and deep understanding.

Thus far in the chapter, we've examined two emphases integral to teaching for understanding: depth versus breath, and explanation. These emphases underscore the importance of intellectual *thoroughness* to teaching for understanding. While thoroughness may not be the most intriguing or compelling virtue, it is central to the activities of asking why or how, seeking and providing explanations, and making connections between seemingly unrelated ideas. It is honed by and helps facilitate the development of understanding.

Multiple Perspectives

Another way to develop an understanding of something is to consider it from multiple perspectives. A concept like evolution, for instance, needn't be studied only from a scientific point of view; it can also be studied from historical, literary, philosophical, or artistic perspectives. Similarly, a historical event can be approached, not merely from the standpoint of the victors, so to speak, but also from the standpoint of other parties affected by the event, including inanimate objects or entities, such as the environment, a political document, or an institution. By exploring concepts or events from multiple perspectives, students are encouraged to develop a more comprehensive grasp of the subject matter.

An example of this is a thinking routine known as Circle of Viewpoints, which "helps learners to identify and consider . . . different and diverse perspectives involved in and around a topic, event, or issue."[18] This protocol begins with the identification of multiple viewpoints from which the relevant topic or issue might be considered. These viewpoints are written in a circle on a whiteboard or a large sheet of paper visible to the entire class. Next, students identify a viewpoint they'd like to explore, which they do by addressing three prompts: (1) "I am thinking of . . . from the viewpoint of . . ." (students name the event or issue they're exploring and the standpoint from which they're exploring it); (2) "I think . . . because . . ." (they describe or comment on the topic from the relevant standpoint and support or explain their reasoning); and (3) "A question or concern I have from this standpoint is . . ." (they consider what someone who occupies the standpoint might be puzzled or curious about). Finally, in small groups or as a class, students share their responses with each other. The responses are then recorded on the whiteboard or sheet of paper. According to Ron Ritchhart and colleagues, this routine fosters "a broader and more complete understanding" of the event or issue being studied.[19]

Another way to foster understanding through a consideration of multiple perspectives involves the use of objections and replies. This won't apply to all subject matters or types of intellectual engagement. But it applies any time students are being asked to defend a thesis or to argue for a particular point of view. One way to help students develop a strong argument is to have them give serious consideration to an opposing view, in particular, to how someone might object to, question, or take issue with their argument.

When engaged in this activity, students must formulate questions or objections that are reasonable. These questions should be ones that an intelligent and informed peer might raise. There is little point in having them come up with objections that can easily be rebutted or refuted. Challenging their own views in this way can be difficult for some students. To illustrate, when I assign philosophical papers, I typically require students to raise and respond to two or three objections to their main argument. I've had countless students come to me asking for help on this part of their papers. They wonder, "If I'm convinced that my argument really supports my thesis, how can I come up with good or powerful objections to it?" In response, I usually say something like "I understand this isn't easy, but I'm confident you can do it. After all, do you believe that no reasonable or informed person could possibly disagree with or have a serious objection to your reasoning?" I don't think I've ever received an affirmative reply to this question.

The idea that considering multiple perspectives can facilitate understanding has obvious ties to the virtue of *open-mindedness*. Indeed, openmindedness simply is a disposition to consider alternative standpoints in the interest of trying to reach the truth or acquire understanding. Like thoroughness, open-mindedness is both enhanced and nurtured by our efforts to understand.

Projects

Another way of teaching for understanding involves the use of projects, or multistage assignments that require students to approach a complex problem or question using a variety of methods or perspectives. Understood in these fairly general terms, projects can be used in different ways and across a range of content areas. They can also be used in conjunction with other types of assignments, assessments, or pedagogical approaches.

To spell out why the use of projects fits well with teaching for understanding, I will focus in particular on project-based learning (PBL).[20] PBL is a fairly specific and comprehensive approach to teaching and learning. If your school does not already practice PBL, this needn't be an issue. In what follows, I'll emphasize aspects of the approach that can be integrated within a diverse range of instructional contexts.

PBL is "a teaching method in which students gain knowledge and skills by working for an extended period of time to investigate and respond to an authentic, engaging, and complex question, problem, or challenge."[21]

For example, with this approach, students might research factors contributing to air pollution in their community and work with local government and public health agencies to develop proposals for improving air quality. Doing so could provide them with opportunities to develop knowledge and skills related to data collection and analysis, environmental science, public health, or local politics.[22]

Numerous books and articles have been written describing the practice of PBL and documenting its effectiveness for promoting student learning.[23] Accordingly, I will limit my attention here to some connections between PBL and teaching for understanding.

It isn't difficult to appreciate why an approach like PBL might be especially conducive to nurturing understanding. First, PBL is a problem-focused method.[24] As such, it is far removed from approaches that favor passive information consumption or the rote application of principles or formulas. Instead, it promotes active, critical thinking. It requires students to struggle and persevere to arrive at a solution. These activities put students in an excellent position to develop a deep and comprehensive grasp of the issues.

Second, PBL involves an application of knowledge to real-world issues and questions.[25] As we've seen, the ability to make this kind of application is a telltale sign of understanding. Moreover, the application of knowledge to new issues or contexts also deepens a person's grasp of the subject matter. In this way, PBL both requires and augments understanding.

In *Setting the Standard for Project Based Learning*, John Larmer and coauthors draw attention to both of the features of PBL just identified: "Problems and questions provide the organizing structure for [PBL] . . . [S]tudents are not just gaining knowledge in order to remember it; they're gaining knowledge in order to use it. By focusing on a problem or question, students not only master new knowledge but also learn when and how this new knowledge can be used."[26]

Third, PBL often involves the incorporation of multiple perspectives.[27] When it comes to troubleshooting real-world problems, the interests of various groups must be considered and weighed against each other. For reasons discussed earlier, this kind of perspective-switching can be an effective way of helping students develop a more comprehensive and nuanced grasp of the material.

We've examined some connections between the methodology of PBL and the outcome of understanding. As Larmer and coauthors note, "PBL is an instructional approach that encourages both students and teachers to dig deeply into a subject, going beyond rote learning and grappling with the concepts and understandings fundamental to the subject and the discipline."[28] The particular aspects of PBL we've drawn attention to are not unique to this approach. Rather, any complex and well-designed project—whether part of a PBL curriculum or not—can manifest and nurture understanding in many ways, including problem-focused attention, the application of knowledge to real-world or otherwise meaningful topics and questions, and the incorporation of multiple perspectives.[29] Indeed, you may already use projects like these as a way of helping your students develop a comprehensive grasp of what they're learning.

Well-designed projects also invite the practice of several intellectual virtues. The focus on problem-solving encourages intellectual *autonomy*. The need to examine the problem from multiple perspectives encourages *open-mindedness*. And the complex and long-term structure of a project encourages intellectual *tenacity* and *perseverance*.

Inquiry

Inquiry-based learning is another familiar pedagogical approach that aligns closely with teaching for understanding.[30] By *inquiry*, I mean a deliberate and sustained attempt to get to the fact of the matter about a particular issue or question (e.g., why the sky is blue, how the pyramids were built, what caused the dinosaurs to go extinct). Inquiry-based learning, as Teresa Coffman describes it, "builds upon students' natural curiosity of the world and embeds relevant real-world problems and issues into the curriculum."[31]

To see why an emphasis on inquiry is essential to teaching for understanding, recall that the teaching for understanding aims to help students grasp the how and why of what they're learning and to do so actively and intelligently; it requires them to wonder, explore, probe, make connections, and apply their knowledge.[32] Inquiry-based approaches to teaching and learning facilitate both of these aims.

First, they emphasize the how and why of the subject matter by structuring learning around a complex question that students are likely to be curious about or find meaningful. As Coffman notes, "The primary goal in inquiry learning is to pose a question that relates to the standards of learning as well as student interests."[33] These are not simply yes-or-no questions. Rather, they are *why* questions, such as "Why is plastic waste a threat to our oceans, and what can we do about it?" or "What is 'fake news,' why is it a problem, and how can it be identified?" Second, an inquiry-based approach requires active and intelligent engagement with the subject matter because it puts the onus on students to research and formulate answers to the guiding question. Students are responsible for digging into and developing a genuine mastery of the topics they're studying.[34]

Inquiry-based learning bears several similarities to PBL.[35] Both allow students' natural interests and questions to influence what is learned. And both place a premium on active learning.[36] A further similarity is that both approaches can be implemented in ways that are more or less comprehensive and systematic.[37] Just as we can use complex, well-designed projects to help our students understand the subject matter more deeply even without comprehensive PBL, we can also help our students engage in inquiry even if our curriculum isn't completely inquiry based. We can create opportunities for students to identify thoughtful questions that interest them, and we can charge them with the thinking and research necessary for answering these questions and support them along the way.

In addition to promoting genuine understanding, the activity of inquiry also helps foster the virtue of *curiosity*. Again, on the approach described here, inquiry is structured around questions that students are likely to find interesting and meaningful. Moreover, students themselves are empowered to seek and find answers to these questions. In this way, inquiry provides students with frequent opportunities to nurture and deepen their intellectual appetites.

CONCLUSION

We have examined five features of teaching and learning that support the development of deep understanding: (1) depth of coverage and engagement, (2) providing explanations (as opposed to mere regurgitation), (3) multiple perspectives, (4) relevant and complex projects, and (5) student-led inquiry. For each of these features, we have also noted important connections with particular intellectual virtues, such as thoroughness, open-mindedness, autonomy, tenacity, and curiosity. The connection between teaching for intellectual virtues and teaching for understanding should now be apparent. In short, teaching for understanding is an indispensable part of teaching for intellectual virtues because it gives students frequent opportunities to practice intellectual virtues. In the chapter that follows, we explore the idea of practicing intellectual virtues in much greater depth.

CHAPTER 8

Practice

> What we need to learn before doing, we learn by doing; for example, we become builders by building, and lyre-players by playing the lyre. So too we become just by doing just actions, temperate by temperate actions, and courageous by courageous actions.
>
> —Aristotle, *Nicomachean Ethics*

For millennia, moral philosophers have taught that the path to virtue is paved with virtuous actions. We become generous by regularly giving of our financial resources, honest by telling the truth, courageous by facing down our fears, and so on. While this seems plausible, it is also a little puzzling: How can we regularly perform virtuous actions if we aren't already virtuous?

In response to this question, Aristotle observed that it is possible to perform virtuous actions without actually *being* virtuous, that is, without possessing a settled *habit* or *disposition* to behave in virtuous ways. For Aristotle, we become virtuous by imitating virtuous individuals. He thought that if we repeatedly behave as a virtuous person would, then over time and with a fair bit of luck, these patterns of behavior will blossom into bona fide virtues.[1]

PRACTICING INTELLECTUAL VIRTUES

This was Aristotle's view of moral virtues. However, the same idea can be applied to intellectual virtues.[2] Author Philip Dow describes the habitual nature of intellectual character—and its practical significance—as follows:

> We tend to think of our choices as isolated moments of decision in which we reason through the pros and cons before making the best choice we can based on the information that we have. In reality, most of the choices we make are not the result of conscious and deliberate reasoning. Whether it is a product of the flood of mental distractions and the frenetic busyness of our modern lives, or simply exhaustion, we end up making most of our choices on mental auto-pilot. We don't reason so much as react, and in this haste we are usually forced to rely on the mental ruts our thinking patterns have produced. These mental ruts that our thinking naturally slips into are our intellectual character. If we have trained our minds in the direction of good thinking habits, our mental auto-pilot will generally produce good choices, and good choices generally produce good outcomes. If we have not actively sought to develop the character of our minds then the prognosis is less encouraging. If these little decisions never amounted to much it wouldn't really matter, but the problem is that it is in the accumulation of these little choices that the trajectory of our lives is set. In other words, the quality of our mental auto-pilot matters a great deal.[3]

How exactly are these "mental ruts" formed? How does a person get from performing intellectually virtuous actions to *being* intellectually virtuous?

As described in chapter 2, for every intellectual virtue, there is a particular kind of mental activity characteristic of this virtue—an activity that differentiates the virtue from other virtues. Intellectual carefulness, for instance, characteristically involves being on the lookout for and avoiding intellectual errors. Open-mindedness involves perspective-switching. And intellectual autonomy involves thinking for oneself. Recall as well that these activities can be practiced and improved on. With practice we can get better at spotting and avoiding potential mistakes, taking up alternative standpoints, and drawing our own conclusions. This is the skill or competence dimension of intellectual virtues.

The proposal, then, is that we cultivate intellectual virtues by regularly practicing the skills or abilities proper to these virtues. Accordingly, if we repeatedly engage in perspective-switching, regularly taking up and giving a fair hearing to points of view very different from our own, we will gradually improve at this activity and eventually develop a habit of open-mindedness.[4]

Tempting as it may be, this picture is an oversimplification. Even if we regularly practice intellectual virtues, there is no guarantee that this activity will take root in our character and develop into a habit.[5] We might ultimately dislike thinking or acting virtuously or find that the costs of doing so are too high. In short, if our own psychological constitution or circumstances don't support virtuous practice, then regularly performing virtuous actions may fail to have a lasting impact on our character.[6]

This limitation underscores the importance of the postures and practices discussed in previous chapters. These postures and practices can be thought of as ways of teaching and being with our students—ways that serve to complement and enhance their practice of intellectual virtues. The postures and practices help create conditions in our students and classrooms whereby, if our students regularly practice intellectual virtues, virtuous habits will be more likely to emerge.[7]

How can we provide our students with ongoing and well-supported opportunities to practice intellectual virtues? This is the main question we will be exploring in this chapter. I will begin by reviewing an exercise aimed at helping you to identify a list of target virtues and to connect these virtues to some of your existing pedagogical practices. Next, I'll focus on thinking routines as a straightforward and concrete way of encouraging your students to practice intellectual virtues. Finally, I'll offer some guidance on how best to implement and use these routines.

Getting Oriented

In this section, we will undertake a reflection exercise aimed at helping you think through how to provide your students with frequent and well-designed opportunities to practice the skills and abilities characteristic of intellectual virtues. The exercise centers around three main questions: Which virtues are you interested in focusing on with your students? What do these virtues look like in practice? And how can you create opportunities for your students to practice these virtues?

Which Virtues Are You Interested in Focusing On?

When addressing these questions, you can begin by identifying a list of *target virtues*, the virtues you most want to help your students cultivate. If you neglect to do this—if your aim, say, is to help your students become more intellectually virtuous in some general or unspecified sense—then your efforts are likely to founder. When we provide students with opportunities to practice intellectual virtues, we are helping them practice the skills characteristic of *particular* virtues like curiosity, attentiveness, intellectual autonomy, and intellectual tenacity. Therefore, if you're unclear about which virtues you'd like to help your students develop, you are likely to struggle with identifying and designing opportunities for them to practice intellectual virtues.

If you are just beginning to experiment with teaching for intellectual virtues, you might want to limit your focus to two or three target virtues. You might begin by asking yourself: Which two or three intellectual virtues am I most interested in giving my students opportunities to practice? To answer this question, you might want to look back at chapter 2, which offers brief sketches of nine intellectual virtues. Or you might look at a book like Nathan King's *The Excellent Mind* or Philip Dow's *Virtuous Minds*, both of which contain lively and accessible profiles of several individual virtues.[8]

As you identify your list of target virtues, keep in mind several points. First, which virtues are most relevant to the subject matter you teach? For instance, if you teach history, you might be drawn to virtues like open-mindedness and intellectual humility. If you teach math, then intellectual carefulness and courage may seem more relevant. Or if you teach science, you might emphasize virtues such as curiosity and intellectual autonomy. Realistically, students need to manifest a range of intellectual virtues to develop a firm grasp of any subject matter. However, this requirement needn't prevent you from identifying and focusing on the virtues most relevant to your content area.

Second, as you select your target virtues, you should be mindful of who your students are—of their personal, cultural, racial, and socioeconomic backgrounds. As noted in chapter 3, if your students come from a background marked by poverty and chronic stress, or if they've been subject to systemic injustice or oppression, then an ongoing emphasis on attending to and owning their intellectual limitations (humility) may be unwise.[9] Instead, they might do better to focus on recognizing and owning their intellectual strengths (autonomy). Conversely, if your students come from a privileged and affluent background or have had minimal exposure to outside perspectives, then it might be advisable to emphasize humility and open-mindedness over virtues like autonomy or tenacity. The point, again, is that your selection of target virtues should be informed by the specific identity or identities of your student population.

Third, it is also a good idea to allow students themselves to weigh in on which virtues they want to work on or would like to cultivate.[10] Of course, the students' preferences may conflict with each other. And the virtues the students select may conflict with what you know about the kind of thinking required by your subject matter. Nevertheless, you can still solicit their input and do your best to incorporate it into your decision-making. Doing so has an obvious benefit: the students are more likely to be enthusiastic about practicing virtues they have identified as important or have expressed an interest in cultivating.

What Do These Target Virtues Look Like in Practice?

Once you've identified a list of target virtues, the next step is to spend some time reflecting on the activities or skills characteristic of these virtues. You can do so by posing questions to your students about each virtue on your list: What does it look like for someone to practice or manifest this virtue? What does a person with this virtue tend to do, think, or feel?

Here too it may be useful to consult the profiles of individual virtues from chapter 2 or other sources. Doing so can help you pinpoint the defining features and activities characteristic of your target virtues. However, this may only get you so far. Most important at this stage is not to imagine how people *in general* might practice your target virtues, but to picture instead how students like yours, engaging with the subject matter you teach, might practice them. This idea can be unpacked along three dimensions.

First, your mental picture of your target virtues must be developmentally informed and appropriate.[11] As we've seen in other chapters, what open-mindedness or intellectual autonomy look like in adults, say, may be considerably different from what they look like in elementary or middle school students. Therefore, as you reflect on your target virtues, be sure to identify expressions of these virtues that reflect the developmental capabilities and limitations of your students. If you've been teaching for a while, you'll likely have a good sense of what these capabilities and limitations are. If not, you may want to do a little research on the topic.[12] In any case, without a developmentally informed idea of what it would look like for your students to practice your target virtues, your efforts to help them practice these virtues are likely to be met with frustration.

Second, here as well, your thinking should be informed by the particular backgrounds and identities of your students. Suppose you're working with students whose cultural background is such that they place a great deal of value on respecting and deferring to their teachers. This background should be taken into account when you consider how your students might practice a virtue like intellectual autonomy or courage. These virtues may express themselves differently in your students than they would in students whose cultural background favors independence or self-reliance. Similarly, if a high percentage of your students have learning disabilities, you might need to rethink your idea of what it would look like for them to practice virtues that touch on these disabilities. If you have several students with ADHD, for instance, you'll need to think carefully about how these students might practice the virtue of attentiveness.

Third, as with your initial list of target virtues, your mental picture of what these virtues look like in practice should also be informed by the subject matter you teach. You should consider how these virtues are likely to express themselves in the kind of thinking or other mental operations demanded by your content area. To do this, you might bring to mind a particular assignment you regularly use in one of your classes and ask yourself: In the context of this assignment, what might it look like for my students to practice one or more of my target virtues? What sorts of things might they do or say? What kinds of mistakes might they avoid by practicing these virtues?

How Can You Create Opportunities for Your Students to Practice Your Target Virtues?

Once you've arrived at a suitable list of target virtues and have a good sense of what they look like in practice, you can turn your attention to two additional questions. First, in what ways are you *already* creating opportunities for your students to practice your target virtues? Here the task is to survey your existing teaching practices and materials (your primary modes of instruction, in-class exercises, homework assignments, projects, etc.) and to identify how you regularly encourage your students to do things like consider multiple perspectives (open-mindedness), wonder and ask thoughtful questions (curiosity), take intellectual risks (courage), and admit their intellectual limitations (humility).

Hopefully this examination of your methods will bring to light several ways in which you are already encouraging the practice of intellectual virtues. If so, this recognition is a good springboard from which to consider a second question: What else might you do to create structured opportunities for your students to practice the mental moves characteristic of your target virtues? How might you tweak your existing teaching methods, exercises, assignments, or other pedagogical activities? What new activities or interventions might you introduce or experiment with?

Suppose, for instance, that your target virtues are curiosity and intellectual autonomy. You might ask yourself: In my day-to-day interactions with my students, how can I create more space for them to pause and wonder about the material we're exploring? How can I give them practice asking thoughtful questions? What can I do to encourage my students to engage in self-directed thinking? How can I create opportunities for them to form their own opinions or to come up with their own ideas or conjectures?

When I began asking questions like this about my own teaching several years ago, the results were decidedly mixed. On the one hand, it was clear that I was giving my students regular opportunities to practice virtues like carefulness and thoroughness. For instance, when assessing my students' performance on written exams, I have always valued accuracy and precision (carefulness) and required my students to explain (rather than merely regurgitate) the material they are discussing (thoroughness). That said, I was also struck and a little embarrassed by my lack of pedagogical imagination, especially with regard to the practice of virtues like curiosity, attentiveness, open-mindedness, and intellectual courage. How often was I creating structured opportunities for my students to practice wondering about what they were learning (curiosity)? What was I doing to invite them to bring their full selves—their hearts as well as their minds—to the learning process (attentiveness)? Was I regularly encouraging them to give a fair hearing to viewpoints they disagree with (open-mindedness)? Was I encouraging intellectual risk-taking, or was I protecting them from taking risks (courage)? My answers to these questions were not very impressive.

At that point in my teaching career, I was still in the grip of the idea that my primary job was to help my students develop a firm understanding of the subject matter and that their primary responsibility was to acquire and demonstrate such an understanding. As a result, my default mode of instruction was lecturing.[13] To be sure, my lectures were interactive: for example, I regularly paused to check for understanding and incorporated elements of Socratic questioning into my lectures. Although I continue to think of skilled, interactive lecturing as *one* effective practice for some teachers, this sort of lecturing was the only tool in my pedagogical toolkit.

Since that time, I have found other ways to encourage my students to practice the virtues of good thinking. As noted elsewhere in the book, I now provide my students with regular opportunities, in class and across various assignments, to spend time formulating thoughtful questions about the material we're exploring (curiosity). I also regularly pause at the beginning of class to take a step back and remind my students of the ultimate purpose of what we are doing and learning in the course. This practice draws my students in by giving them space to think, connecting what we are doing or learning to other things they care about, and inviting them to be personally present (attentiveness). When discussing controversial issues, I regularly ask my students to explore and defend a position they reject. This exercise helps them see both sides of the issue and recognize some of the limitations of their own perspectives (open-mindedness and humility).

In this section, we've examined three steps you can take to begin providing your students with ongoing and well-designed opportunities to practice intellectual virtues. First, create a list of target virtues. Second, form a clear and concrete idea of what it would look like for your students to practice these virtues. And finally, reflect on what you are already doing and what else you might do to encourage your students to engage in this practice.

THINKING ROUTINES

One effective way of encouraging students to practice intellectual virtues is *thinking routines*, which are structured protocols that elicit the mental moves characteristic of intellectual virtues. As Ron Ritchhart explains, thinking routines "consist of a few steps, are easy to teach and learn, are easily supported, and get used repeatedly."[14] To provide a more precise idea of what thinking routines involve and how they are related to teaching for intellectual virtues, I will describe a few routines in some detail. In doing so, I will lean heavily on Ritchhart and colleagues' excellent and extensive work on this topic.[15]

Step Inside

A thinking routine called Step Inside is similar to the Circle of Viewpoints routine discussed in chapter 7. While both routines revolve around perspective-taking, Step Inside is designed to go deeper and to elicit a more empathic response.[16] The routine begins with the teacher introducing an item of source material to the students. The item could be an image, a video clip, a story, a question, or any other item that contains two or more perspectives capable of being explored cognitively or emotionally.[17]

Students are then led through the following steps:

1. First, they are asked to identify the various perspectives embedded in the source material and to select one perspective they would like to explore in greater depth. Alternatively, the teacher can assign each student to a particular perspective. The teacher can also decide whether to have the students explore the perspectives individually, in small groups, or together as a class.
2. Students probe their assigned perspectives by reflecting on and recording their responses to the following four questions: (1) What might a person whose perspective you are exploring see, observe, or notice? (2) What might the person know, understand, hold true, or believe? (3) What might he or she care about? (4) What might the person wonder about or question?
3. The teacher then engages students in a discussion of their answers. The nature of the discussion will depend on whether the students have explored the perspectives individually or as a group. The aim of the discussion is for students to reflect on their thinking and to articulate what they have learned or how their thinking has changed.

Step Inside has obvious applications to the study of historical figures and events and to the exploration of characters in a novel or play. But it can also be useful for examining things like a painting, photograph, social or political issue, or proposed governmental policy.[18] Like Circle of Viewpoints, Step Inside can also be used to explore the "perspectives" of inanimate objects. This flexibility underscores the routine's broad applicability. For example, in an environmental science course, students might be encouraged to step inside the various perspectives embodied in the Great Barrier Reef to better understand the effects of climate change. In *Making Thinking Visible*, Ritchhart and his coauthors describe how Step Inside was used by one elementary teacher in a unit on electricity:

[The teacher] asked her students to think about what they had learned about circuits and the various circuits they had explored, such as lights and doorbells. Students then selected one aspect of the circuit: the wire, the electrons, the light bulb filament, and so on, to Step Inside. After the students had written their responses to the question prompts, the class played a game in which a student read his or her responses without revealing the chosen perspective, and the rest of the class tried to guess the viewpoint they had chosen.[19]

Step Inside encourages the practice of several intellectual virtues. The most obvious one is open-mindedness. However, to practice open-mindedness in the empathic way required by this routine, students must bring their "full selves" to the activity, including their powers of imagination (attentiveness). What students learn from entering empathically into the perspective of another can also be an occasion for intellectual humility, since this new knowledge might bring to light limitations or flaws in their own perspectives. Finally, like Circle of Viewpoints, Step Inside allows students to dig deeper into an issue or a problem and to gain a more comprehensive or explanatory understanding of it. Consequently, Step Inside encourages intellectual thoroughness.

What Makes You Say That?

What Makes You Say That? is a routine aimed at encouraging students to reflect on their own beliefs and thought processes. It consists simply of posing the question "What makes you say that?" In contrast to Step Inside, this routine needn't take the form of a separate exercise in the overall flow of a lesson. Instead, it can be woven throughout different classroom interactions and activities.

Like the rest of us, students often form and hold beliefs unreflectively. As a result, they sometimes lack good reasons or support for their beliefs. What Makes You Say That? provides an opportunity for students to step back and consider why they believe what they believe. This thinking routine can be applied to beliefs about any number of topics, such as why a physical phenomenon has occurred, how a character in a book should respond to a challenge, why a historical event unfolded as it did, or whether a particular mathematical conjecture is true. Because the routine invites students to consider the grounds or evidence for their beliefs, it also promotes *evidential reasoning*, an important cognitive skill.[20]

By encouraging students to grasp the connection between the evidence and their beliefs, What Makes You Say That? can help them cultivate an appropriate confidence in their beliefs. However, it can also be an occasion for recognizing that one or more of their beliefs are not well founded. Notice, in this respect, that the question "What makes you say that?" is not identical to the question "Can you support your claim with evidence?" The latter encourages students to immediately begin searching for evidence in support of what they already believe, even if this evidence has little to do with why they hold the belief or beliefs in question. It can, in some cases, encourage rationalization or post hoc justification of their beliefs. By contrast, the question "What makes you say that?" invites a broader type of reflection. In response to this question, a student might be led to conclude, "I guess I made that remark largely out of fear," "I believe this because that's what my parents believe," or "I thought I couldn't succeed at this because I've failed at it in the past."

Accordingly, the goal of What Makes You Say That? isn't so much to challenge students' beliefs. Nor is it even to compel them to defend their beliefs (though it may often and appropriately have this effect). Rather, it is to help them develop a habit of self-reflection, in particular, a habit of reflection on the reasons, motives, or other factors that underlie their thinking.

In doing so, this routine provides students with opportunities to practice several virtues. Where the routine uncovers rational support for a belief, it encourages the practice of intellectual autonomy. Where it uncovers a lack of support, it encourages the practice of intellectual humility. Because looking honestly at the basis of our beliefs can be unsettling, even disturbing, this routine also helps students practice intellectual courage. Finally, by inviting students to think deeply and carefully about the basis of their beliefs—to probe why they believe what they believe—the routine also encourages intellectual thoroughness and carefulness.

What Makes You Say That? is a good example of a routine that can be initiated not only by teachers but also by students. In a classroom discussion or debate, one student might make an effort to better understand the viewpoint of another by asking, "What makes you say that?" This question can also be posed by students to their teachers, for example, when a student doesn't understand a point the teacher is making or when a student is intrigued by something the teacher has said. In this way, What Makes You Say That? can also provide opportunities to practice *curiosity*.

See-Think-Wonder

A third routine, See-Think-Wonder, is designed to "draw on students' close looking and intent observation as the foundation for greater insights, grounded interpretations, evidence-based theory building, and broad-reaching curiosity."[21] Like Step Inside, it can be used to explore a diverse range of objects, such as paintings, photographs, artifacts, complex mathematical equations, video clips, political cartoons, maps, charts, and graphs. It is important, however, that the object be complex, interesting, or ambiguous enough to evoke thoughtful reflection and engagement.

To initiate the routine, the teacher ensures that the immediate environmental conditions (e.g., light, noise, arrangement of furniture) are conducive to close and careful observation. The teacher then introduces the object to the students and gives them two or three minutes to observe it in silence. After this period of quiet observation, the teacher guides them through the following three steps:

1. Students are asked to look intently at the object and to articulate, as concretely and specifically as possible, what they *see*. Their responses at this point should be strictly descriptive (not evaluative or interpretive). The goal is for students simply to report what they perceive with their senses. Time permitting, it can also be useful for the teacher or students to record these observations.

2. Once several observations have been made, the teacher invites students to explain or interpret the "data" they have collected. What do

the students *think* might be going on or happening with the object? To illustrate, if the object were a painting, the students would begin, in the previous step, by describing as many visual details of the painting as possible. Then, in the present step, they would begin to identify possible explanations or interpretations of these details. Although this second step builds on the first, the steps must be undertaken separately. If students jump too quickly to offering explanations or interpretations, they may fail to notice (and therefore to explain or comprehend) several important details. This step also presents an opportunity to probe students' thinking: Why are they inclined to interpret or explain the data in the relevant way? What is the basis for their thinking? Accordingly, this step can also be an opportunity to combine See-Think-Wonder with the What Makes You Say That? routine.

3. Having made careful observations of the object and proffered multiple explanations and interpretations of it, the students are then invited to take a step back and *wonder*. Here the teacher might ask questions like these: What remains unclear? What else does the painting (or other object) make you think about? Why do you think the artist (or author, etc.) made it the way she or he did? The point of this step, Ritchhart and colleagues explain, is to ensure that students "have had time to take in new information through careful observation, think about and synthesize this information, and then identify additional wonderings." It also has the potential to "open up whole new areas of exploration and thinking initiated by the students themselves."[22]

As indicated, this routine is designed to separate certain mental moves or processes that students otherwise might be tempted to combine. By asking students first to observe and then to interpret or explain, the teacher encourages them to collect all the relevant data before making conjectures or drawing conclusions about what they're viewing. One advantage of this routine is that it has a "low floor" and a "high ceiling." It has a low floor because *all* students are capable of making observations about the appearance of the object ("see"). It has a high ceiling because the "think" and "wonder" steps invite a level of intellectual engagement and reflection that is open-ended and potentially quite sophisticated.[23]

See-Think-Wonder enables students to practice at least five intellectual virtues. First, it provides an opportunity to practice attentiveness. Students are encouraged to focus intently on the object, looking closely and identifying subtle details and patterns. For a similar reason, it also invites the practice of intellectual carefulness. Again, the routine encourages students to avoid overlooking important details and to refrain from drawing premature conclusions. By requiring students to formulate their own interpretations and explanations of what they observe, the routine also encourages intellectual autonomy. Similarly, by encouraging students to probe for deeper meaning and to explain what they observe, it promotes intellectual thoroughness. And by inviting them to wonder and ask questions about the object, it provides an opportunity to practice curiosity.

Adapting and Creating Your Own Routines

While the thinking routines just described are tried-and-true, having been used and written about by seasoned practitioners and researchers, you can also modify these routines or come up with routines of your own. In doing so, you can ensure that your students are given opportunities to practice the thinking moves specific to your target virtues.

Sentence-Phrase-Word is a routine that pairs well with reading assignments.[24] It asks students to read an article, a chapter, or another text and to highlight one sentence, one phrase, and one word that struck them as significant. I use this routine with my undergraduate students for reading selections assigned as homework. To provide my students with additional opportunities to practice curiosity, I've added a fourth step, which requires formulating at least one thoughtful question inspired by the reading. This Sentence-Phrase-Word-Wonder routine encourages students to engage in reflective reading and to reread the assigned material. It also provides a useful structure for in-class discussions of the material.

In some of my more advanced undergraduate and graduate courses, I use a routine I call Agree-Disagree-Wonder. When reading and assessing philosophical texts and arguments, students often benefit from identifying points of agreement and disagreement. They also benefit from wondering and asking questions about the text or argument. I created this routine to encourage my students to practice this sequence of thinking moves. When assigning a reading selection for homework or analyzing a passage in class, I ask the students to read the text all the way through and then go back and identify (1) one part of the author's argument they *agree* with (and why), (2) one part they *disagree* with (and why), and (3) one thing the argument caused them to *think about* or *wonder*. Like Sentence-Phrase-Word, Agree-Disagree-Wonder serves as a useful springboard for in-class discussions. It also encourages the practice of several virtues, including open-mindedness, autonomy, and curiosity.

GUIDELINES FOR USING THINKING ROUTINES

Thinking routines provide students with opportunities to practice and thereby to cultivate a wide range of intellectual virtues. However, the effectiveness of these routines depends in no small part on how they are implemented. In this final section, I will briefly describe a few guidelines for the effective use of thinking routines.

Identify and Make Consistent Use of a Limited Number of Routines

Precisely because there are so many routines to choose from, it can be tempting to bounce around from one routine to another. Although you may need to experiment with several routines to identify the ones most appropriate to you, your students, and your subject matter, it is best to make frequent use of only a few routines.[25] As the name suggests, thinking routines are intended to become *routine* or *habitual*. At first, they may take some getting used to, for you and your students. The goal, however, is for the thinking moves required by the routines to become so familiar that your students begin making them with only minimal prompting. This habit is most likely to develop if the number of routines they're called on to practice is relatively small.

The power of thinking routines is on wide display at the Intellectual Virtues Academy. Across content areas and grade levels, thinking routines have a pervasive presence in the way that IVA students are taught. Directives like "Let's do a See-Think-Wonder on this" or "This would be a good opportunity for Claim-Support-Question" are as common in IVA classrooms as are statements like "Take out your notebooks and begin taking notes" or "It's time for a pop quiz" at many other schools. IVA students are habituated to engage in the varieties of thinking called for by thinking routines. It is simply what's expected of them and the way learning goes at the school.

Expectations of this sort are unlikely to form when teachers make inconsistent use of thinking routines or attempt to use too many of them. Therefore, one important guideline is to identify a small number of suitable routines and to incorporate these routines on a frequent and consistent basis. Again, the goal of doing so is for the kinds of thinking elicited by the routines to become a familiar and habitual part of how our students think and learn.

Provide Appropriate Scaffolding and Encouragement

A second guideline is related to the first. As students grow accustomed to using thinking routines, teachers should provide them with appropriate scaffolding and encouragement.[26] What this looks like will vary from one classroom to another, depending on the subject matter, the ages and abilities of the students, and the routine or routines in question. But the basic principle is straightforward: until these routines become habitual, they won't simply take care of themselves. We must pay attention, be patient, and gently assist our students as they gain familiarity with and competence in the relevant thinking moves. Often this assistance will involve carefully and authentically modeling these moves for our students. And for most of us, it will involve a good bit of trial and error.

Offer Meaningful and Constructive Feedback

A third guideline is to provide students with useful feedback on their use of thinking routines.[27] When students practice a routine, they reveal something of their intellectual character. In particular, they reveal their proficiency (or lack thereof) in the skills or abilities specific to various intellectual virtues. For this reason, providing our students with meaningful and constructive feedback on their use of thinking routines can be an opportunity to support their intellectual character development. It can also help them become more skilled at asking thoughtful questions (curiosity), considering multiple perspectives (open-mindedness), taking intellectual risks (courage), and so on. Such feedback also acknowledges their growth in these or related intellectual skills.

CONCLUSION

Our focus in this chapter has been on helping our students cultivate intellectual virtues by providing them with ongoing and well-supported opportunities to practice these virtues.[28] We have given special attention to thinking routines as one way of doing this. However, as valuable as thinking routines are, they aren't the only way of encouraging our students to practice the virtues of good thinking. Knowing yourself, your students, and your subject matter as you do, you may be in the best position to identify how to encourage your students to practice your target virtues. Therefore, I'll restate two questions posed earlier in the chapter and encourage you to consider them again: In what ways are you already providing your students with opportunities to practice specific virtues? How might you build on these efforts to provide your students with even better or more frequent opportunities of this sort?

CHAPTER 9

Modeling

> Children have never been very good at listening to their elders,
> but they have never failed to imitate them. They must, they
> have no other models.
>
> —James Baldwin, *Nobody Knows My Name*

In the previous chapter, we explored the importance of providing our students with ongoing and well-supported opportunities to practice the virtues of good thinking. We saw that such opportunities are a way of helping students develop the skills or abilities characteristic of intellectual virtues, skills like perspective-switching, thinking for oneself, asking thoughtful questions, and persisting in the face of intellectual struggle.

However, as we observed in chapter 2, intellectual virtues also have a motivational dimension. To possess intellectual tenacity, for instance, a person must not only be skilled at persisting in the face of intellectual struggle but also be motivated to use this skill when the situation calls for it. The same point applies to other intellectual virtues: each virtue involves an element of skill and an element of motivation.[1]

While providing our students with opportunities to practice intellectual virtues may serve them well along the skill dimension of intellectual character growth, it may have little impact along the motivational dimension. Suppose I succeed at teaching my students how to switch perspectives or how to formulate thoughtful and insightful questions. They may or may not use this skill once they leave my classroom. Equipping students with virtuous abilities is no guarantee that they will develop virtuous motivation.

In their research on "epistemic cognition," Clark Chinn, Ronald Rinehart, and Luke Buckland make a related observation: "The large body of research aimed at improving students' thinking does so without explicitly considering whether students *value* knowledge and truth or how these values might be cultivated through well-designed instruction." They argue that "encourage[ing] students to *care* about and seek the truth . . . even if the truth should prove inconvenient" is a "seriously neglected instructional issue."[2] In other words, we must pay closer attention to the motivational aspects of learning.

As teachers interested in helping our students experience the fullness of intellectual character growth, what can we do about this? What practices can we engage in to help nurture our students' intellectual motivation? One such practice consists of authentically modeling intellectual virtues. This practice is the focus of the present chapter.

WHY MODEL INTELLECTUAL VIRTUES?

Why, exactly, should our modeling of intellectual virtues be related to the intellectual motivation of our students? More precisely, why should our own display of qualities like curiosity, open-mindedness, and intellectual humility have an impact on our students' desire or inclination to cultivate similar qualities? To begin working our way toward an answer, we must return once more to the deeply personal nature of good teaching.

Education and Human Connection

Recall that in its *least* transformative or life-giving forms, education tends to be transactional and hypercognitive. It is driven by the dubious idea that a teacher's primary job is to deposit knowledge into the heads of students and that the role of students is to passively receive this deposit.[3] While the transmission of knowledge is one important educational aim, this vision badly neglects a deeply human dimension of teaching and learning.

By contrast, in its most vital and reorienting forms, education is a personal and intimate experience. At its center is an open and vulnerable meeting of two or more people, a meeting that is distinctively and mysteriously human. As Parker Palmer, who has written extensively on this topic, observes, "Reduce teaching to intellect, and it becomes cold abstraction; reduce it to emotions, and it becomes narcissistic; reduce it to the spiritual, and it loses its anchor to the world. Intellect, emotion, and spirit depend on one another for wholeness. They are interwoven in the human self and in education at its best."[4]

At various points in this book, I've noted that many of us who teach do so because we were deeply moved or inspired by our own best teachers. In their presence, we experienced deep connection, if not with them personally, then with who they were or what they stood for, cared about, or excelled at. In my own case, the call to teach came when, in the company of one extraordinary teacher, I found myself thinking in crystal-clear terms, "If I could do what he does in the classroom, *that's what I'd do.*" These encounters at the intersection of teaching and learning have transformative power. They are the source of many great goods: a passion for learning, love for a particular subject matter, newfound self-confidence, hope, and purpose. For some of us, they even lay bare a new career path or vocation. In every case, they imprint themselves on our identities as learners.

I teach at a university sponsored in part by the Jesuit religious order, whose founder was Saint Ignatius of Loyola (1491–1556). An Ignatian educational and pedagogical framework contains a similar view of the interpersonal and formative dimensions of teaching and learning. In a famous address, delivered on the four hundredth anniversary of the *Ratio Studiorum* (a document outlining the defining features of a Jesuit education), the Reverend Peter Hans Kolvenbach, SJ, described the aim of Jesuit education as "the fullest possible development of every dimension of the person" and "the formation of the balanced person with a personally developed philosophy of life that includes ongoing habits of reflection." He also described teachers as the primary agents of this formation: "The teacher is at the service of the students, alert to detect special gifts or special difficulties, personally concerned, and assisting in the development of the inner potential of each individual student."[5]

The Value of Modeling Intellectual Virtues

How are these aspects of education related to the importance of modeling intellectual virtues? Or to the impact that such modeling can have on the motivation of our students? As we've seen at several points in the book, intellectual virtues are deeply personal qualities. They speak to the fundamental concerns, attitudes, values, and habits of the people who possess them. They are admirable and compelling. They can elicit new desires and loves and can inspire their likeness in the minds and hearts of others.

Hence the motivational power of modeling intellectual virtues for our students. When we encounter people who are curious, attentive, openminded, intellectually autonomous, or intellectually courageous, it is only natural for us to want to be like them—to emulate their concerns and dispositions. What is true of us is also true of our students.

Indeed, a significant body of empirical research points to the motivational power of modeling intellectual virtues. Over the past several decades, researchers have found that children whose parents and teachers model qualities like curiosity, open-mindedness, and intellectual humility are more likely to manifest these qualities themselves.[6] As curiosity researcher Wendy Ostroff notes, "Supporting curious children is best achieved when teachers themselves are curious, when they are excited, involved, self-directed, and trying new things."[7]

The value of modeling intellectual virtues isn't limited to its motivational effects. It can also help students develop the skills proper to intellectual virtues. Simply telling my students how to switch perspectives, think for themselves, or take intellectual risks is unlikely to be sufficient for their development of these skills. At a minimum, I must also give my students opportunities to practice switching perspectives, thinking for themselves, and so on. However, even this may be insufficient if my students haven't witnessed the skills in action. By modeling intellectual virtues for our students, we provide them with this additional guidance.

Educational psychologist Ron Ritchhart describes the dual importance of modeling intellectual virtues—or what he calls "thinking dispositions"—as follows: "In learning any new behavior or skill, one often begins by attempting to replicate the actions of someone more expert. However, when one works to acquire a disposition, models serve as more than exemplars of skills. By demonstrating congruence between attitude and behavior, a respected model's ongoing presence also imparts values and serves to cultivate not only one's ability but also one's general inclination toward a particular behavior."[8]

The Inescapability of Modeling

The discussion thus far might give the impression that modeling intellectual character is optional. It is not. We cannot help but model our own intellectual concerns and habits of mind. Whether strong or weak, good or bad, they are always on display. As John Dewey observes, "Everything the teacher does, as well as the manner in which he does it, incites the child to respond in some way or another, and each response tends to set the child's attitude in some way or other."[9] The question, then, isn't about *whether* we will model attributes of intellectual character; it is rather about *which* attributes we will model—whether excellences or defects, virtues or vices.[10]

Dewey's observation underscores a further and related point. Just as virtuous habits of mind are admirable and attractive, less-than-virtuous habits of mind can be alienating or repelling. If I am intellectually careless, arrogant, indifferent, superficial, distracted, narrow-minded, or dogmatic, my students are unlikely to take me or what I have to say seriously. While they might, to get the grade, dutifully memorize and regurgitate what I say in class, their engagement with the subject matter is likely to remain impersonal and superficial. Dewey touches on this point as well: "Example is more potent than precept; and a teacher's best conscious efforts may be more than counteracted by the influence of personal traits which he is unaware of or regards as unimportant."[11]

WHAT DOES IT LOOK LIKE TO MODEL INTELLECTUAL VIRTUES?

The idea that we must model intellectual virtues for our students may feel like a heavy burden. We are already required to do so much as teachers. The idea that we must also *be* a certain way—that we must possess and model intellectual virtues for our students—can feel overwhelming. This feeling may be especially prevalent if you have doubts about the quality of your own intellectual character. You might find yourself thinking, My own intellectual character isn't so virtuous. In fact, it's pretty defective. How, then, am I supposed to genuinely or authentically model intellectual virtues for my students?

This is a reasonable concern. Three points may help ease it. First, recall that intellectual virtues come in degrees. As limited and imperfect beings, none of us possesses even a single virtue in its complete or ideal form. Instead, we are open-minded or intellectually careful or attentive only more or less, to a greater or lesser extent. We must, then, avoid judging ourselves too harshly or holding ourselves to an unrealistic standard. Second, being virtuous in some respects doesn't require being virtuous in all respects. A teacher or student might be strong in autonomy and courage, say, but relatively weak in humility and open-mindedness. Alternatively, a person might be intellectually thorough without being especially careful. Or strong in curiosity but lacking in tenacity. If your intellectual character is a mixed bag, you are in excellent company. Fortunately, a lack of perfection needn't prevent you from embracing and modeling the intellectual character strengths you do possess. Third, as IVA math teach Cari Noble has told me, only imperfect teachers can model intellectual growth for their students: "The best exemplar for students is one who shows growth. Sure, a completely formed very virtuous teacher would be an awesome role model, but they would not be good at modeling how to improve. Only a teacher with flaws they are working on can authentically model how to make a virtue goal and work towards it."[12]

Intellectual Humility

In fact, our intellectual flaws and limitations as teachers have an additional and related silver lining. They are an opportunity to model one of the most important intellectual virtues: namely, intellectual humility. Intellectually humble teachers are aware of their intellectual limitations and mistakes. They don't bend over backward to conceal them; they are willing to admit what they don't know. Because they're aware of and comfortable with their intellectual limitations, these teachers are eager to learn from others, including their students.

To illustrate how intellectual humility can, as it were, make a virtue out of a teacher's intellectual limitations and weaknesses, imagine that a student of mine asks me a question I've never thought about before and don't know the answer to. Or suppose it's a question I'm familiar with and should know the answer to, but don't. How might I respond? I could attempt to bluff my way through an answer. Or I could try to turn the question back on the inquisitive student or her classmates: "What do *you* think the answer is?" Alternatively, I could simply admit my ignorance: "Wow, I've never thought about that before. I'm really not sure what to think." Or, "That's something I should know the answer to, but don't. I will track down the answer and have it for you next time we meet."

Like all humans, we teachers frequently make mistakes, some small and insignificant, others more glaring and consequential. Because we are the putative experts in the room, it can feel difficult—even wrong—to admit when we've committed an error or when we're ignorant about something. Nevertheless, a willingness to model intellectual humility in the company of our students can be extremely powerful.

A friend of mine, a retired university president, tells the story of an experience he had as a graduate student at Harvard University. He had graduated at the top of his undergraduate class and arrived at Harvard with multiple scholarships. In one of his classes, a student asked a question to which the professor responded, "I don't know. Let me think about it and get back to you." Of this experience, my friend says:

> It was the first time that I could remember a teacher saying "I don't know," and this man was one of the leading scholars in the world . . . From then on I began to feel that it was all right not to know. I no longer had to pretend to know. From then on I began to think things through. I wanted to know not what someone else thought, but what I thought. I realized it was ok to be wrong for a time while searching for the truth. Of course this was just the beginning of the journey, but it had begun. The fact that I still vividly remember these moments some 50 years later shows how powerful these moments were.[13]

The esteemed scholar's response is an excellent illustration of intellectual humility. It is also a powerful example of the impact intellectual humility can have on a student. After witnessing his professor's willingness to admit what he didn't know, my friend began—for the first time in his life—to feel comfortable owning his own intellectual limitations. This shift in his intellectual character wasn't limited to intellectual humility. As his comments illustrate, it also freed him up to begin practicing other virtues, including intellectual autonomy: "I wanted to know not what someone else thought, but what I thought."

Many school and classroom environments are marked by a spirit of competition. This spirit can incentivize strength and invulnerability. It can also discourage a willingness to admit ignorance, ask for help, or take intellectual risks; it is fodder for a perfectionist mentality. When we model intellectual humility for our students, we create a different kind of environment: one in which we appear refreshingly human and our students feel comfortable taking intellectual risks and admitting when they need help. In modeling intellectual humility, we manifest a healthier and more fruitful way of thinking and feeling about our intellectual limitations. This eliminates some of the pressure and anxiety of competitive classroom environments and encourages our students to embrace learning with greater freedom and whole-heartedness.

To be sure, modeling intellectual humility for our students can require intellectual courage. It can be frightening or anxiety-provoking to expose our intellectual limitations and flaws to others, particularly to our students. There are, of course, limits to how, or how much, we should be up front about our weaknesses with our students. As with any virtue, discretion and good judgment are a necessity. However, the potential of some core elements of intellectual humility to induce fear or to be misused doesn't make this disposition any less of a virtue or any less important to model for our students.

Intellectual Thoroughness

We now consider what it might look like to model the virtue of intellectual thoroughness. This virtue involves a willingness to dig deeper, to probe for or demonstrate deep understanding. Thorough thinkers make connections between the various things they know. And they are capable of explaining their knowledge to others.

Viewed in this way, the virtue of thoroughness is closely tied to cognitive mastery, to having a firm personal command of an idea or a body of knowledge. It involves knowing the ins and outs of something and the ability to apply and extend this knowledge. Such mastery is an impressive and distinctively human achievement. Consequently, modeling thoroughness can serve as a compelling invitation to our students to plunge deeper into the learning process—to push beyond mere appearances or easy answers, and to probe for greater understanding. It can make rigorous intellectual engagement look and feel attractive.

How do we model intellectual thoroughness for our students? For one, we can give verbal expression to some of the fine-grained details of our own thinking. A professor of mine in graduate school did this especially well. He rarely presented carefully worked-out modules of content. Rather, he taught philosophy by modeling philosophical thinking, and he modeled philosophical thinking largely by thinking out loud.[14] One of the more striking features of his thinking was his tendency to probe: to ask why and how, to draw careful distinctions, to consider a range of different views, objections to these views, and responses to these objections. He continually pushed deeper and deeper, trying to get to the nub of what he was thinking about. As his student, I was deeply impressed by his command of the material: by the way he could come at the material from different angles, explain it, reexplain it, and connect it to other things we were learning about. What captured my imagination wasn't the breadth or quantity of his knowledge; it was rather his command of what he knew. His rigorous pursuit of understanding—his intellectual thoroughness—had a powerful effect on me. It made me want to become a more thorough thinker myself.

Comprehensive mastery of a subject matter can seem like a rare and exotic aim in today's intellectual climate, which prizes what philosopher Michael Lynch has called "Google-knowing" over deep understanding.[15] This shift is evident, among other ways, in the decline of book reading among teenagers.[16] As another author explains:

> For some people, the very idea of reading a book has come to seem old-fashioned, maybe even a little silly—like sewing your own shirts or butchering your own meat. "I don't read books," says Joe O'Shea, a former president of the student body at Florida State University and a 2008 recipient of a Rhodes Scholarship. "I go to Google, and I can absorb relevant information quickly." O'Shea, a philosophy major, doesn't see any reason to plow through chapters of text when it takes but a minute or two to cherry-pick the pertinent passages using Google Book Search. "Sitting down and going through a book from cover to cover doesn't make sense," he says. "It's not a good use of my time, as I can get all the information I need faster through the Web." As soon as you learn to be "a skilled hunter" online, he argues, books become superfluous.[17]

With so much information available at our fingertips, and with information technology and social media platforms that favor pithy assertions and catchy sound bites, real-life examples of intellectual thoroughness seem to be fading fast. This is all the more reason for us to model deeper and more complex ways of thinking and communicating for our students. Given the connection between intellectual thoroughness and complex understanding, and the importance of understanding to the overall aims of education, modeling intellectual thoroughness is of critical importance today.

Curiosity

The modeling of curiosity also can have a powerful effect on our students. As students, many of us witnessed in our best teachers an infectious love for what they were teaching. Something about this passion was compelling. It called forth its likeness in us. We became more curious on account of their curiosity.

In similar fashion, we can help nurture our students' curiosity by consciously modeling a love and fascination for our subject matter. Pause for a moment and ask yourself some questions: Would your students consider you a curious thinker? If so, why? What concrete evidence of your curiosity have you offered them? If you haven't offered much but regard yourself as a curious thinker, what else might you do to authentically model this quality for your students?

Curiosity is fundamentally about asking thoughtful and insightful questions. Therefore, one way of modeling curiosity mirrors the way of modeling thoroughness just described: it involves thinking and wondering out loud. As teachers, questions often occur to us while we are instructing our students. We notice a possible implication of something we've said. Or we identify a discrepancy that gives us pause. If our primary role as teachers is to transmit knowledge and information, we might see little point in giving expression to these questions. However, if part of our role is to model an active and inquisitive mind, then wondering aloud makes good sense. In doing so, we needn't feel pressure to answer the questions we articulate. We can simply register what we find interesting or puzzling and move on.

Part and parcel of wondering out loud is permitting our questions to take hold of us at an affective, or emotional, level. There's a big difference between a question asked in a detached or indifferent way and a question asked with genuine passion and wonder. While we don't always have immediate control over our emotions, we can control how much we allow ourselves to feel what we are wondering and how we give expression to these feelings. Given how infectious a teacher's curiosity can be, we must be mindful of how we can share and model this virtue.

In his *Letters to a Young Poet*, Rainer Maria Rilke speaks to some of the affective aspects of wrestling with big questions: "Have patience with everything unresolved in your heart and try to love the questions themselves as if they were locked rooms or books written in a very foreign language. Don't search for the answers, which could not be given to you now, because you would not be able to live them. And the point is, to live everything. Live the questions now. Perhaps, then, someday far in the future, you will gradually, without ever noticing it, live your way into the answer."[18]

Why should a teacher's display of curiosity have an impact on students? There is, in fact, something deeply and distinctively human about the capacity for wonder. As Aristotle observed long ago, "All humans by nature desire to know."[19] Accordingly, our modeling of curiosity, like our modeling of intellectual humility, can have a humanizing effect on how our students experience us. When they see us wonder, they see that while we may be the "experts" in the room, we are far from having it all figured out. They experience us as fellow learners and inquirers. Over time, this view can inspire them to begin formulating, being moved by, and "living" questions of their own.

Creating space in ourselves or our lessons to model curiosity for our students can be challenging. We might feel too pressed for time to indulge in the kind of intellectual exploration that modeling curiosity requires. Or perhaps we've been teaching the same material year after year, and it no longer sparks much curiosity or wonder in us. While we must be honest with ourselves about these challenges, they don't absolve us of doing what we can to consistently and authentically model curiosity for our students. Instead, they demonstrate that modeling curiosity may take a certain amount of intentionality and preparation on our part. Before teaching or designing a lesson plan, I might need to step back and ask myself: What is there to wonder about in the material we'll be covering? What do I find puzzling or interesting about it? If I struggle to answer this question, it may be time for me to seek out some fresh perspectives on my content area, for example, by spending some time during the summer learning about new developments in the field or by retooling old lesson plans in ways that better reflect some of my current intellectual interests and passions.

SOME GUIDING PRINCIPLES

We've considered what it might look like to model three virtues: intellectual humility, intellectual thoroughness, and curiosity. Of course, these aren't the only virtues worth modeling for our students. Open-mindedness, attentiveness, intellectual carefulness, and other virtues also can be modeled to powerful effect. Regardless of which virtues we choose to model, our modeling efforts must adhere to certain principles, three of which I turn now to discuss.

The Importance of Authenticity

Although I have alluded to authenticity throughout the chapter, the idea bears special emphasis: our modeling of intellectual virtues must be authentic. In his work on teaching for virtuous intellectual character, Ritchhart draws a distinction between "demonstration modeling" and "authentic modeling." He says that demonstration modeling "often feels artificial and lacks the real convictions of someone engaged in a spontaneous act," whereas authentic modeling "enculturates values by showing students what the teacher deems important and worthwhile" and "fosters ability by showing a technique in context." He adds, "When I speak of modeling, it is more in the context of the teacher acting as a role model, someone worth emulating, than as a demonstrator. When you are in the presence of such models, you get the sense of the teacher as a thinker and not as a teacher of thinking."[20]

It can be tempting to think that authentically modeling intellectual virtues for our students rules out the possibility of intending or planning to do so—that an authentic modeling of intellectual virtues must be entirely natural and spontaneous. This supposition isn't quite right. Authenticity isn't synonymous with naturalness or spontaneity. To illustrate, when working on a lesson for an upcoming class period, I might pause to consider, Which virtues would it be natural for me to practice during this lesson? What would it look like for me to do so? Might there also be other virtues I could practice? This brief imaginative exercise can prime me to notice and seize opportunities to model specific virtues for my students. And it needn't make my modeling of these virtues any less authentic than it would be if it were entirely spontaneous.[21]

That said, we need to avoid modeling virtues in ways that seem forced or didactic. If our students get the impression that we are faking it or that we are trying to teach them a lesson about intellectual humility, open-mindedness, or any other virtue, our efforts are likely to be in vain. In keeping with this principle, we should be cautious about trying to model virtues we don't possess at least to some extent. Our modeling of intellectual virtues will be convincing and inspiring only if we are at least minimally competent in the skills specific to the virtues in question and only if this competence is at least somewhat integrated into our ordinary ways of thinking and communicating.

The Importance of Self-Awareness

This discussion of authenticity leads to a second important principle. To get a sense of which virtues we should consider modeling for our students, we must have a keen and well-informed sense of our own intellectual character strengths and limitations. Such knowledge isn't guaranteed; it isn't something we automatically or necessarily possess. To know our intellectual character strengths and limitations, we must spend some time reflecting on the geography of our own minds.

One way of doing this involves reflecting on questions like the following: Which intellectual virtues do I already model for my students? What does this look like? How do I make these virtues visible to my students? Which intellectual virtues do I struggle to exhibit in the classroom? What does this struggle tend to look like? Why do I struggle in these ways? To complement this exercise, we might also engage in one of the self-assessment exercises described in chapters 6 or 10. Another approach might be to reread the profiles of individual virtues in chapter 2 or to read a short book on intellectual virtues, paying close attention to passages that seem to describe our own habits of mind. To ensure some objectivity in this process, we might also consider asking people who know us well, including one or more colleagues, to tell us what they would identify as some of our chief intellectual character strengths and limitations and to support their answers with concrete examples where possible. Even better, we might survey our students about which virtues they've seen us model over the year or semester.[22]

Knowledge of our intellectual character strengths and limitations cannot be acquired in a day. It takes time to get to know the terrain of our own minds. Nonetheless, if we are intent on modeling intellectual virtues for our students, we should at least be paying closer attention to, and trying to develop an understanding of, the stronger and weaker points of our mental character.

Creating an Ethos of Trust and Acceptance

I'll conclude the chapter by drawing attention to a third principle, which concerns the dynamic between intellectual virtues and moral virtues. While authentically modeling intellectual virtues like curiosity and thoroughness can have an impact on the intellectual character development of our students, this potential can be squandered if we don't also practice certain moral virtues. If I am demonstrably passionate about my subject matter, or skilled at offering comprehensive explanations, but am also rude, condescending, or insensitive to my students, then the potential influence of my intellectual virtues will be undercut by my moral shortcomings. I don't have to be a moral saint to inspire a love of learning in my students, but my students will be more likely to accept my invitation to deeper learning if they feel supported and respected in my classroom.

As discussed in chapter 4, a caring and receptive pedagogical posture amplifies the benefits of modeling intellectual virtues. When we feel cared for by others, we are more willing to follow them to where they are trying to lead us. We are more receptive to what they have to say. We may even be inspired to adopt some of their values and ways of being. When the people in question are our teachers, this can have a significant impact on our development of intellectual virtues. It can affect our desire to learn, how we think, and the kinds of thinkers and learners we aspire to be. As Palmer notes, "The practice of intellectual rigor in the classroom requires an ethos of trust and acceptance."[23] For these reasons, our modeling of intellectual virtues must be supplemented by a genuine commitment to and concern for the general well-being of our students.

CHAPTER 10

Assessment

> Teachers need to enhance their evaluation skills about the
> effects that they are having on students. Only then are teach-
> ers best equipped to know what to do next to enhance students'
> improvement.
>
> —John Hattie, *Visible Learning for Teachers*

Over the past several chapters, we've explored a wide range of pedagogical
principles, postures, and practices aimed at helping students cultivate the
character strengths of good thinkers and learners. In this chapter, we turn
our attention to a challenging but critical question: How, if at all, should
we attempt to *assess* the intellectual character of our students? Is such assessment possible? Is it advisable? If so, how should it be done?

We'll begin by looking at why intellectual character assessment is worthwhile. We will then consider some points of caution and some additional
guiding principles. Next, we'll examine three types of intellectual character assessments: student self-assessments, teacher assessments, and other
behavioral assessments (including assessments by parents and peers). The
aim of this chapter is to provide you with a clear rationale for evaluating
the intellectual character of your students as well as some practical guidance and concrete examples of how to do so.

WHY ASSESSMENT IS IMPORTANT

Many teachers suffer from assessment fatigue. It feels as though we are called on to document, track, and report on the impact of almost everything we do. Often enough, the very things we are asked to do (or avoid doing) are dictated by whether they can be assessed in narrow and quantifiable terms. It's a familiar case of the tail wagging the dog.

I share these feelings and concerns. Nevertheless, when it comes to teaching for intellectual virtues, we still need to pay attention to, and make some effort to assess, the intellectual character of our students. Doing so is important for a few reasons.

First, paying close attention to the intellectual character of our students is critical to preserving a kind of practical or professional integrity. If I tell you that I'm committed to helping my students make progress in intellectual virtues, and you learn that I pay little or no attention to their intellectual character strengths and limitations or to how these might be developing over time, you would be right to question my commitment. Thus, while our ability to know the intellectual character of our students may be limited, if we're serious about trying to help them grow in intellectual virtues, we cannot ignore the issue of assessment.

Assessment of intellectual character can also inform and sharpen our pedagogical aims and practices. As we'll see later in the chapter, evaluating our students in terms of a particular virtue requires a clear and concrete sense of what it would look like for our students to manifest this virtue in a classroom setting. Such knowledge is valuable in a couple of ways. It can provide us with a more refined grasp of the character-based goals we have for our students. It can also alert us to when our students are struggling to make progress toward these goals. Either way, this knowledge can lead to helpful recalibration. For example, if curiosity is one of my target virtues, my assessment efforts might reveal that several of my students are struggling to develop the skill of asking thoughtful and insightful questions. This knowledge could, in turn, help me adjust my pedagogical goals or practices to better support my students' development of curiosity.

The information we glean from efforts like these can also be parlayed into meaningful and supportive feedback for our students. As we've noted many times in this book, intellectual virtues are admirable and compelling personal qualities; they are qualities that many if not all of our students would like to possess or ways they'd like to be. Therefore, if we can provide our students with rich and specific feedback about their intellectual character strengths or about the progress they're making with respect to particular virtues, this knowledge may bolster their commitment to growing in intellectual virtues.[1]

POINTS OF CAUTION

While efforts to assess the intellectual character of our students are worthwhile, these efforts are a precarious undertaking. Indeed, some ways of proceeding may end up impeding rather than nurturing our students' intellectual character development. Let's consider a few cautionary points.

Most of us are not social scientists trained in experimental design and data collection. For this reason, we lack the skills, knowledge, and other resources necessary for creating scientifically rigorous character assessments. While this limitation doesn't mean we are incapable of obtaining any useful information about the intellectual character of our students, it does suggest that we should be careful about placing too much confidence or stock in our evaluations. Instead, we should approach them with intellectual humility and tentativeness, and we should encourage our students to do the same.[2]

Furthermore, unless we're careful, our assessment efforts may backfire. For example, once our students know we'll be evaluating their intellectual character, their motivation to practice intellectual virtues may change. They may begin asking thoughtful questions, taking intellectual risks, and so on, as a way of securing whatever extrinsic incentive they perceive to be at stake, such as gaining our approval or outscoring their peers. These external incentives are problematic given that *intrinsic* intellectual motivation is an important element of intellectual virtues and that extrinsic motivation crowds out or diminishes intrinsic motivation.[3] In light of this discussion, we should be reluctant to assign "character grades" or to allot class points based on how our students do on character-based assessments.

In a similar vein, unless we exercise significant discretion in how we convey the results of our assessments, our students may end up feeling personally criticized and sour on the very idea of intellectual virtues. Again, our intellectual character says something about who we are as persons, about our very identity. Therefore, we should use the information we gather to encourage and build up our students—never to criticize or tear them down. This approach needn't prevent us from providing constructive character-based feedback on exams, papers, or related coursework (e.g., "Try to show a bit more open-mindedness in how you describe this point of view," "This answer could be more thorough," "Aim for greater carefulness next time," or "Keep working at developing your own ideas and opinions"). However, it does mean that we should categorically avoid "shaming and blaming" our students for (what we perceive to be) their lack of intellectual virtue. Comments like "You're closed-minded" or "You're not gritty enough" should be off the table.

SHARPENING THE FOCUS

There are a few more things to keep in mind as we begin taking steps to assess the intellectual character of our students. One is to maintain a relatively narrow focus. Our aim should not be to determine whether our students are becoming intellectually virtuous in some generic or unspecified sense. Rather, we should focus on their development relative to a limited number of target virtues.

When designing or choosing an assessment, we should also be mindful of the different dimensions or aspects of intellectual virtues. These dimensions may need to be measured or assessed in different ways. In the case of open-mindedness, for instance, it is easier to discern whether our students are developing the ability to switch perspectives (skill dimension) than it is to determine why they are using this ability (motivational dimension) or whether they can reliably identify opportunities to use this ability across different contexts (judgment dimension). Therefore, we should be attentive to questions like the following: Am I most interested in assessing my students along the skill, motivational, or judgment dimension of my target virtues? Are the assessment tools I'm using well suited to provide me with this information?

Finally, to develop a well-rounded picture of our students' intellectual character, we should do what we can to incorporate input from multiple sources and perspectives. On the one hand, our students have special or privileged access to certain features of their intellectual character (e.g., their own beliefs, desires, and inclinations, as thinkers and learners). This special access points to the value of self-reflection and self-assessment. On the other hand, self-assessment also has some well-known limitations.[4] Moreover, there may be other features of our students' intellectual character that we, as their teachers, are uniquely capable of perceiving—features that even our students are unaware of. Something similar may be true of our students' parents or peers. Therefore, as we'll see later in the chapter, we should aim to incorporate a combination of self-report and third-person behavioral assessments.

So far in this chapter, I have noted several guidelines for assessing students' intellectual character. I have suggested that we should: (1) approach the process and our findings with intellectual humility; (2) avoid doing anything that might diminish the intrinsic motivation of our students; (3) use the information we collect in ways that are positive and supportive; (4) adopt a relatively narrow and specific focus; (5) be mindful of the different dimensions of intellectual virtues; and (6) incorporate input from multiple sources or perspectives.

ASSESSMENT ACTIVITIES

In this section, we will consider several ways of trying to assess the intellectual character of our students. These assessments are of three types: (1) student self-assessments; (2) teacher assessments; and (3) additional behavioral assessments (e.g., by parents or peers). This collection of assessments is merely a representative sample. The particular assessments we examine may or may not be suitable for you or your students. If nothing else, I hope they might inspire you to find or create alternative assessments that better fit your needs and interests.[5]

Student Self-Assessments

Assessments in the first category can be more or less complex and demanding. I will begin with a less demanding self-assessment exercise and then turn to some exercises that are a little more rigorous. Any of these exercises can be administered on a single occasion (e.g., at the beginning of the year as part of a brief lesson on intellectual virtues) or more than once (e.g., at the beginning and end of the school year or semester).

In the first exercise, students receive a list of target virtues along with a brief definition or description of each virtue. They are given approximately five minutes to read and reflect on the list without writing anything down. Next, they're asked to reflect on and answer the following questions: (1) Of the listed virtues, which one *best* characterizes your own thinking? Why? How does this virtue tend to influence your thinking, either at school or in other areas of your life? What are some specific examples that support your response? (2) Of the listed virtues, which one *least* characterizes your own thinking? Why? How does the absence of this virtue affect your thinking, either at school or in other areas of your life? What are some specific examples that support your response? Students are then invited to share some of their reflections in small groups or with the entire class.

This exercise is aimed at helping students (and their teachers) develop an understanding of the landscape of their own minds.[6] Moreover, it encourages them to think about this landscape not in abstraction but in connection with their actual experience as thinkers and learners. While the probative value of this exercise may be limited, it can provide us with an initial picture of some of our students' intellectual character strengths and limitations. If used at multiple points in a given semester or year, the exercise can also indicate whether these factors are changing over time.

A second exercise is a little more complex. It involves the use of self-assessment surveys, which ask students to record their level of agreement with several first-person statements corresponding to specific virtues. Some sample statements include: "My classes often leave me wondering about the topics we discussed" (curiosity), "I have a hard time coming up with my own ideas" (autonomy), and "I go back over by assignments before turning them in" (carefulness). Surveys for several intellectual virtues can be found online, in appendix B of this book, or in various scholarly journals.[7] Alternatively, you may wish to create survey items of your own. One advantage of creating your own items is that you can closely align the items with how you're thinking of your target virtues and how they are likely to be manifested by your students. A potential downside of this approach is that the items may not track your target virtues as reliably as would items vetted by trained researchers.

There are multiple ways in which these surveys can be administered and used. At the Intellectual Virtues Academy, every student takes a self-assessment survey containing items specific to the school's nine key virtues at the beginning and end of each school year. Data from these surveys, along with considerable qualitative feedback from teachers, goes into an annual "intellectual character report" for each student.[8] Students are also given regular opportunities to reflect on and discuss this feedback in weekly advisory groups.

Another example of a self-assessment tool is one that I use in most of my freshman-level courses.[9] As explained in chapter 5, I begin each semester with a mini unit that introduces the class to intellectual virtues and how they are related to the aims of the course and of education in general. Because I feel comfortable talking about and teaching for a wide range of intellectual virtues, I provide my students with definitions, slogans, and examples of all nine virtues explored in chapter 2 (see also appendix A). After the mini unit, I administer a thirty-six-item self-assessment survey (four items per virtue) to help my students begin to apply what they have learned about intellectual virtues to their understanding of themselves as thinkers and learners. The items are listed on the front side of an 8½ × 11-inch sheet of paper, with no indication of which items correspond to which virtues. Students respond to the items using a Likert-type scale (where 1 = "Very different from me," 2 = "Different from me," 3 = "Neither different from me nor like me," 4 = "Like me," and 5 = "Very much like me"). After recording their responses to all thirty-six items, they turn the sheet of paper over and tally their scores for each virtue. Next, they use this information to create a simple bar graph depicting their intellectual strengths and limitations (with virtues on the x-axis and survey scores on the y-axis). Finally, they spend some time reflecting on and responding to several questions, such as the following: (1) According to the assessment, what are your greatest intellectual character strengths? Which virtues do you most need to work on? (2) Do you think these results are mostly accurate? Why or why not? Do any of the results surprise you? Why or why not? (3) Up to this point in your life, how have your intellectual character strengths served you well? Support your answer with some specific examples. (4) How have your intellectual character limitations made life more difficult? Support your answer with some specific examples. Between their scores on the survey and their written responses to the reflection questions, this exercise gives me a helpful window into the intellectual character strengths and limitations of many of my students.

A third self-assessment exercise, also discussed earlier, is suitable mainly for older (secondary or postsecondary) students. It consists of character-based self-reflection papers. In connection with the mini unit just noted, I sometimes have my students write two short (1,000- to 1,500-word) papers in which they reflect on their intellectual character in light of a series of readings about intellectual virtues.[10] Like the previous exercise, this assignment has several goals. One of these goals is to give students an opportunity to learn about intellectual virtues and to apply this knowledge to how they understand themselves as thinkers and learners. A second goal is to provide students and me with a sense of their intellectual character strengths and limitations, including how (if at all) these have changed over the semester. Each paper asks the students to discuss several key points from the readings and to reflect on how these points relate to their own character and experiences as learners. Again, the students are encouraged to be specific in their answers, illustrating their reflections with concrete and real-life examples.

These papers provide me with information about my student's intellectual histories, experiences, and habits that I otherwise wouldn't acquire.

While this information is helpful from an assessment standpoint, I also use it when deciding which virtues to emphasize in my teaching, for example, which virtues to model or to give my students more frequent opportunities to practice.

Although these papers are graded, they are worth only a few points (usually around 5 percent of the overall grade). Students are not, of course, graded on the apparent quality of their intellectual character. Rather, when evaluating their papers, I use criteria such as the following: Does the paper conform to all the requirements stated in the prompt? Is it clear that the student read the material carefully and thoroughly? Did the student clearly engage in thoughtful reflection on how the material relates to her or his intellectual character? Are these reflections supported and illustrated with concrete and real-life examples?

We've considered three ways of using self-assessments to gain insight into the intellectual character of our students and how their character might be changing over time. However, as noted above, self-assessments do have certain drawbacks and limitations. In particular, we aren't always reliable informants about our own inner states and dispositions. Self-reflection and self-reporting are susceptible to a host of biases, blind spots, and other distorting factors. Therefore, we should consider other forms of intellectual character assessment as well.

Teacher Assessments

One of these other forms involves making our own observations about the intellectual character of our students. Here as well, we can pursue approaches that are more or less complex and demanding.

The first option is straightforward and should require little additional work if you are already building opportunities to practice the skills specific to your target virtues into your regular assignments, exercises, exams, and other instructional activities. If that is the case, then when it comes to evaluating your students' performance on these activities, you'll automatically be gaining insight into whether they are developing the skills in question.

To illustrate, when students in my courses write argumentative papers, I require them to consider two or three objections to their argument and then to modify or defend their argument in light of these objections. In doing so, they must practice the skills specific to virtues like intellectual humility and open-mindedness. The objections students come up with must be forceful—they mustn't be careless, misinformed, or uncharitable. This requirement encourages students to practice identifying and articulating the limitations and potential vulnerabilities of their own reasoning (intellectual humility). It also encourages them to enter into and give a fair representation of the perspectives of people who disagree with them (open-mindedness). Accordingly, when grading these papers, part of what I am looking for is whether my students possess the skills specific to at least two important virtues. Because my students normally have to write multiple papers during a semester, this assignment also shows me whether their proficiency in these skills is improving over time.

Of course, the fact that students can identify the limitations of their own perspectives or give a fair hearing to alternative viewpoints is no guarantee of intellectual humility or open-mindedness. The students might, among other things, have these skills but be unmotivated to use them in most situations. As a consequence, the results of teacher assessments are somewhat limited in their significance. Nevertheless, given that possessing the skills specific to intellectual virtues is one important part of possessing the virtues themselves, the information provided by this kind of assessment does count for something.

Notably, many teachers already assess their students with respect to virtues like intellectual carefulness and thoroughness. These teachers expect their students to avoid careless mistakes, demonstrate precision in their thinking and writing, make connections between ideas, and demonstrate that they have a firm understanding of the material they're discussing. In doing so, the teachers build opportunities to practice carefulness and thoroughness into their graded assignments, the evaluation of which tells them something about their students' progress in these virtues.

A somewhat more demanding but potentially more probative form of assessment consists of recording qualitative observations about students' intellectual conduct, in particular, conduct that expresses (or seems to express) their intellectual character. For instance, you might keep a special notebook (or computer file) in which you periodically record how you've seen your students manifest one or more dimensions of your target virtues. Though it's more demanding, you might also commit to sitting down once or twice each semester or year and, for each of your students and target virtues, jotting down some observations and remarks. For example, suppose your target virtues are curiosity, open-mindedness, and intellectual courage. At each of the relevant intervals, and for each of your students, you could record some brief notes about whether the student has asked thoughtful questions (curiosity), demonstrated an interest in or an ability to explore multiple perspectives (open-mindedness), and shown a willingness to take intellectual risks (courage).[11]

The qualitative information acquired from this type of exercise can provide you with a sense of the intellectual character strengths and limitations of your students. Again, if conducted multiple times over a year or semester, it can also help you identify changes in their intellectual character.

Information of this sort can be useful in other ways as well. As suggested at the outset of the chapter, if you find that very few of your students are practicing one of your target virtues, this might mean they haven't been given sufficient opportunities to practice this virtue. If so, you might consider adjusting your pedagogical practices accordingly. The information can also form the basis of useful and constructive feedback. For instance, at IVA, character-based feedback is incorporated into students' report cards. In contrast with comments like "a pleasure to have in class," this feedback describes the intellectual character of students in concrete detail, affirming their strengths and gently pointing out areas for improvement. The following two comments are taken from one IVA student's report card:

[The student] works thoroughly and carefully (and efficiently!). I would love to see him participate even more in class discussions. I know that he has great thoughts in there! I want to hear more of his "wonders"!

[The student] is extremely thorough in his work, particularly in his writing. He is often able to think through the third, fourth, and fifth angle of a question, whereas many students are tempted to stop at the first or second

. . . [The student] seems to be a highly curious person, especially when it comes to books. I often see him reading outside of class. I would like to see that curiosity more in the classroom . . . I would like to see him "wonder" more about the subject matter, asking more open-ended questions.

Notice that these remarks, which were written by different teachers, present a uniform picture of the student's intellectual character as strong in virtues like carefulness and thoroughness and having room for improvement in curiosity. The constructive feedback offered also illustrates nicely how a teacher can call attention to a student's intellectual limitations and encourage the student to try to develop in these areas, without doing so in a critical or shaming manner. While you may not be in a position to incorporate feedback like this into your students' actual report cards, this limitation needn't prevent you from sharing it in a different format (e.g., in a personal email or periodic "character comments").[12]

Additional Behavioral Assessments

When we are trying to understand the intellectual character of our students, it can also be helpful to incorporate input from other parties who are close enough to them to regularly observe their intellectual activity. Potential candidates include parents or guardians and peers. One benefit of incorporating input from these sources is that they are in a position to observe the intellectual activity of our students outside of an academic context. As such, they can help round out and deepen our understanding of how our students are disposed as thinkers and learners.

While gathering input from these sources does take additional work, creating the relevant assessments needn't be especially demanding. Some of the assessments just described can easily be adapted for use by parents or peers. For example, a student's parents or peers might be given a list of several target virtues along with corresponding definitions or descriptions and be asked to explain which virtues they think best describe the student and why. To make their feedback more concrete, they could also be asked to support their judgments with specific examples.[13]

Alternatively, we might consider converting the self-report surveys discussed earlier to behavioral measures by changing the point of view of the survey items from first person to third person.[14] For instance, instead of "I am eager to explore new things" or "I am an independent thinker," the items might read "The student is eager to explore new things" and "The student is an independent thinker." This kind of revision wouldn't work in every case, since some of the first-person items likely will pertain to aspects of the student's psychology to which parents and peers don't have immediate access (e.g., the student's feelings, attitudes, or beliefs about learning). That said, with items that pertain to observable behavior, such a revision can be relatively straightforward.

LIMITATIONS OF ASSESSMENT TOOLS

Most of the assessment tools described thus far, while capable of shedding some light on the intellectual character of our students, have not undergone rigorous psychometric evaluation. Therefore, we can't be certain that the information they provide is accurate. They might fail to register how our students are growing in intellectual virtues. Or they might give us the impression that our students are growing in intellectual virtues when in reality they are not. Thus, the need for intellectual humility remains.

One way to get around some of these limitations would be to enlist the expertise and resources of a trained researcher. Such opportunities are not easy to come by. And they can make significant demands on the time and energy of teachers and students. However, given the higher quality of feedback that experts can provide, this is an option worth considering. Alas, there is no single tried-and-true way of seeking out or identifying opportunities to collaborate with academic researchers. Perhaps a professor you know from your teacher credentialing program would be willing to work with you to design a study of your pedagogical practices and their effects on the thinking dispositions of your students. Or perhaps this person could put you in contact with other scholars already conducting research in this area.[15]

CONCLUSION

Evaluating the intellectual character of our students is an important if tricky part of teaching for intellectual virtues. However, as the quote from education researcher John Hattie at the beginning of the chapter makes clear, such evaluation is essential to knowing "what to do next." In this chapter, we have considered several ways of assessing our students' intellectual character. We must approach these assessments with a spirit of intellectual humility, being mindful of their limitations. We must also recognize how our efforts to assess our students' intellectual character can affect their intellectual motivation, including their motivation to practice and grow in intellectual virtues. Here as well, we must make every effort to approach the process of assessment in ways that edify our students and support their development as learners.

CHAPTER 11

Beginning

> If you can't fly then run, if you can't run then walk, if you can't
> walk then crawl, but whatever you do you have to keep mov-
> ing forward.
>
> —Martin Luther King Jr., "Keep
> Moving from This Mountain"

This book began by calling attention to an unfortunate and lamentable disconnect between what originally drew many of us into the teaching profession and what we find ourselves preoccupied with and teaching for on a daily basis. Chapters 1 and 2 presented the construct of intellectual virtues as a useful way of fleshing out at least part of that original motivating vision. Chapters 3 through 9 examined the principles, postures, and practices aligned with teaching for intellectual virtues. And chapter 10 considered ways of assessing the intellectual character of our students.

We come now to the conclusion of the book. Having been exposed to a new and challenging terrain, you may feel a little overwhelmed or disoriented. Perhaps you're convinced that teaching for intellectual virtues is a good idea but feel at a loss about where to begin. What are some initial steps you might take to begin reorienting your beliefs, attitudes, and practices to the goal of helping your students experience meaningful growth in intellectual virtues?

This is the question we'll be exploring in this chapter. I will describe five steps you can take to begin teaching for intellectual virtues in a more deliberate way. Each of the steps is explored in greater detail in one or more of the preceding chapters. Therefore, my descriptions of these steps will be brief. I will, however, make reference to the chapters where additional details can be revisited. Finally, bear in mind that these steps are just a beginning. They do not capture the fullness of what it looks like to teach for intellectual virtues. Rather, they are intended as a relatively simple and manageable entry point.

STEP ONE: IDENTIFY AND REFLECT ON YOUR TARGET VIRTUES

We've seen that it can be tempting to think in overly general and nonspecific terms about nurturing the intellectual character growth of our students. Accordingly, we should fix our attention on a limited number of intellectual virtues. In chapter 5, I suggested starting with two or three target virtues.[1]

To identify a suitable list of target virtues, I recommend perusing a list of intellectual virtues and reflecting on the following sorts of questions: Which intellectual virtues are most relevant to my content area? That is, which virtues does my content area call on students to practice most frequently? Which virtues are most relevant to the identity or identities of my students, for example, to their cultural, socioeconomic, racial, or ethnic backgrounds? Which virtues do my students think are most valuable? Which ones do they think they need to grow in most?[2]

Once you've formulated your list, you'll want to gain a clear and concrete grasp of what each virtue looks like in practice. You might begin by doing a little reading about your target virtues, so that you accurately identify their characteristics and avoid confusing them with other intellectual virtues. To this end, you could reread the profiles of the nine virtues in chapter 2 or investigate other introductory books or online resources.[3]

After securing a firm understanding of your target virtues, you'll want to consider, more precisely, what it would look like for your students to manifest these virtues in one of your classes. To do this, you might try the following exercise. For each of your target virtues, spend some time thinking about and describing the specific beliefs, actions, and feelings that a student of yours who possesses this virtue might possess or perform. For instance, if open-mindedness is one of your virtues, you might ask yourself several questions: (1) What sorts of *beliefs* would open-minded students in one of my classes be likely to have? What might they believe about the value of learning? About the specific topics or issues we are studying? About themselves? Their peers? (2) How would open-minded students in one of my classes be inclined to *act*, both mentally and physically? What mental moves would they make? What sorts of things might they say or do? Or refrain from saying or doing? (3) What would open-minded students tend to *feel*? What would excite them? What would make them feel uncomfortable? In reflecting on these questions, you'll want to be very specific in your thinking, formulating concrete examples whenever possible.

Related to this, and in keeping with the discussion of Aristotle's doctrine of the mean in chapter 2, you might also spend some time reflecting on the states of excess and deficiency corresponding to your target virtues. By looking closely at what these virtues are *not*, you can gain a deeper understanding of what they *are* and why they are valuable. Suppose, again, that one of your target virtues is open-mindedness. You might consider a variety of questions: What would closed-mindedness (deficiency) look like if manifested by students in my classes? What do closed-minded students often believe (about learning, the subject matter, themselves, their peers, etc.)? How do they behave? What do they say? What mental moves do they make? What feelings do closed-minded students tend to have? What do they enjoy? What do they dislike? You could then turn to the state of being overly open-minded (excess) and reflect on similar questions. Again, you might ask yourself: What sorts of things would excessively open-minded students in my classes tend to believe, do, or feel?

These are some indirect ways of trying to specify and understand—from the inside, so to speak—how your students might manifest your target virtues. Such knowledge is extremely important, for as discussed in chapter

5, if our character-based goals for our students aren't realistic, or if these goals fail to match who our students are or where they are developmentally, then our best efforts may amount to very little and may even be harmful.

STEP TWO: INTRODUCE YOUR STUDENTS TO YOUR TARGET VIRTUES

In chapter 5, we explored the importance of introducing our students to, and making regular use of, the language and concepts of intellectual virtue. We saw that doing so can have various benefits, including increasing our students' awareness of opportunities to practice intellectual virtues and bolstering their motivation to seize these opportunities. Thus, a second initial step involves introducing your students to your target virtues.

You can introduce these virtues in a variety of ways, for example, with a mini unit on intellectual character, a series of brief homework assignments, or online videos. However, when developing this material, you should keep a couple of points in mind. First, for each virtue, you will want to provide a brief description or definition that is concrete and can easily be understood by your students. You might also think about formulating a catchy slogan or icon for each virtue (see appendix A). Second, you should also be sure to highlight the value, relevance, and attractiveness of each virtue and to do so in ways that your students are likely to find interesting and compelling. Again, this can play an important role in nurturing your students' motivation to practice and grow in these virtues. One way of doing this involves supplementing your descriptions or definitions with concrete examples. These can be taken from history, current events, movies, TV shows, novels, social media, or elsewhere. The goal, again, is to share examples that illustrate the substance and attractiveness of your target virtues.

STEP THREE: GIVE YOUR STUDENTS OPPORTUNITIES TO REFLECT ON THEIR INTELLECTUAL CHARACTER

A third step follows closely on the heels of the second. Once your students have a basic understanding of your target virtues, you'll need to give them opportunities to begin applying this knowledge to how they think about and understand themselves as thinkers and learners. As we saw in chapter 6, students can acquire this understanding of themselves through a process of self-reflection.

Opportunities for self-reflection can take a variety of forms (see "Self-Reflection Exercises" and "Self-Reflection Project" in chapter 6). For example, after you introduce your target virtues, you might give your students a chance to reflect on whether, or in what ways, the relevant definitions, slogans, and examples accurately describe some of their own habits or dispositions as thinkers and learners. You might have them respond to questions like the following: Which of these target virtues best describes your intellectual character? Why? Which of the virtues least describes your intellectual character? Why?

With an exercise like this, a couple of things are worth keeping in mind. First, students' self-assessments should be as specific and concrete as possible. Thus, students should be encouraged to provide real-life examples or other forms of evidence in support of their assessments. Second, when students begin reflecting on their intellectual character, they don't always like what they find. Therefore, you'll want to make clear to them that all of us have intellectual character flaws and limitations, that these drawbacks aren't immutable, and that we can take steps to improve our intellectual character. You should also frame the exercise in positive terms, for example, as an opportunity for your students to increase their self-awareness and to position themselves for intellectual growth.

Another approach would be to use a self-assessment tool like the one described in chapters 6 and 10. With this tool, students evaluate themselves in connection with several carefully constructed survey items, graph their scores, and reflect on the results. An even more ambitious approach, also described in chapter 6, involves a series of readings and two short self-reflection papers.

In thinking about how to execute and interpret the results of these assessments, you'll want to bear in mind two additional points. First, one goal of the assessments is to increase your students' motivation to practice your target virtues. This motivational change is more likely to occur if your students see and appreciate the *value* of these virtues. Accordingly, it may also be helpful to have your students reflect, not just on the attributes of their own thinking habits, but also on the *implications* and *consequences* of these habits. For example, they could think about whether a particular thinking habit makes their life easier or more difficult, how the habit is related to their personal or professional goals, or how it bears on the kinds of thinkers or persons they aspire to be. Second, as explained in chapter 6, none of us has perfect or exhaustive introspective access to the truth about the state of our intellectual character. Indeed, many of us are prone to think too highly of ourselves and to avoid looking at the weaker and less flattering features of our mental geography. This tendency underscores the importance of creating a classroom environment in which students feel cared for and supported enough to engage in honest introspection. It also highlights the importance of not treating the results of these assessments as the final word about the students' intellectual character.

STEP FOUR: CONDUCT A SURVEY OF YOUR PEDAGOGICAL PRINCIPLES, POSTURES, AND PRACTICES

In chapters 3 through 9, we explored the pedagogical principles, postures, and practices at the heart of teaching for intellectual virtues. As you set out to teach in ways that will help your students make progress in these virtues, you'll want to spend some time reflecting on your own pedagogical principles, postures, and practices, and on how well they align with the principles, postures, and practices discussed earlier in this book.

You might begin by revisiting the ten principles described in chapter 3. How well do these capture your own fundamental beliefs about teaching and learning? To begin answering this question, you might first identify three to five principles that you endorse but feel like you could do a better job of adhering to in your teaching. For each one, you might spend some time reflecting on questions like the following: Why do I accept this principle? What support or evidence do I have for thinking it is correct? How do my current teaching practices already embody or reflect its content?

How might I adjust my current practices to bring them into better alignment with this principle?

You could take a similar approach to reflecting on your pedagogical postures. As we saw in chapter 4, students are more likely to be open to deep learning and intellectual character growth if they feel seen, heard, and cared for by their teachers. The postures discussed in chapter 4 are a way of establishing this kind of connection with our students, of showing them that we are personally present and concerned with who they are and what they have to contribute as thinkers and learners.

So, again, for two or three of these postures, you might spend some time reflecting on how they compare with the "self" you tend to bring to the classroom. Concerning the posture of presence, for instance, you might ask yourself: When I am with my students, am I really *with* them? Or am I often distracted or preoccupied? Concerning the posture of humility, you might consider: Am I comfortable accepting my limitations as a teacher? Do I feel as if I need to control exactly what and how my students learn? How do I tend to think and feel when things in my classroom don't go as planned?

As with the other questions discussed in this chapter, it is important to be honest with yourself and to support your judgments with concrete evidence or examples whenever possible. To help ensure the objectivity and accuracy of your thinking, you might also consider enlisting your students in this process. For example, you might occasionally administer an anonymous survey that briefly describes several postures and invites the students to identify which ones they think best describe you as a teacher.

Finally, you should also spend some time reflecting on your pedagogical practices. So, once more, for each of the practices discussed in chapters 5 through 9, consider jotting down some ways in which you are already implementing this practice and some ways in which you are not implementing it but could be. Take, for instance, the practice of modeling intellectual virtues, which was the focus of chapter 9. For each of your target virtues, you might ask yourself questions such as: How frequently do I model this virtue for my students, and what does this look like? Is my modeling of this virtue authentic? How else might I go about modeling this virtue? How might doing so benefit or otherwise affect my students? Or consider the practice of teaching for understanding, which was explored at some length in chapter 7. Here you might ask: How are my teaching methods and routines already aligned with helping my students develop a deep understanding of the material? Do any aspects of my teaching encourage my students to simply memorize and regurgitate? What possible changes either to how I teach or to my assignments and assessments might better support my students' development of deep understanding?

Conducting a comprehensive survey of your pedagogical principles, postures, and practices is no small task. To motivate yourself to do it, and to do it well, you might consider joining forces with one or more like-minded colleagues, friends, or acquaintances. Doing so can provide you with the necessary motivation and introduce an element of objectivity to your reflection. Indeed, this point holds for all the steps discussed in this chapter and for teaching for intellectual virtues in general. Because this approach often involves swimming against the local current and because it is aimed, ultimately, at a unique and idealistic end, we are better off practicing the approach with people who are able to give and receive support, encouragement, and insight along the way.

STEP FIVE: CREATE OPPORTUNITIES FOR YOUR STUDENTS TO PRACTICE YOUR TARGET VIRTUES

As noted throughout the book, every intellectual virtue has a skill or competence that distinguishes it from other intellectual virtues. Because skills are developed through practice and repetition, if we desire to cultivate a particular virtue, we must practice and become proficient in its characteristic skill. To grow in open-mindedness, we must practice perspective-switching; to grow in intellectual courage, we must practice facing down our intellectual fears; to grow in intellectual autonomy, we must practice making our own judgments and drawing our own conclusions; and so on.

In light of these aspects of virtue formation, one of the most important steps to take as you begin teaching for intellectual virtues is to create frequent and well-supported opportunities for your students to practice the skills characteristic of your target virtues (as explored at length in chapter 8). In keeping with several of the steps discussed previously, you might begin by thinking about how you're already providing these opportunities. In your ordinary lessons and interactions with students, which target virtues do you routinely encourage your students to practice? And how do you support their practice of these virtues? You might also consider posing similar questions to your students: Which virtues do they believe they are regularly called on to practice in your classes? When they practice these virtues, do they receive helpful assistance and feedback?

Hopefully your answers to these questions will be a source of encouragement. It might also be helpful to ask yourself some more challenging questions, such as: How might I inadvertently be *blocking* or *suppressing* opportunities for students to practice my target virtues? In what ways do I neglect to support or provide helpful feedback when they do practice these virtues? What motivates me to do these things? Your answers to these questions may prove humbling but illuminating. In my own case, I had been interested for years in helping my students cultivate greater curiosity before I realized, after a little self-reflection, that I was rarely providing them with structured opportunities to sit back and wonder or puzzle about the material at hand. When I reflected on why this might be the case, I quickly realized that providing these opportunities was at odds with my penchant for efficiency and control in the classroom.

This initial course of reflection should put you in a good position to consider how you might build on, improve, or add to your existing efforts to encourage your students to practice your target virtues. Again, for each of these virtues, you might begin by considering: What are some additional ways I can encourage my students to practice this virtue? How might I tweak some of my existing exercises, assignments, or assessments to this end? Which thinking routines might I begin using regularly? How might I support and provide my students with helpful feedback as they practice these routines? For more on these issues and on thinking routines in particular, see chapter 8.

CONCLUSION

We've considered five initial steps you can take as you set out to teach for intellectual virtues in a more focused and systematic way: (1) identify and reflect on your target virtues; (2) introduce your students to your target virtues; (3) give your students an opportunity to reflect on their intellectual character strengths and limitations; (4) conduct a comprehensive survey of your pedagogical principles, postures, and practices; and (5) begin creating frequent and well-supported opportunities for your students to practice your target virtues. Again, these steps are just a beginning. As the semester or year progresses, you'll also want cultivate a caring and respectful rapport with your students, encourage them to further reflect on their intellectual character, take steps to ensure that you are teaching for deep understanding, think about how best to model your target virtues, make regular and constructive use of the language of the virtues, continue to give your students opportunities to practice intellectual virtues, and identify ways of learning about and assessing their intellectual character.[4]

At several points throughout the book, I've made reference to the allegory of the cave from Plato's *Republic*. In this story, Socrates compares our capacity to learn with our inability to visually perceive what is immediately behind us. To see what is behind us, we must turn our entire body around. Similarly, Socrates says, education is concerned with the "turning around" of the whole person, so that that the mind can perceive "that which is and the brightest thing that is, the one we call the good."[5] In keeping with this Platonic vision, I have argued in these pages that teaching at its best has the power to reshape and reorient some of our students' fundamental beliefs, attitudes, and desires. It can help them become more curious, open-minded, intellectually tenacious, autonomous, careful, and courageous. It can nurture and mature their intellectual character.

This is, of course, a pedagogical ideal. However, if we allow this ideal to guide and inform why and how we teach, and to do so in ways that are sensible and realistic, it can imbue our work as teachers with a sense of meaning and purpose, which can help sustain us as we encounter the slings and arrows of classroom teaching.

Nine Key Virtues: Descriptions and Slogans

This table provides descriptions and slogans for the nine intellectual virtues discussed in chapter 2 and throughout the rest of the book. With some minor exceptions, these are also the descriptions and slogans adopted by the Intellectual Virtues Academy of Long Beach, California. See http://www .ivalongbeach.org/academics/master-virtues.

Virtue	*Description*	*Slogan*
Curiosity	A disposition to wonder, ponder, and ask why. A thirst for understanding and a desire to explore.	Ask questions!
Autonomy	A capacity for active, self-directed thinking. An ability to think and reason for oneself.	Admit what you don't know!
Humility	A willingness to own one's intellectual limitations and mistakes. Unconcerned with intellectual status or prestige.	Think for yourself!
Attentiveness	A readiness to be "personally present" in the learning process. Keeps distractions at bay. Notices important details.	Look and listen!
Carefulness	A disposition to notice and avoid intellectual pitfalls and mistakes. Strives for accuracy.	Get it right!
Thoroughness	A disposition to seek and provide explanations. Unsatisfied with mere appearances or easy answers. Probes for deeper meaning and understanding.	Go deep!

Virtue	*Description*	*Slogan*
Open-mindedness	An ability to think outside the box. Gives a fair and honest hearing to competing perspectives.	Think outside the box!
Courage	A readiness to persist in thinking or communicating in the face of fear, including fear of embarrassment or failure.	Take risks!
Tenacity	A willingness to embrace intellectual challenge and struggle. Keeps its eyes on the prize and doesn't give up.	Embrace struggle!

APPENDIX B

Virtue-Based Self-Assessments

The following are self-assessment scale items for the nine intellectual virtues discussed in chapter 2. Responses to the scale items can be conveyed using a Likert-type scale (e.g., 1 = "Very different from me," 2 = "Different from me," 3 = "Neither different from me nor like me," 4 = "Like me," and 5 = "Very much like me"). An asterisk (*) indicates items that should be reverse-scored (these items describe an *absence* of the virtue in question). (These items were coauthored with Steve Porter.)

CURIOSITY

_____ My classes often leave me wondering about the topics we discussed.

_____ I wonder about how things work.

_____ I often ask "what-if" questions like "What if something else had happened?"

_____ The world is a fascinating place to discover.

_____ I ask a lot of "why" questions.

_____ I like to study things I already know rather than learn something new.*

_____ I rarely think of questions about what we are learning in class.*

_____ Learning is boring.*

INTELLECTUAL AUTONOMY

———————   I am an independent thinker.

———————   Sometimes I disagree with what my parents or teachers think.

———————   I think differently from my classmates.

———————   When someone gives me advice, I like to think it through for myself.

———————   It bothers me when I am not given a chance to express my opinion.

———————   I find it difficult to come up with my own ideas.*

———————   When I get stuck on a problem, I immediately ask my parents or teachers for help.*

———————   I have a hard time figuring things out on my own.*

INTELLECTUAL HUMILITY

———————   I feel comfortable asking for help when I don't understand something.

———————   I have a lot to learn.

———————   Some of my friends are smarter than I am.

———————   It is easy for me to admit when I am wrong.

———————   I like to impress others with what I know.*

———————   I like to correct my classmates' mistakes.*

———————   I feel as if I don't know anything.*

———————   I am right about most things.*

ATTENTIVENESS

———————   I enjoy paying attention.

———————   I like to look closely at things.

———————   I tend to notice details that other people miss.

———————   I could spend a very long time looking at a detailed image.

———————   I am able to focus on the important parts of a topic.

———————   My mind is always wandering.*

_____   I often have to ask for instructions to be repeated because I missed something the first time.*

_____   I am often distracted when I should be paying attention.*

INTELLECTUAL CAREFULNESS

_____   I like to be accurate.

_____   I check my work for errors before turning it in.

_____   I take the time I need to get the answer right.

_____   I avoid jumping to conclusions.

_____   I start working on assignments before I read the instructions.*

_____   I like to finish assignments quickly even if this means getting a few answers wrong.*

_____   I make careless errors in my school work.*

_____   I am terrified of making mistakes.*

INTELLECTUAL THOROUGHNESS

_____   I like to get to the bottom of things that interest me.

_____   When I don't understand something, I try to find out more about it.

_____   It bothers me when I don't understand what the teacher is talking about.

_____   It is more important to understand what I am learning than to get a good grade.

_____   I like to make connections between the different things I'm learning about.

_____   I like to know just enough to do well on the test.*

_____   I have a difficult time explaining what I know to other people.*

_____   When someone goes into detail about a topic, I often get bored.*

OPEN-MINDEDNESS

_____   I like to hear different perspectives.

_____   I am open to considering new evidence.

_____   I enjoy learning why other people believe what they believe.

_____ I am willing to change my beliefs.

_____ I am a flexible thinker.

_____ I find it difficult to think outside the box.*

_____ I feel uncomfortable around people who see things differently than I do.*

_____ I often ignore perspectives I don't agree with.*

INTELLECTUAL COURAGE

_____ I am willing to answer a question even if I think my answer might be wrong.

_____ I stand up for what I believe in.

_____ I speak up in class even when I am nervous about doing so.

_____ I am willing to take risks to learn more.

_____ When my answer is different from everyone else's, I avoid speaking up.*

_____ Fear often prevents me from learning more.*

_____ If I think my friends might laugh at me, I keep my opinion to myself.*

_____ I don't ask questions in class, because I don't want to be embarrassed.*

INTELLECTUAL TENACITY

_____ Even if a class is boring, I work hard to pay attention and learn.

_____ I continue thinking about difficult problems even when I can't find a solution.

_____ I work hard at school.

_____ I enjoy mental challenges.

_____ When I am frustrated with a problem, I try hard to stick with it.

_____ I get discouraged when something doesn't make sense the first time.*

_____ When I can't figure out a problem, I quit trying.*

_____ I avoid challenging assignments and problems.*

Notes

Introduction

1. On the power and potential influence of individual teachers, see John Hattie, *Visible Learning* (London: Routledge, 2009), chap. 11.

2. According to the 29th annual Met Life Survey of the American Teacher, from 2008 to 2013, the percentage of US teachers who were very satisfied with their jobs decreased 23 points, from 62 percent to a mere 39 percent, the lowest level in twenty-five years. See Valerie Strauss, "U.S. Teachers' Job Satisfaction Craters—Report," *Washington Post*, February 20, 2013, https://www.washingtonpost.com/news/answer-sheet/wp/2013/02/21/u-s-teachers-job-satisfaction-craters-report.

3. The need for this kind of project is evident in a recent comprehensive study by Jal Mehta and Sarah Fine, *In Search of Deeper Learning: The Quest to Remake the American High School* (Cambridge, MA: Harvard University Press, 2019). Mehta and Fine found that while the teachers they interviewed wanted to create intellectually vibrant and challenging classrooms, this was rarely accomplished. They conclude, "To close the gap between espoused values and enacted practices, schools need a *specific and granular vision of deep learning and a carefully crafted organizational design that enables them to realize it*" (41; emphasis added). My aim in this book is to provide a granular vision of an important educational ideal and a carefully crafted account of how teachers can pursue and make progress toward this ideal.

4. Parker Palmer, *The Courage to Teach* (San Francisco: Jossey-Bass, 1998), 17.

5. See especially Ron Ritchhart, *Intellectual Character: What It Is, Why It Matters, and How to Get It* (San Francisco: Jossey-Bass, 2002). Ritchhart's book is informed by earlier research conducted by Ritchhart and others at Project Zero, an education research center at the Harvard Graduate School of Education. See, for instance, Shari Tishman, Eileen Jay, and David Perkins, "Teaching Thinking Dispositions: From Transmission to Enculturation," *Theory into Practice* 32 (1993): 147–153. For some more recent work on this topic, see Daniel Lapsley and Dominic Chaloner, "Post-Truth and Science Identity: A Virtue-Based Approach to Science Education," *Educational Psychologist* 55 (2020): 132–143; Sarit Barizilai and Clark Chinn, "On the Goals of Epistemic Education: Promoting Apt Epistemic Performance," *Journal of the Learning Sciences* 27 (2018): 353–389; Clark Chinn, Luke Buckland, and Ala Samarapungaven,

"Expanding the Dimensions of Epistemic Cognition: Arguments from Philosophy and Psychology," *Educational Psychologist* 46 (2011): 141–167.

6. See William Hare, *In Defence of Open-Mindedness* (Kingston: McGill-Queen's University Press, 1985); Israel Scheffler, *In Praise of the Cognitive Emotions* (New York: Routledge, 1991); Bertrand Russell, *On Education* (New York: Routledge Classics, 2010), chap. 14; David Carr, *Educating the Virtues* (London: Routledge, 2011); Kristjan Kristjansson, *Aristotelian Character Education* (New York: Routledge, 2015); Hugh Sockett, *Knowledge and Virtue in Teaching and Learning* (New York: Routledge, 2012); and Harvey Siegel, *Education's Epistemology* (Oxford: Oxford University Press, 2017).

7. See Tishman, Jay, and Perkins, "Teaching Thinking Dispositions"; Arthur L. Costa and Bena Kallick, *Learning and Leading with Habits of Mind: 16 Essential Characteristics for Success* (Alexandria, VA: Association for Supervision and Curriculum Development, 2008); Ellen Langer, *The Power of Mindful Learning* (Cambridge, MA: DaCapo Press, 1997); Angela Duckworth, Christopher Peterson, Michael D. Matthews, and Dennis Kelly, "Grit: Perseverance and Passion for Long-Term Goals," *Journal of Personality and Social Psychology* 92 (2007): 1087–1101; Richard Ryan and Edward Deci, *Self-Determination Theory* (New York, Guilford Press, 2017); Richard Ryan and Edward Deci, "Intrinsic and Extrinsic Motivations: Classic Definitions and New Directions," *Contemporary Educational Psychology* 25 (2000): 54–67; Kazuhiro Ohtani and Tetsuya Hisasaka, "Beyond Intelligence: A Meta-Analytic Review of the Relationship Among Metacognition, Intelligence, and Academic Performance," *Metacognition and Learning* 13 (2018): 179–212; Carl Benware and Edward L. Deci, "Quality of Learning with an Active Versus Passive Motivational Set," *American Educational Research Journal* 21 (1984): 755–765; Xin Tang Ming-Te Wang, Jiesi Guo, and Katariina Salmela-Aro, "Building Grit: The Longitudinal Pathways between Mindset, Grit, and Academic Outcomes," *Journal of Youth and Adolescence* 48 (2019): 850–863; Joseph Durlak, Celene E. Domitrovich, Roger P. Weissberg, and Thomas P. Gullotta, *Handbook of Social and Emotional Learning* (New York: Guilford Press, 2015); and Richard Paul and Linda Elder, *Critical Thinking* (Upper Saddle River, NJ: Pearson, 2002).

8. There are different strands of virtue epistemology. This book draws from so-called responsibilist virtue epistemology, which focuses on the *character* strengths of good thinkers and inquirers. For an overview of virtue epistemology, see John Turri, Mark Alfano, and John Greco, "Virtue Epistemology," in *Stanford Encyclopedia of Philosophy*, fall 2019 edition, ed. Edward Zalta, https://plato.stanford.edu/archives/fall2019/entries/epistemology-virtue.

9. Jason Baehr, *The Inquiring Mind: On Intellectual Virtues and Virtue Epistemology* (Oxford: Oxford University Press, 2011); and Jason Baehr, ed., *Intellectual Virtues and Education: Essays in Applied Virtue Epistemology* (New York: Routledge, 2016).

10. For additional work at the intersection of virtue epistemology and education, see Ronald Barnett, "Knowing and Becoming in Higher Education Curriculum," *Studies in Higher Education* 34 (2009): 429–440; James MacAllister, "Virtue Epistemology and the Philosophy of Education," *Journal of the Philosophy of Education* 46 (2012):

251–270; Heather Battaly, "Teaching Intellectual Virtues: Applying Virtue Epistemology in the Classroom," *Teaching Philosophy* 29 (2006): 191–222; Patrick Frierson, *Intellectual Agency and Virtue Epistemology: A Montessori Perspective* (London: Bloomsbury Academic, 2020); Ben Kotzee, *Education and the Growth of Knowledge: Perspectives from Social and Virtue Epistemology* (Malden, MA: Wiley-Blackwell, 2013); Randall Curren, "Virtue Epistemology and Education," in *The Routledge Handbook of Virtue Epistemology*, ed. Heather Battaly (New York: Routledge, 2019), 470–482; Duncan Pritchard, "Educating for Intellectual Humility and Conviction," *Journal of Philosophy of Education* 54 (2020): 398–408; Lani Watson, "The Epistemology of Education," *Philosophy Compass* 11 (2016): 146–159; Ryan Byerly, "Teaching for Intellectual Virtues in Logic and Critical Thinking Classes," *Teaching Philosophy* 42 (2019): 1–27; and Jason Baehr, "Educating for Intellectual Virtues: From Theory to Practice," *Journal of the Philosophy of Education* 47 (2013): 248–262.

11. See Intellectual Virtues Academy, home page, http://www.ivalongbeach.org.

12. In 2016, an Intellectual Virtues Academy High School opened in Long Beach. While my role in its founding and operations has been limited by comparison with my involvement with the IVA middle school, its leaders (especially James McGrath and Summer Sanders) and teachers are doing excellent and innovative work. To learn more about the high school, see https://www.academylongbeach.org.

13. Samuel Johnson, *Selected Essays*, ed. David Womersly (London: Penguin Books, 2003), 11.

Chapter 1

1. Though I will here be speaking of educational ideals, my primary concern is with the aims of *teaching* in particular (as opposed to the aims of education in general). This distinction is noteworthy given that education at large has aims that go beyond the aims of teaching.

2. See Common Core State Standards Initiative, "About the Standards," http://www .corestandards.org/about-the-standards (emphasis added). The more recently adopted Next Generation Science Standards (www.nextgenscience.org) are equally focused on knowledge and intellectual skills.

3. E. D. Hirsch, *Cultural Literacy: What Every American Needs to Know* (Boston: Houghton and Mifflin Company), xvi.

4. Core Knowledge, "What is the Core Knowledge Sequence?," https://www.coreknowledge .org/our-approach/core-knowledge-sequence/. For more on the distinctively "epistemic" aims of education, including aims that go beyond knowledge and skills, see Emily Robertson, "The Epistemic Aims of Education," in *The Oxford Handbook of Philosophy of Education*, ed. Harvey Siegel (Oxford: Oxford University Press, 2009), 11–34.

5. Mortimer Adler, *The Paideia Program: An Educational Syllabus* (San Francisco: Institute for Philosophical Research, 1984), 39.

6. Daniel Willingham, *Why Don't Students Like School* (San Francisco: Jossey Bass, 2009), 28–29. For an exchange on the relationship between thinking skills and knowledge, see Robert Ennis, "Critical Thinking and Subject Specificity," *Educational Researcher* 18 (1989): 4–10; and John McPeck, "Critical Thinking and Subject Specificity: A Reply to Ennis," *Educational Researcher* 19 (1990): 10–12.

7. Hugh Sockett, *Knowledge and Virtue in Teaching and Learning* (New York: Routledge, 2012), 177.

8. Thomas Lickona, *Educating for Character: How Our Schools Can Teach Respect and Responsibility* (New York: Bantam Books, 1991), 5.

9. Martin Luther King Jr., *The Strength to Love* (Minneapolis: Fortress Press, 1963), 5–6.

10. Collaborative for Academic, Social, and Emotional Learning (CASEL), "What Is SEL?," https://casel.org/what-is-sel.

11. CASEL, "SEL: What Are the Core Competence Areas and Where Are They Promoted?," December 20, 2020, https://casel.org/core-competencies.

12. Ban Ki-Moon, quoted in Center for Universal Education at the Brookings Institution, *Measuring Global Citizenship Education: A Collection of Practices and Tools* (Washington, DC: Brookings Institution, 2017), https://www.brookings.edu/wp-content/uploads/2017/04/global_20170411_measuring-global-citizenship.pdf.

13. David Leonhardt, "Is College Worth It? Clearly, New Data Say," *New York Times*, May 27, 2014, https://www.nytimes.com/2014/05/27/upshot/is-college-worth-it-clearly-new-data-say.html.

14. Ellen Ruppel Shell, "College May Not Be Worth It Anymore," *New York Times*, May 16, 2018, https://www.nytimes.com/2018/05/16/opinion/college-useful-cost-jobs.html. Notably, this claim is made only in connection with students who are born into poverty. It acknowledges that for other students, college remains financially advantageous.

15. See James Heckman and Tim Kautz, "Hard Evidence on Soft Skills," *Labour Economics* 19 (2012): 451–464.

16. Marcel M. Robles, "Executive Perceptions of the Top 10 Soft Skills Needed in Today's Workplace," *Business Communication Quarterly* 75 (2012): 453–465.

17. Battelle for Kids, "Partnership for 21st Century Learning, a Network of Battelle for Kids," http://www.battelleforkids.org/networks/p21.

18. Philosophers of education have long acknowledged that education should instill in students a proper *care* for and *commitment* to knowledge and skills. See Harvey Siegel, D. C. Phillips, and Eamonn Callan, "Philosophy of Education," in *Stanford Encyclopedia of Philosophy*, winter 2018 edition, ed. Edward N. Zalta, https://plato.stanford.edu/archives/win2018/entries/education-philosophy.

19. On the personal or characterological dimension of good thinking, see Shari Tishman, David Perkins, and Eileen Jay, *The Thinking Classroom: Learning and Teaching in a Culture of Thinking* (Boston: Allyn and Bacon, 1995), 38–40.

20. See John Dewey, *How We Think* (Lexington, MA: D.C. Heath, 1910), 66.

21. Ron Ritchhart, *Intellectual Character: What It Is, Why It Matters, and How to Get It* (San Francisco: Jossey-Bass, 2002), 229.

22. Dewey, *How We Think*, 6, 26.

23. Dewey, 26.

24. Dewey, 28.

25. Daeun Park, Eli Tsukayama, Geoffrey P. Goodwin, Sarah Patrick, and Angela L. Duckworth, "A Tripartite Taxonomy of Character: Evidence for Intrapersonal, Interpersonal, and Intellectual Competencies in Children," *Contemporary Educational Psychology* 48 (2017), 25.

26. Park et al., "Tripartite Taxonomy," 26.

27. Angela Duckworth, *Grit: The Power of Passion and Perseverance* (New York: Scribner), 273.

28. On the first point, see Duckworth, *Grit*, 273–274; on the second, see Walton Family Foundation, "A Q&A with Character Lab's Dr. Angela Duckworth," September 15, 2017, https://www.waltonfamilyfoundation.org/stories/k-12-education/a-q-a-with-character-labs-dr-angela-duckworth; and on the third, see Duckworth, *Grit*, 274. For some additional resources published by Duckworth's Character Lab, see Character Lab, "Character," 2021, https://characterlab.org/character; and Character Lab, "Curiosity," 2021, https://characterlab.org/playbooks/curiosity.

29. David Whyte, "The Conversational Nature of Reality," interview by Krista Tippett, transcript, *On Being with Krista Tippett*, April 7, 2016; updated December 12, 2019, https://onbeing.org/programs/david-whyte-the-conversational-nature-of-reality/.

30. The need for this language is nicely illustrated by the results of a study by Susan Engel, who found that when teachers were presented with a list of twenty-five qualities they might want to nurture in their students, 75 percent of respondents circled "curiosity," but that when they were asked to come up with their own list of qualities, few mentioned curiosity. See Susan Engel, "Children's Need to Know: Curiosity in Schools," *Harvard Educational Review* 81 (2011): 638.

31. Arthur L. Costa and Bena Kallick, *Learning and Leading with Habits of Mind: 16 Essential Characteristics for Success* (Alexandria, VA: Association for Supervision and Curriculum Development, 2008).

32. While there isn't a substantial body of empirical research focused immediately and explicitly on the academic benefits of intellectual virtues or the pedagogical practices aimed at this goal, indications of such benefits aren't difficult to find. For instance, in a comprehensive study of twenty-four character strengths and their relationship to various positive outcomes, intellectual virtues or virtue-like qualities including "curiosity," "love of learning," "persistence," and "perspective/wisdom" were significantly correlated with outcomes such as a higher GPA and college satisfaction. See John W. Lounsbury, Leslee A. Fisher, Jacob J. Levy, and Deborah P. Welsh, "An Investigation of Character Strengths in Relation to the Academic Success of College Students," *Individual Differences Research* 7 (2009): 52–69. Similarly, some research

suggests that noncognitive skills such as self-efficacy and certain Big Five personality traits, including openness to experience and conscientiousness, contribute significantly to academic performance. See Myint Swe Khine and Shaljan Areepattamannil, eds., *Non-Cognitive Skills and Factors in Educational Attainment* (Rotterdam: Sense Publishers, 2016). Given the similarity between these qualities and virtues like curiosity, open-mindedness, carefulness, autonomy, and tenacity, it is reasonable to think that said virtues might also contribute to academic success. Finally, as we will explore in more detail in later chapters, several of the practices central to teaching for intellectual virtues coincide with so-called metacognitive strategies and active learning, both of which have been shown to yield significant academic benefits (e.g., grades, conceptual mastery, intrinsic motivation, and knowledge transfer). See Patricia Chen, Omar Chavez, Desmond C. Ong, and Brenda Gunderson, "Strategic Resource Use for Learning: A Self-Administered Intervention That Guides Self-Reflection on Effective Resource Use Enhances Academic Performance," *Psychological Science* 28, no. 6 (2017): 1–12; and Carl Benware and Edward Deci, "Quality of Learning with an Active Versus Passive Motivational Set," *American Educational Research Journal* 21 (1984): 755–765.

33. See Common Core States Standards Initiative, "Read the Standards," http://www .corestandards.org/read-the-standards; and Next Generation Science Standards, "The Standards," https://www.nextgenscience.org/standards/standards. For more on intellectual virtues and critical thinking, see John Passmore, "On Teaching to Be Critical," in *The Concept of Education*, ed. R.S. Peters (London: Routledge & Kegan Paul, 1967), 192–212; Harvey Siegel, "Critical Thinking and the Intellectual Virtues," in *Intellectual Virtues and Education: Essays in Applied Virtue Epistemology*, ed. Jason Baehr (New York: Routledge, 2016), 95–112; and Jason Baehr, "Intellectual Virtues, Critical Thinking, and the Aims of Education," in *Routledge Handbook of Social Epistemology*, ed. Peter Graham et al. (New York: Routledge, 2019), 447–457.

34. For more on this point, see Nathan L. King, *The Excellent Mind: Intellectual Virtues for Everyday Life* (New York: Oxford University Press, 2021), chap. 1; and James Montmarquet, *Epistemic Virtue and Doxastic Responsibility* (Lanham, MD: Rowman & Littlefield, 1993).

35. Philip Dow, *Virtuous Minds: Intellectual Character Development* (Downers Grove, IL: IVP Academic, 2013), 22.

36. Sabrina Tavernise and Aidan Gardiner, "'No One Believes Anything': Voters Worn Out by a Fog of Political News," *New York Times*, November 18, 2019, https://www .nytimes.com/2019/11/18/us/polls-media-fake-news.html.

37. This is not, of course, a total solution to the relevant problems, many of which are systemic and merit a systemic response. For recent discussions of this point, see King, *Excellent Mind*, chap. 1; and Daniel Lapsley and Dominic Chaloner, "Post-truth and Science Identity: A Virtue-Based Approach to Science Education," *Educational Psychologist* 55 (2020): 132–143.

38. Laszlo Block, quoted in Thomas L. Friedman, "How to Get a Job at Google," *New York Times*, February 2, 2014, https://www.nytimes.com/2014/02/23/opinion/sunday/friedman-how-to-get-a-job-at-google.html.

39. Block, "Job at Google."

40. Block.

41. Plato, *Republic*, Book VII (514a–517a), in *Complete Works*, ed. John M. Cooper, trans. G. M. A. Grube, rev. C. D. C. Reeve (Indianapolis, IN: Hackett Publishing, 1997).

42. Plato, *Republic*, Book VII (518b-d), in *Complete Works*, ed. John M. Cooper, trans. G. M. A. Grube, rev. C. D. C. Reeve (Indianapolis, IN: Hackett Publishing, 1997), 1135–1136 (emphasis added).

43. Parker Palmer, *The Courage to Teach* (San Francisco: Jossey-Bass, 1998), 6.

Chapter 2

1. Aristotle, *Nicomachean Ethics*, Book I, Chapter 2, trans. Roger Crisp (Cambridge: Cambridge University Press, 2000), 4. Aristotle's thinking was not as egalitarian as this remark about the good for "human beings" might suggest. Like many of his contemporaries in the ancient world, Aristotle (384–322 BCE) did not regard women or slaves as morally or intellectually on par with free men. This reprehensible lacuna in his ethical thought has played a role in perpetuating sexist and racist thinking in many parts of the Western world. While his blind spots were severe and not to be discounted, it remains that Aristotle was gifted with insight about character and virtue—insight that applies broadly (not merely to free men) and remains true for us today. I will be drawing on these insights throughout the book (while also remaining mindful of the limitations and defects of other parts of Aristotle's philosophy).

2. For a helpful conceptual discussion of character, see Scott Seider, *Character Compass: How Powerful School Culture Can Point Students Toward Success* (Cambridge, MA: Harvard Education Press, 2012), chap. 1.

3. For some philosophical treatments of intellectual virtues understood in this way, see Linda Zagzebski, *Virtues of the Mind: An Inquiry into the Nature of Virtue and the Ethical Foundations of Knowledge* (Cambridge: Cambridge University Press, 1996); Robert Roberts and Jay Wood, *Intellectual Virtues: An Essay in Regulative Epistemology* (Oxford: Oxford University Press, 2007); and Jason Baehr, *The Inquiring Mind* (Oxford: Oxford University Press, 2011).

4. To date, intellectual vices have received considerably less attention from philosophers than intellectual virtues have. However, this is beginning to change. See, for example, Quassim Cassam, *Vices of the Mind* (Oxford: Oxford University Press, 2019); and Ian J. Kidd, Heather Battaly, and Quassim Cassam, eds., *Vice Epistemology* (New York: Routledge, forthcoming).

5. For a related view, see Christian Miller, *Moral Character: An Empirical Theory* (Oxford:

Oxford University Press, 2013). Miller's view differs from the view defended here because he thinks few people possess virtues or vices of any sort.

6. Put another way, people aren't *responsible* for their possession of ADHD or similar learning disabilities. For some of the challenges involved with trying to explicate this notion of responsibility, see Heather Battaly, "Vice Epistemology Has a Responsibility Problem," *Philosophical Issues* 29 (2019): 24–36.

7. For example, curiosity is a paradigm intellectual virtue but is not widely recognized as a moral virtue (indeed, some have regarded it as an intellectual *vice*). The relationship between intellectual virtues and moral virtues is another challenging philosophical problem. For more on the issue, see Baehr, *Inquiring Mind*, appendix. For an account of different types of character, see David Light Shields, "Character as the Aim of Education," *Phil Delta Kappan* 92 (2011): 48–53.

8. I defend a *four*-dimensional model of intellectual virtues in Baehr, "The Four Dimensions of an Intellectual Virtue," in *Moral and Intellectual Virtues in Western and Chinese Philosophy*, ed. Chienkuo Mi, Michael Slote, and Ernest Sosa (New York: Routledge, 2015), 86–98. The fourth dimension is an *affective* one. It consists of virtuous or appropriate feelings and related affective states. I omit this dimension here both for the sake of simplicity and because I think it is less important from an educational standpoint (albeit not completely so). For similar models of thinking dispositions, see Shari Tishman, Eileen Jay, and David Perkins, "Teaching Thinking Dispositions: From Transmission to Enculturation," *Theory into Practice* 32, no. 3 (1993): 147–153; and Ron Ritchhart, *Intellectual Character: What It Is, Why It Matters, and How to Get It* (San Francisco: Jossey-Bass, 2002), chap. 3.

9. On the importance of a motivational, or care, dimension of epistemic cognition, see Clark Chinn, Ronald Rinehart, and Luke Buckland, "Epistemic Cognition and Evaluating Information: Applying the AIR Model of Epistemic Cognition," in *Processing Inaccurate Information: Theoretical and Applied Perspectives from Cognitive Science and the Educational Sciences* (Cambridge, MA: MIT Press, 2014), 446.

10. We will take a closer look at the motivational dimension of intellectual virtues in chapter 9. For a fuller defense of the point about intrinsic motivation, see Baehr *Inquiring Mind*, chap. 6. For more on intrinsic motivation in a learning context, see Richard Ryan and Edward Deci, "Intrinsic and Extrinsic Motivations: Classic Definitions and New Directions," *Contemporary Educational Psychology* 25 (2000): 54–67; and Deborah Stipek, *Motivation to Learn: Integrating Theory and Practice*, 4th ed. (New York: Pearson, 2001).

11. This doesn't mean, of course, that ideally intellectually virtuous people care about epistemic goods *strictly* or *exclusively* for their own sake. They might also be interested in these goods for other, more practical reasons (e.g., for securing gainful employment, creating an innovative piece of software, or discovering a lifesaving drug).

12. See Shari Tishman, "Why Teach Habits of Mind?," in *Discovering and Exploring Habits of Mind: 16 Essential Characteristics for Success*, ed. Arthur L. Costa and Bena

Kallick (Alexandria, VA: Association for Supervision and Curriculum Development, 2000), 45–47.

13. Aristotle, *Nicomachean Ethics*, Book II, Chapter 6. Aristotle defended this theory in connection with his account of moral virtues. However, moral virtues as he understood them are structurally similar to how we're thinking about intellectual virtues, so the doctrine applies equally well to intellectual virtues.

14. For definitions and slogans of each virtue, see Intellectual Virtues Academy, "Master Virtues," http://www.ivalongbeach.org/academics/master-virtues. For blog posts on each of the virtues discussed in chapter 2, see various authors, "Posts on Master Virtues," Intellectual Virtues Academy, http://www.ivalongbeach.org/library/blog/posts-on-master-virtues.

15. For an alternative and more expansive taxonomy, see Baehr, *Inquiring Mind*, chap. 2.

16. Edward Deci and Richard Ryan, "Intrinsic Motivation," in *The Corsini Encyclopedia of Psychology*, 4th ed., ed. Irving Weiner and Edward Craighead (Hoboken, NJ: John Wiley & Sons, 2010), 868. See also Richard Ryan and Edward Deci, *Self-Determination Theory: Basic Psychological Needs in Motivation, Wellness, and Development* (New York: Guilford Press, 2018); Edward Deci and Richard Ryan, *Intrinsic Motivation and Self-Determination in Human Behavior* (New York: Plenum Press, 1985).

17. Aristotle, *Metaphysics*, trans. C. D. C. Reeve (Indianapolis, IN: Hackett Publishing, 2016), 2.

18. Cf. the distinction between natural curiosity and what the author calls "scientific curiosity" in William James, *The Principles of Psychology*, vol. 2 (New York: Holt, 1950 [1890]), 429–430. See also John Dewey, *How We Think* (Boston: D.C. Heath & Co. Publishers, 1910), 30–34.

19. Virtuously curious thinkers can also wonder about topics that are worthwhile rather than trivial, salacious, or dodgy. For more on this issue, see the discussion of deep understanding in chapter 7.

20. Nenad Miscevic, "Curiosity: The Basic Epistemic Virtue," in *Moral and Intellectual Virtues in Western and Chinese Philosophy*, ed. Chienkuo Mi, Michael Slote, and Ernest Sosa (New York: Routledge, 2015), 145–163. For discussions of the psychological literature on curiosity, see George Loewenstein, "The Psychology of Curiosity: A Review and Reinterpretation," *Psychological Bulletin* 116 (1994): 75–98; and Amanda Markey and George Loewenstein, "Curiosity," in *The International Handbook of Emotions in Education*, ed. Reinhard Pekrun and Lisa Linnenbrink-Garcia (New York: Routledge, 2014), 228–245.

21. For a comparison of curiosity and inquisitiveness, see Lani Watson, "Curiosity and Inquisitiveness," in *The Routledge Handbook of Virtue Epistemology*, ed. Heather Battaly (New York: Routledge, 2019), 155–166.

22. The term *heteronomy* comes from *hetero* ("other, different") and *nomos* ("law"). For a related discussion, see Dewey, *How We Think*, 23.

23. Richard Paul and Linda Elder, *Critical Thinking: Tools for Taking Charge of Your Professional and Personal Life* (Upper Saddle River, NJ: Pearson, 2002), 33.

24. Dewey, *How We Think*, 63.

25. Dewey, 64.

26. For a philosophical exploration of this view of intellectual humility, see Dennis Whitcomb, Heather Battaly, Jason Baehr, and Daniel Howard-Snyder, "Intellectual Humility: Owning Our Limitations," *Philosophy and Phenomenological Research* 94, no. 3 (2017): 509–539. For a different account of intellectual humility, see Roberts and Wood, *Intellectual Virtues*, chap. 9. For psychological treatment of intellectual humility, see Mark R. Leary, "Cognitive and Interpersonal Features of Intellectual Humility," *Personality and Social Psychology Bulletin* 43, no. 6 (2017): 793–813. For discussions of humility in an educational context, see Patrick Frierson, *Intellectual Agency and Virtue Epistemology* (London: Bloomsbury Academic, 2020), chap. 10; and Ian Kidd, "Educating for Intellectual Humility," in *Intellectual Virtues and Education: Essays in Applied Virtue Epistemology*, ed. Jason Baehr (New York: Routledge, 2016), chap. 4.

27. Maria Montessori, quoted in Frierson, *Intellectual Agency*, 205.

28. Tenelle Porter, "The Benefits of Admitting When You Don't Know," *Greater Good Magazine*, July 16, 2018, https://greatergood.berkeley.edu/article/item/the_benefits_of _admitting_when_you_dont_know, which is a summary of the findings in Tenelle Porter and Karina Schumann, "Intellectual Humility and Openness to the Opposing View," *Self and Identity* 17 (2018): 139–162. See also Tenelle Porter, Karina Schumann, Diana Selmeczy, and Kali Trzesniewski, "Intellectual Humility Predicts Master Behaviors When Learning," *Learning and Individual Differences* 80 (May 2020): 101888. For similar findings, see Elizabeth J. Krumrei-Mancuso, Megan C. Haggard, Jordan P. LaBouff, and Wade C. Rowatt, "Links Between Intellectual Humility and Acquiring Knowledge," *Journal of Positive Psychology* 15, no. 2 (2020): 155–170.

29. Shinzen Young, "What Is Mindfulness: A Contemplative Perspective," in *Handbook of Mindfulness in Education*, ed. Kimberly Schonert-Reichl and Robert Roeser (New York: Springer, 2016), 34.

30. For a related discussion, see Frierson's illuminating treatment of Montessori's view of active attention and perception in *Intellectual Agency*, chap. 2.

31. Ellen Langer, "Mindful Learning," *New Directions in Psychological Science* 9, no. 6 (2000): 220.

32. For more on the application of Langer's work to education, see Ellen Langer, *The Power of Mindful Learning* (Cambridge, MA: DeCapo Books, 1997). See also Kimberly Schonert-Reichl and Robert Roeser, eds., *The Handbook of Mindfulness in Education* (New York: Springer, 2016).

33. Mary Oliver, "Low Tide," *Amicus Journal* 18 (1997), 34.

34. Israel Scheffler, *In Praise of Cognitive Emotions and Other Essays in the Philosophy of Education* (New York: Routledge, 1991), 5.

35. Thanks to Pamela Paresky for helping me see that carefulness isn't just about avoiding mistakes. The distinction between avoiding errors and getting things just right is important in an educational context, where a fear of failure can run rampant. For

related discussions, see Bertrand Russell, *On Education* (New York: Routledge Classics, 2010), 156–159; and Dewey, *How We Think*, 57–58.

36. Fyodor Dostoevsky, *The Idiot*, trans. David McDuff (London: Penguin, 2004), 644.

37. For a defense of this way of thinking about open-mindedness, see Baehr, *Inquiring Mind*, chap. 8.

38. For a semicritical perspective on teaching for open-mindedness, see Peter Gardner, "Should We Teach Children to Be Open-Minded? Or, Is the Pope Open-Minded About the Existence of God?," *Journal of Philosophy of Education* 27 (1993): 39–43. For a response, see William Hare and T. McLaughlin, "Four Anxieties About Open-Mindedness: Reassuring Peter Gardner," *Journal of Philosophy of Education* 32 (1998): 283–292.

39. William Hare, "The Ideal of Open-Mindedness and Its Place in Education," *Journal of Thought* 38 (2003): 3–10. For more on open-mindedness and education, see William Hare, *Open-Mindedness and Education* (Montreal: McGill-Queen's University Press, 1985); and William Hare, "Open-Mindedness in the Classroom," *Journal of Philosophy of Education* (1985): 251–259.

40. For more on the relationship between open-mindedness and intellectual humility, see James Spiegel, "Open-Mindedness and Intellectual Humility," *Theory and Research in Education* 10 (2012): 27–38.

41. Philip Dow, *Virtuous Minds: Intellectual Character Development* (Downers Grove, IL: IVP Academic, 2013), 73.

42. Dewey, *How We Think*, 13.

43. Carol Dweck, "Even Geniuses Work Hard," *Educational Leadership* 68, no. 1 (2010): 17, http://www.ascd.org/publications/educational-leadership/sept10/vol68/num01/Even-Geniuses-Work-Hard.aspx.

44. Angela Duckworth, *Grit: The Power of Passion and Perseverance* (New York: Scribner, 2016), 272.

45. Duckworth, *Grit*, 269. See also Angela Duckworth, Christopher Peterson, Michael D. Matthews, and Dennis R. Kelly, "Grit: Perseverance and Passion for Long-Term Goals," *Journal of Personality and Social Psychology* 92, no. 6 (2007): 1087–1101.

46. Duckworth et al., "Grit," 1098.

47. See, for example, Paul Tough, *How Children Succeed: Grit, Curiosity, and the Hidden Power of Character* (New York: Houghton, Mifflin, Harcourt, 2012), chap. 1.

48. This doesn't mean there aren't other things we can do as teachers to help our students cultivate grit. Along these lines, see Steven Porter, "A Therapeutic Approach to Intellectual Virtue Formation in the Classroom," in *Intellectual Virtues and Education: Essays in Applied Virtue Epistemology*, ed. Jason Baehr (New York: Routledge, 2016), 221–239.

49. As Nathan King argues, we can view intellectual character as a species or type of intellectual perseverance. See his "Perseverance as an Intellectual Virtue," *Synthese* 191 (March 2014): 3501–3523.

50. Angela Duckworth, *Grit*, 180. For a similar perspective, see Yukun Zhao, Gengfeng

Niu, Hanchao Hou, Guang Zeng, Liying Xu, Kaiping Peng, and Feng Yu, "From Growth Mindset to Grit in Chinese Schools: The Mediating Roles of Learning Motivations," *Frontiers in Psychology* 9 (October 2018): 1–7.

51. Thus tenacity and courage are what I have elsewhere described as "facilitating virtues." See Baehr, *Inquiring Mind*, 173.

Chapter 3

1. On the effectiveness of active-learning strategies, see Michael Prince, "Does Active Learning Work? A Review of the Research," *Journal of Education Engineering* 93 (2004): 223–231; Carl Benware and Edward Deci, "Quality of Learning with an Active Versus Passive Motivational Set," *American Educational Research Journal* 21 (1984): 755–765; and Scott Freeman, Eileen O'Connor, John W. Parks, Matthew Cunningham, David Hurley, David Haak, Clarissa Dirks, Mary Pat Wenderoth, and Martha Grossel, "Prescribed Active Learning Increases Performance in Introductory Biology," *CBE—Life Sciences Education* 6, no. 2 (2007): 132–139.

2. Aristotle, *Nicomachean Ethics*, Book 2, Chapter 1, trans. Roger Crisp (Cambridge: Cambridge University Press, 2000), 23.

3. Bertrand Russell, *On Education* (New York: Routledge Classics, 2010), 163.

4. Patrick Frierson, *Intellectual Agency and Virtue Epistemology* (London: Bloomsbury Academic, 2020), 27 (emphasis in original).

5. For a recent study comparing the effectiveness of lecturing and several active-learning strategies, see Louis Deslauriers, Logan S. McCarty, Kelly Miller, Kristina Callaghan, and Greg Kestin, "Measuring Actual Learning Versus Feeling of Learning in Response to Being Actively Engaged in the Classroom," *Proceedings of the National Academy of Sciences of the United States of America* 116, no. 39 (2019): 19,251–19,257.

6. On the importance of depth versus breadth to high-quality learning and to students' formation as thinkers and learners, see Jal Mehta and Sarah Fine, *In Search of Deeper Learning: The Quest to Remake the American High School* (Cambridge, MA: Harvard University Press, 2019), chap. 8. See also Marc S. Schwartz, Philip M. Sadler, Gerhard Sonnert, and Robert H. Tai, "Depth Versus Breath: How Content Coverage in High School Science Courses Related to Later Success in College Science Coursework," *Science Education* 93, no. 5 (2009): 798–826.

7. On this topic, see Martha Stone Wiske, ed., *Teaching for Understanding: Linking Research with Practice* (San Francisco: Jossey-Bass, 1998).

8. Ron Ritchhart, *Intellectual Character: What It Is, Why It Matters, and How to Get It* (San Francisco: Jossey-Bass, 2002),

9. Susan Engel, *The Hungry Mind: The Origins of Curiosity in Childhood* (Cambridge, MA: Harvard University Press, 2018), 190.

10. Parker Palmer, *To Know as We Are Known* (San Francisco: HarperCollins, 1983).

11. It is also contestable whether education is principally an academic enterprise. See

David Light Shields, "Character as the Aim of Education," *Phi Delta Kappan* 92 (2011): 48–53.

12. See John Hattie, *Visible Learning for Teachers* (London: Routledge, 2012), 187–188.

13. For an insightful and persuasive defense of this claim, see Steven Porter, "A Therapeutic Approach to Intellectual Virtue Formation in the Classroom," in *Intellectual Virtues and Education: Essays in Applied Virtue Epistemology*, ed. Jason Baehr (New York: Routledge, 2016), 221–239. For more on the relationship between secure relational attachments and virtues like curiosity, intellectual humility, autonomy, courage, and tenacity, see chapter 4.

14. Mehta and Fine, *In Search of Deeper Learning*, 351–352.

15. See Scott Seider, *Character Compass: How Powerful School Culture Can Point Students Toward Success* (Cambridge, MA: Harvard Education Press, 2012), 219–224.

16. On this point, see Dennis Whitcomb, Heather Battaly, Jason Baehr, and Daniel Howard-Snyder, "The Puzzle of Humility and Disparity," in *The Routledge Handbook of the Philosophy of Humility*, ed. Mark Alfano, Michael Lynch, and Alessandra Tanesini (New York: Routledge), 72–83.

17. This is a familiar point from the literature on traditional (moral/civic) character education. See, for example, Marvin Berkowitz, Melinda Bier, and Brian McCauley, "Toward a Science of Character Education: Frameworks for Identifying and Implementing Effective Practices," *Journal of Character Education* 13 (2017): 33–51. A similar point is made in research on teaching for critical thinking. Here see Deanna Kuhn, "A Developmental Model of Critical Thinking," *Education Researcher* 28 (1999): 16–26.

18. See Daniel Siegel and Tina Payne Bryson, *The Whole-Brain Child* (New York: Bantam Books, 2012); Daniel Siegel, *The Developing Mind: How Relationships and the Brain Interact to Shape Who We Are* (New York: Guilford Press, 2012); and Frances Jensen, *The Teenage Brain: A Neuroscientist's Survival Guide to Raising Adolescents and Young Adults* (New York: HarperCollins, 2015).

19. Naturally, some discretion may be required here, as our students' answers to these questions may be somewhat off target. Still, we should seek to be as flexible as possible in allowing their input to shape at least some of the relevant decisions.

20. Student buy-in and empowerment are central features of successful programs in traditional (moral/civic) character education. See, for example, Berkowitz, Bier, and McCauley, "Science of Character Education"; Marvin Berkowitz, "What Works in Values Education," *International Journal of Educational Research* 50 (2011): 153–158; and Kevin Ryan and Karen Bohlin, *Building Character in Schools* (San Francisco: Jossey-Bass, 2003), chap. 7.

21. Edward Deci and Richard Ryan, "Intrinsic Motivation," in *The Corsini Encyclopedia of Psychology*, 4th ed., ed. Irving Weiner and Edward Craighead (Hoboken, NJ: John Wiley & Sons, 2010), 868. See also Edward Deci, Gregory Betley, James Kahle, Linda Abrams, and Joseph Porac, "When Trying to Win: Competition and Intrinsic Motivation," *Personality and Social Psychology Bulletin* 71 (1981): 79–83;

and Richard Ryan and Edward Deci, *Self-Determination Theory: Basic Psychological Needs in Motivation, Wellness, and Development* (New York: Guilford Press, 2018). This is not to say, of course, that any element of competition in a classroom setting is always bad.

22. See Carol Dweck, *Mindset: The New Psychology of Success* (New York: Random House, 2006); Dweck, "Even Geniuses Work Hard," *Educational Leadership* 68, no. 1 (2010): 16–20, http://www.ascd.org/publications/educational-leadership/sept10/vol68/num01/Even-Geniuses-Work-Hard.aspx; and Lisa Blackwell, Kali Trzesniewski, and Carol Dweck, "Implicit Theories of Intelligence Predict Achievement Across an Adolescent Transition: A Longitudinal Study and an Intervention," *Child Development* 78 (2007): 246–263.

23. Dweck, "Even Geniuses Work Hard," 16.

24. Yukun Zhao, Gengfeng Niu, Hanchao Hou, Guang Zeng, Liying Xu, Kaiping Peng, and Feng Yu, "From Growth Mindset to Grit in Chinese Schools: The Mediating Roles of Learning Motivations," *Frontiers in Psychology* 9 (October 2018): 6.

25. For some recent empirical research that addresses the relationship between intellectual humility and a growth mind-set, see Tenelle Porter, Karina Schumann, Diana Selmeczy, and Kali Trzesniewski, "Intellectual Humility Predicts Mastery Behaviors When Learning," *Learning and Individual Differences* 80 (May 2020): 101888.

26. Hattie, *Visible Learning*, 184.

27. Maria Popova, "Hope, Cynicism, and the Stories We Tell Ourselves," *Brain Pickings*, https://www.brainpickings.org/2015/02/09/hope-cynicism.

28. See Jason Baehr, "Is Intellectual Character Growth a Realistic Educational Aim?," *Journal of Moral Education* 45(2016): 117–131. This sober-minded assessment is not meant to discount the significant body of empirical evidence suggesting that the postures and practices described in this book can have a meaningful impact on the intellectual character of many of our students. This evidence includes but isn't limited to classroom-based, ethnographic case-studies and several controlled empirical studies. For more on these points, see chapters 4 through 9.

Chapter 4

1. Relevant here is the distinction between "states" and "traits" in psychology (though I am not thinking of intellectual virtues as traits in the strong sense). Again, a person can be in a state of humility, say, without possessing a stable trait of humility. On this distinction, see William Chaplin, Oliver John, and Lewis Goldberg, "Conceptions of States and Traits: Dimensional Attributes with Ideals as Prototypes," *Journal of Personality and Social Psychology* 54 (1988): 541–557.

2. The claim that intellectual virtue-possession is not under our *direct* voluntary control is consistent with the (much more plausible) claim that it is or can be under our *indirect* voluntary control. For more on this point, see Jason Baehr, *The Inquiring*

Mind: On Intellectual Virtues and Virtue Epistemology (Oxford: Oxford University Press, 2011), chap. 2.

3. This doesn't imply that intellectual virtues don't have an "others-regarding" dimension. They do. But the moral dimension here is broader and different. See Baehr, *Inquiring Mind*, appendix.

4. A prime example is negligence. Negligence is *morally* problematic; however, it is typically the result of a person's failure to *think* in intellectually virtuous ways (e.g., carefully, attentively, etc.). For more on the relationship between intellectual virtues and morally responsible action, see Jason Baehr, "Virtue Epistemology, Virtue Ethics, and the Structure of a Virtue," *The Routledge Handbook of Virtue Epistemology*, ed. Heather Battaly (New York: Routledge, 2018), 144–162.

5. Lola Hill, "What Does It Take to Change Minds? Intellectual Development of Preservice Teachers," *Journal of Teacher Education* 51 (2000): 50–62.

6. Alfred North Whitehead, *The Aims of Education* (New York: Free Press, 1929), 30.

7. Presence, as described here, bears obvious similarities to the virtue of attentiveness, as described earlier in the book. Indeed, while the scope of attentiveness, understood as an intellectual virtue, is somewhat narrower than that of the posture of presence (the focus of attentiveness being distinctively epistemic), attentiveness involves the intelligent and habitual practice of certain aspects of presence (i.e., being fully present in a learning context).

8. David Whyte, "What to Remember When Waking," in *The House of Belonging* (Langley, WA: Many Rivers Press, 2016).

9. Teaching from a posture of presence bears similarities to some of the themes and practices associated with contemplative pedagogy. For more on this approach and some of the pedagogical practices associated with it, see Jane Dalton, Kathryn Byrnes, and Elizabeth Hope Dorman, eds., *The Teaching Self: Contemplative Practices, Pedagogy, and Research in Higher Education* (Lanham, MD: Rowman & Littlefield, 2018). For additional resources, see Columbia Center for Teaching and Learning, "Contemplative Pedagogy," https://ctl.columbia.edu/resources-and-technology/resources/contemplative -pedagogy/.

10. As suggested earlier in the chapter, the posture of humility is broader than the posture (and likewise the virtue) of *intellectual* humility: it involves a willingness to own not merely our intellectual limitations but our other limitations as well. For an exploration of humility understood along these lines, see Nancy Snow, "Humility," *The Journal of Value Inquiry* 29 (1995): 203–216.

11. Like all aspects of teaching, this recommendation to admit our uncertainty and intellectual mistakes requires some discretion. Although some teachers may occasionally need to avoid letting their students "see them sweat," we must not overestimate how often this is the case.

12. As the name suggests, this posture has two distinct aspects: being *open* to one's students and being willing to *receive* what they have to offer. I treat openness and

receptivity as a single posture because of how intimately these two aspects are related to each other.

13. John Hattie, *Visible Learning for Teachers* (London: Routledge, 2012), 187.

14. Gregory Boyle, *Barking to the Choir: The Power of Radical Kinship* (New York: Simon & Schuster), 54.

15. David Whyte, *Consolations* (Langley, WA: Many Rivers Press), 94.

16. For a seminal work in attachment theory, see John Bowlby, *Parent-Child Attachment and Healthy Human Development* (New York: Basic, 1988). On attachment security and virtues like courage, autonomy, humility, and integrity, see Deborah Finfgeld, "Courage as a Process of Pushing Beyond the Struggle," *Qualitative Health Research* 9 (1999): 803–814; Annie Rogers, "Voice, Play, and a Practice of Ordinary Courage in Girls' and Women's Lives," *Harvard Educational Review* 63 (1993): 265–295; and Omri Gillath, Amanda K. Sesko, Phillip R. Shaver, and David S. Chun, "Attachment, Authenticity, and Honesty: Dispositional and Experimentally Induced Security Can Reduce Self- and Other-Deception," *Journal of Personality and Social Psychology* 98 (2010): 841–855. On attachment security and grit, which in turn is closely related to intellectual tenacity and perseverance, see Jaclyn Levy and Howard Steele, "Attachment and Grit: Exploring Possible Contributions of Attachment Styles (from Past and Present Life) to the Adult Personality Construct of Grit," *Journal of Social and Psychological Science* 4 (2011): 16–49; Toni Mandelbaum, "The Relationship Between Attachment and Grit in Lower Income Adolescents," *Journal of Character Education* 14 (2018): 59–74; and Carissa Dwiwardini, Peter C. Hill, Richard A. Bollinger, Lashley E. Marks, Justin R. Steele, Holly N. Doolin, Sara L. Wood, Joshua Hook, and Don Davis, "Virtues Develop from a Secure Base: Attachment and Resilience as Predictors of Humility, Gratitude, and Forgiveness," *Journal of Psychology & Theology* 42 (2014): 83–90. On attachment security and curiosity, see Susan Engel, "Children's Need to Know: Curiosity in Schools," *Harvard Educational Review* 81 (2011): 625–645; and Susan Engel, *The Hungry Mind: The Origins of Curiosity in Childhood* (Cambridge, MA: Harvard University Press, 2015), chap. 2. Finally, the importance of positive relational experiences to character formation is also widely recognized within traditional (moral/civic) character education. See Marvin Berkowitz, Melinda Bier, and Brian McCauley, "Toward a Science of Character Education: Frameworks for Identifying and Implementing Effective Practices," *Journal of Character Education* 13 (2017): 33–51; and Marvin Berkowitz, "What Works in Values Education," *International Journal of Educational Research* 50 (2011): 153–158.

17. Justin Westbrook, "Attachment and the Virtuous Life: Early Attachment's Effect on Virtue Development" (PhD diss., Graduate School of Psychology, Fuller Theological Seminary, 2013), 11. For a similar perspective, see Ross Thompson, "The Development of Virtue: A Perspective from Developmental Psychology," in *Cultivating Virtue: Perspectives from Philosophy, Theology, and Psychology*, ed. Nancy Snow (Oxford: Oxford University Press, 2015), 279–306.

18. Steven Porter, "A Therapeutic Approach to Intellectual Virtue Formation in the Classroom," in *Intellectual Virtues and Education: Essays in Applied Virtue Epistemology*, ed. Jason Baehr (New York: Routledge, 2016), 232.

Chapter 5

1. Tim Van Gelder, "Teaching Critical Thinking: Some Lessons from Cognitive Science," *College Teaching* 53 (2005): 44.

2. Accordingly, at IVA, the language of the of virtues is used more frequently with sixth and seventh graders than it is with eighth graders. Ironically, but perhaps not surprisingly, Principal Jacquie Bryant has observed that when eighth graders with apparent "virtue fatigue" are asked to describe what they like most about IVA, they usually end up describing its emphasis on intellectual character formation (albeit not in those terms).

3. For more on this topic, see Ron Ritchhart, *Creating Cultures of Thinking* (San Francisco: Jossey-Bass, 2015), chap. 3; and Ron Ritchhart, *Intellectual Character: What It Is, Why It Matters, and How to Get It* (San Francisco: Jossey-Bass, 2002), chap. 6.

4. Aristotle, *Nicomachean Ethics*, Book I, Chapter 2, trans. Roger Crisp (Cambridge: Cambridge University Press, 2000), 4.

5. Quoted in Andrew Del Banco, *College: What It Was, Is, and Should Be* (Princeton, NJ: Princeton University Press, 2012), 33.

6. On the importance of purpose to personal and intellectual development, see William Damon, *The Path to Purpose: Helping Our Children Find Their Calling in Life* (New York: Free Press, 2008); and William Damon, "The Why Question: Teachers Can Instill a Sense of Purpose," *Education Next* 9 (2009): 84–94.

7. Julia Leonard, Andrea Garcia, and Laura Schulz, "How Adults' Actions, Outcomes, and Testimony Affect Preschoolers' Persistence," *Child Development* 91 (2020): 1254–1271.

8. Angela Duckworth, "Preach What You Practice," Character Lab, March 1, 2020, https://characterlab.org/tips-of-the-week/preach-what-you-practice (emphasis in original).

9. For more on the idea of thick concepts, see Pekka Väyrynen, "Thick Ethical Concepts," *The Stanford Encyclopedia of Philosophy*, fall 2019 edition, ed. Edward N. Zalta, https://plato.stanford.edu/archives/sum2019/entries/thick-ethical-concepts.

10. Character.org, "11 Principles Framework," https://www.character.org/11-principles-framework.

11. Ritchhart, *Creating Cultures of Thinking*, chap. 3. See also Scott Seider, *Character Compass: How Powerful School Culture Can Point Students Toward Success* (Cambridge, MA: Harvard Education Press, 2012), chap. 8.

12. Deanna Kuhn, "A Developmental Model of Critical Thinking," *Education Researcher* 28 (1999): 17.

13. For related discussions, see Shari Tishman, David Perkins, and Eileen Jay, *The Thinking Classroom: Learning and Teaching in a Culture of Thinking* (Boston: Allyn and Bacon, 1995), chaps. 2–3: and Ritchhart, *Intellectual Character*, chap. 6.

14. This practice is widely endorsed in traditional (moral/civic) character education. See, for instance, Marvin Berkowitz, Melinda Bier, and Brian McCauley, "Toward a Science of Character Education," *Journal of Character Education* 13 (2017): 33–51; and Thomas Lickona and Matthew Davidson, *Smart and Good High Schools: Integrating Excellence and Ethics for Success in School, Work, and Beyond* (Washington, DC: Character Education Partnership, 2005).

15. For an inquiry into the role of literature and literary examples in character education, see Karen Bohlin, *Teaching Character Education Through Literature* (New York: Routledge, 2005). See also Heather Battaly, "Responsibilist Virtues in Reliabilist Classrooms," in *Intellectual Virtues and Education: Essays in Applied Virtue Epistemology*, ed. Jason Baehr (New York: Routledge, 2016), 174–182.

16. See Philip Dow, *Virtuous Minds: Intellectual Character Development* (Downers Grove, IL: IVP Academic, 2013). Dow's book is written for a religious audience; however, one needn't be religious to agree with most of what Dow says about particular virtues. See also Nathan L. King, *The Excellent Mind: Intellectual Virtues for Everyday Life* (New York: Oxford University Press, 2021). I've had the good fortune of reading and using earlier drafts of King's book in some of my courses over the past several years.

17. Because the focus of these papers is ancillary to the main academic content of most of the courses in question, I make them worth a very small percentage of students' overall grades.

18. Ritchhart, *Intellectual Character*, 136–137.

19. Ron Ritchhart, Mark Church, and Karin Morrison, *Making Thinking Visible: How to Promote Engagement, Understanding, and Independence for All Learners* (San Francisco: Jossey-Bass, 2011), 29 (emphasis added).

Chapter 6

1. Plato, *Apology*, 38a-b, in *Complete Works*, ed. John Cooper, trans. G. M. A. Grube, rev. C. D. C. Reeve (Indianapolis, IN: Hackett Publishing, 1997), 33.

2. This maxim was inscribed on the Temple of Delphi in ancient Greece. Although it is mentioned by Socrates in Plato's *Protagoras*, 343b, in *Complete Works*, 774, neither Socrates nor Plato is its original source.

3. See, for example, David Dunning, *Self-Insight: Roadblocks and Detours on the Path to Knowing Thyself* (New York: Psychology Press, 2005); and Anthony Greenwald, "The Totalitarian Ego: Fabrication and Revision of Personal History," *American Psychologist* 35 (1980): 603–618.

4. Simine Vazire, "Who Knows What About a Person? The Self-Other Knowledge Asymmetry (SOKA) Model," *Personality Processes and Individual Differences* 98 (2010): 281–300.

5. Though I won't explore the point in detail here, the kind of self-reflection at issue may also be conducive to other important academic outcomes. This connection is suggested by research on two adjacent topics: metacognition and social and emotional learning. As we'll see later, metacognitive activities overlap significantly with several of the reflective aims and practices discussed in this chapter. Therefore, the well-documented academic benefits of metacognition (e.g., on grades, exams scores, memory, reading comprehension, and knowledge transfer) may also extend to some of the practices discussed in this chapter. On the benefits of metacognitive strategies, see Patricia Chen, Omar Chavez, Desmond C. Ong, and Brenda Gunderson, "Strategic Resource Use for Learning: A Self-Administered Intervention that Guides Self-Reflection on Effective Resource Use Enhances Academic Performance," *Psychological Science* 28, no. 6 (2017): 1–12; Kazuhiro Ohtani and Tetsuya Hisasaka, "Beyond Intelligence: A Meta-Analytic Review of the Relationship Among Metacognition, Intelligence, and Academic Performance," *Metacognition and Learning* 13 (2018): 179–212; Kevin Ford, Daniel A. Weissbein, Eleanor M. Smith, Stanley M. Gully, Eduardo Salas, "Relationships of Goal Orientation, Metacognitive Activity, and Practice Strategies with Learning Outcomes and Transfer," *Journal of Applied Psychology* 83, no. 2 (1998): 218–233; and Gavriel Salomon and David Perkins, "Rocky Roads to Transfer: Rethinking Mechanisms of a Neglected Phenomenon," *Educational Psychologist* 24 (1989): 113–142. One of the main competencies social and emotional learning programs seek to foster is self-awareness. Like metacognitive strategies, social and emotional learning strategies have been shown to boost academic performance and other valuable outcomes. We might, then, expect some of the self-reflection practices discussed here to lead to similar outcomes. See Joseph Durlak, Roger P. Weissberg, Allison B. Dymnicki, Rebecca D. Taylor, and Kriston B. Schellinger, "The Impact of Enhancing Students' Social and Emotional Learning: A Meta-Analysis of School-Based Universal Interventions," *Child Development* 82, no. 1 (2011): 405–432.

6. Steven Porter, "A Therapeutic Approach to Intellectual Virtue Formation in the Classroom," in *Intellectual Virtues and Education: Essays in Applied Virtue Epistemology*, ed. Jason Baehr (New York: Routledge, 2016), 228. Porter's chapter provides a useful treatment of how flawed internal working models can inhibit intellectual character growth and what teachers can do to help change these messages. His discussion dovetails with the discussion of postures in chapter 4.

7. Porter, "Therapeutic Approach," 233.

8. See Carol Dweck, *Mindset: The New Psychology of Success* (New York: Ballantine Books, 2007). For a discussion of intelligence as dispositional, or characterological, see Shari Tishman, "Why Teach Habits of Mind?," in *Discovering and Exploring Habits of Mind*, ed. Arthur L. Costa and Bena Kallick (Alexandria, VA: Association for Supervision and Curriculum Development, 2000), 41–52.

9. Nathan Ballantyne, "Epistemic Trespassing," *Mind* 128, no. 510 (2019): 367–395.

10. John Bransford, Ann Brown, and Rodney Cocking, eds., *How People Learn: Brain, Mind, Experience, and School* (Washington, DC: National Academies Press, 2000), 18.

11. Paul Pintrich, "The Role of Metacognitive Knowledge in Learning, Teaching, and Assessing," *Theory into Practice* 41 (2002): 219–225.

12. Pintrich, "Metacognitive Knowledge," 220.

13. Pintrich, 221–222. For more on the connection between intellectual virtues and metacognition, see Daniel Lapsley and Dominic Chaloner, "Post-Truth and Science Identity: A Virtue-Based Approach to Science Education," *Educational Psychologist* 55 (2020): 132–143.

14. Shari Tishman, Eileen Jay, and David Perkins, *The Thinking Classroom: Learning and Teaching in a Culture of Thinking* (Boston: Allyn and Bacon, 1995), 65.

15. For some related ideas and suggestions, see Arthur L. Costa and Bena Kallick, *Learning and Leading with Habits of Mind: 16 Essential Characteristics for Success* (Alexandria, VA: Association for Supervision and Curriculum Development, 2008), chap. 12.

16. Parker Palmer, *The Courage to Teach* (San Francisco: Jossey-Bass, 1998), 10–11.

17. A comment like this is unlikely to have much of an effect if the student doesn't experience me as a caring and supportive presence. This observation underscores an important connection between our ability to help our students engage in honest self-reflection and the postures discussed in chapter 4. Nor is a comment of this sort likely to open the floodgates of self-knowledge. It can, however, lead to the beginning of self-reflection, especially if the student has been primed for it by the other practices described in this book.

18. Palmer, *Courage to Teach*, 6.

19. Most of this selection is quoted in Porter, "Therapeutic Approach," 236. The original source is Ted Fleming, "A Secure Base for Adult Learning: Attachment Theory and Adult Education," *The Adult Learner: The Journal of Adult and Community Education in Ireland* 25 (2008): 33–53.

20. So far in this chapter, the scope of self-reflection, as we've been thinking about it, has included one's entire identity as a learner, not merely one's intellectual character strengths and limitations.

21. See chapter 10, endnote 7, for links to some online resources. For a sampling of self-assessments published in academic journals, see Mark R. Leary, Kate J. Diebels, Erin K. Davisson, Katrina P. Jongman-Sereno, Jennifer C. Isherwood, Kaitlin T. Raimi, Samantha A. Deffler, and Rick H. Hoyle, "Cognitive and Interpersonal Features of Intellectual Humility," *Personality and Social Psychology Bulletin* 43, no. 6 (2017): 793–813; Elizabeth Krumrei-Mancuso and Steven Rouse, "The Development and Validation of the Comprehensive Intellectual Humility Scale," *Journal of Personality Assessment* 98 (2015): 209–221; Megan Haggard, Wade C. Rowatt, Joseph C. Leman, Benjamin Meagher, Courtney Moore, Thomas Fergus, Dennis Whitcomb, Heather Battaly, Jason Baehr, and Dan Howard-Snyder, "Finding the Middle Ground Between Intellectual Arrogance and Intellectual Servility: Development and Assessment of the Limitations-Owning Intellectual Humility Scale," *Personality and Individual Differences* 124 (April 2018): 184–193; Todd Kashdan, "The Five-Dimensional Curiosity Scale: Capturing the Bandwidth of Curiosity and Identifying Four Unique

Subgroups of Curious People," *Journal of Research in Personality* 73 (2017): 130–149; and Keith Stanovich and Richard West, "Reasoning Independently of Prior Belief and Individual Differences in Actively Open-Minded Thinking," *Journal of Educational Psychology* 89 (1997): 342–357.

22. They could, however, be adapted for a younger audience. For additional self-reflection activities, at least some of which are suitable for younger students, see later in this chapter.

23. Several items from these scales have been used in the development of measures by research psychologists, and we've been told that the items have held up well under psychometric evaluation. See, for example, Rick H. Hoyle, Erin K. Davisson, Kate J. Diebels, and Mark Leary, "Holding Specific Views With Humility: Conceptualization and Measurement of Specific Intellectual Humility," *Personality and Individual Differences* 97 (June 2016): 165–172; and Haggard et al., "Finding Middle Ground."

24. For this exercise, I've adapted the scale items used in the IVA survey to better reflect the psychology of postsecondary students.

25. In contrast with the discussion of identity in chapter 3, identity understood in the present way need not be a function of a person's cultural, racial, or socioeconomic background. Nor should it be confused with the metaphysical notion of personal identity as discussed in philosophy.

26. In their six-year study of thirty American high schools, Jal Mehta and Sarah Fine found that the schools most successful at fostering deeper learning had a deliberate and significant impact on the identity of their students. Students at these schools "came to see their core selves as vitally connected to what they were learning and doing." See Jal Mehta and Sarah Fine, *In Search of Deeper Learning: The Quest to Remake the American High School* (Cambridge, MA: Harvard University Press, 2019), 6. On the connection between "science identity" and intellectual virtues, see Lapsley and Chaloner, "Post-Truth and Science Identity," 139–140.

27. For the books, I typically use either Philip Dow, *Virtuous Minds: Intellectual Character Development* (Downers Grove, IL: IVP Academic, 2013) or Nathan L. King, *The Excellent Mind: Intellectual Virtues for Everyday Life* (New York: Oxford University Press, 2021). As mentioned in an earlier note, Dow's book is written for a religious audience but has wide appeal. While King's book was only recently published, King has allowed me to use drafts of it in several recent classes.

28. Two additional points address potential worries or questions about an assignment like this. First, I make this project worth only a small portion of my students' overall grades (usually around 5 percent). In my experience, this minor weighting does not diminish their interest in the assignment or their willingness to take it seriously. Second, while there is a subjective aspect to the assignment, I've found that the criteria embedded in questions like the following generally result in a fairly wide distribution of scores: Did the student follow all the instructions, answering all the questions and meeting all the specified requirements? Has the paper been carefully proofread, and does it employ proper grammar, mechanics, diction, spelling, and so forth? More

importantly, are the student's reflections well developed? Do they demonstrate that the student read the chapters carefully and engaged in deep, thoughtful, and honest reflection? Are the student's examples and goals concrete and realistic?

Chapter 7

1. For some useful resources on this topic, see Martha Stone Wiske, ed., *Teaching for Understanding: Linking Research with Practice* (San Francisco: Jossey-Bass, 1998); Tina Blythe, with the researchers and teachers of the Teaching for Understanding Project, *The Teaching for Understanding Guide* (San Francisco: Jossey-Bass, 1998); Kenneth Leithwood, Pat McAdie, Nina Bascia, and Anne Rodrigue, eds., *Teaching for Deep Understanding: What Every Educator Should Know* (Thousand Oaks, CA: Corwin Press, 2006); and Grant Wiggins and Jay McTighe, *Understanding by Design*, 2nd ed. (Alexandria, VA: Association for Supervision and Curriculum Development, 2005).

2. P. H. Hirst and R. S. Peters, *The Logic of Education* (London: Routledge, 1970), 19.

3. I will alternate between the terms *understanding* and *deep understanding* throughout the chapter, but my main concern is deep understanding, not mere linguistic comprehension.

4. It is possible to conceive of understanding as something like an attribute of personal character, as when we say that someone is an "understanding person." See Stephen Grimm, "Understanding as an Intellectual Virtue," in *Routledge Handbook of Virtue Epistemology*, ed. Heather Battaly (New York: Routledge), 340–351.

5. This statement doesn't mean that intellectually virtuous people are unconcerned with intellectual virtues. Nor does it imply that an interest in intellectual virtues never informs these people's thinking or conduct; surely it does. However, being intellectually virtuous is not their primary focus or concern.

6. For a sampling of views, see Dennis Whitcomb, "Epistemic Value," in *The Continuum Companion to Epistemology*, ed. Andrew Cullison (London: Continuum, 2012), 270–287; Robert Roberts and Jay Wood, *Intellectual Virtues: An Essay in Regulative Epistemology* (Oxford: Oxford University Press), chap. 6; and Stephen Grimm, "What Is Interesting?" *Logos & Episteme* 2 (2011): 515–542.

7. For more on this point, see Jason Baehr, *The Inquiring Mind: On Intellectual Virtues and Virtue Epistemology* (Oxford: Oxford University Press, 2011), chap. 6.

8. Douglas Newton, "Helping Children to Understand," *Evaluation & Research in Education* 15, no. 3 (2001): 120.

9. Blythe, *Teaching for Understanding Guide*, 13.

10. See Ron Ritchhart, *Intellectual Character: What It Is, Why It Matters, and How to Get It* (San Francisco: Jossey-Bass, 2002), 75–79, 222–224.

11. Patrick Frierson, *Intellectual Agency and Virtue Epistemology: A Montessori Perspective* (London: Bloomsbury Academic, 2020), 30. For a related discussion of understanding as a cognitive achievement, see Duncan Pritchard, "Epistemic Virtue and the Epistemology of Education," in *Education and the Growth of Knowledge: Perspectives*

from Social and Virtue Epistemology, ed. Ben Kotzee (Malden, MA: Wiley Blackwell, 2014), 92–105.

12. For more on the centrality of depth to teaching for understanding, see these two chapters in Kenneth Leithwood, Pat McAdie, Nina Bascia, and Anne Rodrigue, eds., *Teaching for Deep Understanding: What Every Educator Should Know* (Thousand Oaks, CA: Corwin Press, 2006): Kenneth Leithwood, Pat McAdie, Nina Bascia, Anne Rodrigue, and Shawn Moore, "Deep Understanding for All Students"; and Carl Bereiter, "Reflections on Depth."

13. See Ron Ritchhart, Mark Church, and Karin Morrison, *Making Thinking Visible* (San Francisco: Jossey-Bass, 2011), chap. 1.

14. David Perkins, "What Is Understanding?," in *Teaching for Understanding: Linking Research with Practice*, ed. Martha Stone Wiske (San Francisco: Jossey-Bass, 1998), 41. See also David Perkins, "Teaching for Understanding," *American Educator* 17 (1993): 28–35, which equates understanding with an ability to perform the relevant activities. Although understanding involves these abilities, it cannot be reduced to such.

15. Of course, this approach requires some knowledge of historical facts, timelines, events, and the like. However, it also requires much more than this (e.g., rigorous and complex thinking about the relevant facts). See, for example, curricular resources from the Stanford History Education Group, available at https://sheg.stanford.edu.

16. Common Core State Standards Initiative, "Common Core State Standards for Mathematics," http://www.corestandards.org/assets/CCSSI_Math%20Standards.pdf.

17. Michigan State University, College of Natural Science, Connected Mathematics Project, "Philosophy," https://connectedmath.msu.edu/curriculum-design/philosophy/#overarchingGoal.

18. Ritchhart, Church, and Morrison, *Making Thinking Visible*, 171. We will explore thinking routines in detail in chapter 8.

19. Ritchhart, Church, and Morrison, 171.

20. For overviews of the literature on project-based learning (PBL), see Dimitra Kokotsaki, Victoria Menzies, and Andy Wiggins, "Project-Based Learning: A Review of the Literature," *Improving Schools* 19 (2016): 267–277; and Johannes Strobel and Angela van Barneveld, "When Is PBL More Effective? A Meta-Synthesis of Meta-Analyses Comparing PBL to Conventional Classrooms," *Interdisciplinary Journal of Problem-Based Learning* 3 (2009): 45–58.

21. Buck Institute for Education, PBL Works, "What Is PBL?," https://www.pblworks.org/what-is-pbl.

22. For some examples of PBL, see Foundry, "Project-Based Learning and Problem-Based Learning (PBL) Ideas, Examples and Activities," Keystone Insights, 2020, https://www.projectfoundry.com/pbl-project-ideas.

23. See, for example, John Larmer, John Mergendoller, and Suzie Boss, *Setting the Standard for Project Based Learning: A Proven Approach to Rigorous Classroom Instruction* (Alexandria, VA: Association for Supervision and Curriculum Development, 2015); Suzie Boss and John Larmer, *Project Based Teaching* (Alexandria, VA: Association

for Supervision and Curriculum Development, 2018); and John Mergendoller, Nan Maxwell, and Yolanda Bellisimo, "The Effectiveness of Problem-Based Instruction: A Comparative Study of Instructional Methods and Student Characteristics," *Interdisciplinary Journal of Problem-Based Learning* 1 (2006): 49–69.

24. Buck Institute for Education, PBL Works, "Gold Standard PBL: Essential Project Design Elements," https://www.pblworks.org/what-is-pbl/gold-standard-project-design.

25. See the discussions of authenticity in Boss and Larmer, *Project Based Teaching*, 3; and Larmer, Mergendoller, and Boss, *Setting the Standard*, 40–41.

26. Larmer, Mergendoller, and Boss, *Setting the Standard*, 37.

27. See Lih-Juan ChanLin, "Technology Integration Applied to Project-Based Learning in Science," *Innovations in Education and Teaching International* 45, no. 1 (2008), 63.

28. Larmer, Mergendoller, and Boss, *Setting the Standard*, 35.

29. These are some of the qualities that distinguish what PBL researchers call "main course projects" from what they refer to as "dessert projects." See Larmer, Mergendoller, and Boss, *Setting the Standard*, chap. 4.

30. For practitioner-oriented work on inquiry-based learning, see Jennifer Watt and Jill Colyer, *IQ: A Practical Guide to Inquiry-Based Learning* (New York: Oxford University Press, 2014); Teresa Coffman, *Inquiry-Based Learning: Designing Instruction* (Lanham, MD: Rowman & Littlefield, 2017); and Teresa Coffman, *Engaging Students Through Inquiry-Oriented Learning and Technology* (Lanham, MD: Rowman & Littlefield, 2009).

31. Coffman, *Inquiry-Based Learning*, 3.

32. On the connection between inquiry and teaching for understanding, see these two chapters in Martha Stone Wiske, ed., *Teaching for Understanding: Linking Research with Practice* (San Francisco: Jossey-Bass, 1998); Martha Stone Wiske, "What Is Teaching for Understanding?," 74–75; and Ron Ritchhart et al., "How Does Teaching for Understanding Look in Practice?," 130–134 and 143–145.

33. Coffman, *Engaging Students*, 19.

34. Coffman, 11.

35. According to Larmer, Mergendoller, and Boss, *Setting the Standard*, chap. 2, two of seven "essential project design elements" of "gold standard PBL" are "student voice and choice" and "sustained inquiry."

36. Coffman, *Engaging Students*, 14.

37. Larmer, Mergendoller, and Boss, *Setting the Standard*, 40.

Chapter 8

1. See Aristotle, *Nicomachean Ethics*, Book II, transl. Roger Crisp (Cambridge: Cambridge University Press, 2000). "Fair bit of luck" is an important qualification. For Aristotle, whether we become virtuous also depends on several factors outside our control, for example, on the parenting we receive, our access to good teachers and role models,

and our status in society. Accordingly, Aristotle's view isn't as simple or straightforward as it might initially seem.

2. Aristotle also discussed *intellectual* virtues, claiming that, unlike moral virtues, intellectual virtues aren't formed by the kind of imitation and practice just noted. See Aristotle, *Nicomachean Ethics*, Book VI. However, Aristotle wasn't thinking of intellectual virtues as we are in this book. He thought of intellectual virtues as truth-conductive cognitive powers or the knowledge such powers make possible, such as scientific knowledge (*episteme*), technical knowledge (*techne*), intuitive reason (*nous*), practical wisdom (*phronesis*), and theoretical wisdom (*sophia*). Accordingly, intellectual virtues as we're conceiving of them bear a closer resemblance to what Aristotle thought of as ethical or moral virtues.

3. Philip Dow, *Virtuous Minds: Intellectual Character Development* (Downers Grove, IL: IVP Academic, 2013), 22–23.

4. For a related perspective from cognitive science, see Tim Van Gelder, "Teaching Critical Thinking: Some Lessons from Cognitive Science," *College Teaching* 53 (2005): 41–48. On the characteristics of high-quality practice, see Angela Duckworth, *Grit: The Power of Passion and Perseverance* (New York: Scribner, 2016), chap. 7.

5. By "practicing intellectual virtues," I mean practicing the *skills* or *activities* characteristic of intellectual virtues. Therefore, a person can practice open-mindedness, say, without actually *being* open-minded, that is, without possessing a settled and intelligent habit or disposition to engage in open-minded activity.

6. For more on how attempts to habituate intellectual virtues can fail, see Steven Porter, "A Therapeutic Approach to Intellectual Virtue Formation in the Classroom," in *Intellectual Virtues and Education: Essays in Applied Virtue Epistemology*, ed. Jason Baehr (New York: Routledge, 2016), 221–239. For a recent interdisciplinary take on how virtues are developed, see Julia Anna, Darcia Narvaez, and Nancy Snow, eds., *Developing the Virtues: Integrating Perspectives* (Oxford: Oxford University Press, 2016).

7. The idea that practicing intellectual virtues can play an important role in their development enjoys considerable empirical support, particularly in connection with virtues like curiosity, open-mindedness, and intellectual humility. For instance, several studies have shown that providing students with well-supported opportunities to engage in good questioning is integral (along with other factors) to their development of curiosity. See, for instance, Robert Saxe and Gary Stallok, "Curiosity and the Parent-Child Relationship," *Child Development* 42 (1971): 373–384; and Barry Zimmerman and Earl Pike, "Effects of Modeling and Reinforcement on the Acquisition and Generalization of Question-Asking Behavior," *Child Development* 43 (1972): 892–907. See also Jamie Jirout, Virginia Vitiello, and Sharon Zumbrunn, "Curiosity in Schools," in *The New Science of Curiosity*, ed. Goren Gordon (Hauppauge, NY: Nova Science Publishers, 2018), 243–266; and Susan Engel, *The Hungry Mind* (Cambridge, MA: Harvard University Press, 2018). While most of this research is focused explicitly on curiosity, several authors adopt views of curiosity that encompass

major elements of open-mindedness and intellectual humility. Thus, their findings arguably bear on the development of these other virtues as well.

8. See Nathan L. King, *The Excellent Mind: Intellectual Virtues for Everyday Life* (New York: Oxford University Press, 2021); and Dow, *Virtuous Minds.*

9. This isn't to say that such students would have no use for intellectual humility. After all, no one is cognitively infallible, and each of us must be mindful of, and take appropriate responsibility for, our intellectual limitations and mistakes. See Dennis Whitcomb, Heather Battaly, Jason Baehr, and Daniel Howard-Snyder, "The Puzzle of Humility and Disparity," in *The Routledge Handbook of the Philosophy of Humility,* ed. Mark Alfano, Michael Lynch, and Alessandra Tanesini (New York: Routledge), 72–83. That said, if we are going to focus on a limited subset of virtues, we should give our attention to the virtues that are most relevant to our students and most likely to benefit them.

10. On the importance, within character education, of empowering students and securing student buy-in, see Marvin Berkowitz, Melinda Bier, and Brian McCauley, "Toward a Science of Character Education: Frameworks for Identifying and Implementing Effective Practices," *Journal of Character Education* 13 (2017): 40–45; Marvin Berkowitz, "What Works in Character Education," *International Journal of Educational Research* 50 (2011): 157; and Thomas Lickona and Matthew Davidson, *Smart & Good High Schools: Integrating Excellence and Ethics for Success in School, Work, and Beyond* (Cortland, NY: Center for the 4th and 5th Rs/Washington, DC: Character Education Partnership, 2005), chap. 4.

11. See Berkowitz, Bier, and McCauley, "Science of Character Education," 40–45. For a similar perspective on fostering critical thinking skills, see Deanna Kuhn, "A Developmental Model of Critical Thinking," *Educational Researcher* 28 (1999): 16–26.

12. For instance, you might consider reading Daniel Siegel and Tina Payne Bryson, *The Whole-Brain Child* (New York: Bantam Books, 2012); or Frances Jensen and Amy Ellis Nutt, *The Teenage Brain* (New York: HarperCollins, 2015).

13. As we have seen, teaching for understanding is one important part of teaching for intellectual virtues. My mistake was in tending to think of understanding as the exclusive educational aim. I was also mistaken in thinking that lecturing (even *interactive* lecturing) was the only or best way of fostering understanding. See Louis Deslauriers, Logan S. McCarty, Kelly Miller, Kristina Callaghan, and Greg Kestin, "Measuring Actual Learning versus Feeling of Learning in Response to Being Actively Engaged in Classroom," *Proceedings of the National Academy of Sciences of the United States of America* 116, no. 39 (2019): 19,251–19,257.

14. Ron Ritchhart, *Intellectual Character: What It Is, Why It Matters, and How to Get It* (San Francisco: Jossey-Bass, 2002), 88.

15. See especially Ron Ritchhart, Mark Church, and Karin Morrison, *Making Thinking Visible: How to Promote Engagement, Understanding, and Independence for All Learners* (San Francisco: Jossey-Bass, 2011); and Ron Ritchhart and Mark Church, *The Power of Making Thinking Visible* (San Francisco: Jossey-Bass, 2020). For a useful online

resource, see Project Zero, "Project Zero's Thinking Routine Toolbox," Harvard Graduate School of Education, 2016, https://pz.harvard.edu/thinking-routines.

16. Ritchhart, Church, and Morrison, *Making Thinking Visible*, 178.

17. For an in-depth discussion of this routine, see Ritchhart, Church, and Morrison, *Making Thinking Visible*, 171–184.

18. Ritchhart, Church, and Morrison, 179.

19. Ritchhart, Church, and Morrison, 180.

20. Ritchhart, Church, and Morrison, 165.

21. Ritchhart, Church, and Morrison, 55.

22. Ritchhart, Church, and Morrison, 55.

23. Thanks to Cari Noble for this point.

24. For more about this routine, see Ritchhart, Church, and Morrison, *Making Thinking Visible*, 207–213.

25. Ritchhart, Church, and Morrison, 268–269.

26. Ritchhart, *Intellectual Character*, chap. 5. See also Engel, *The Hungry Mind*, 191.

27. Ritchhart, *Intellectual Character*, chap. 5. See also Lisa Tsui, "Fostering Critical Thinking Through Effective Pedagogy," *Journal of Higher Education* 73 (2002): 740–763.

28. Practicing intellectual virtues can also contribute to deeper learning and to the development of other important intellectual skills and abilities. To illustrate, providing our students regular and well-supported opportunities to practice intellectual virtues is a prime example of "active learning," which has been shown to promote a wide range of academic outcomes, such as short-term and long-term recall, conceptual mastery, increased intrinsic motivation, exam scores, and grades. See, for example, Michael Prince, "Does Active Learning Work? A Review of the Research," *Journal of Education Engineering* 93 (2004): 223–231; Carl Benware and Edward Deci, "Quality of Learning with an Active Versus Passive Motivational Set," *American Educational Research Journal* 21 (1984): 755–765; and Scott Freeman, Eileen O'Connor, John W. Parks, Matthew Cunningham, David Hurley, David Haak, Clarissa Dirks, Mary Pat Wenderoth, and Martha Grossel, "Prescribed Active Learning Increases Performance in Introductory Biology," *CBE—Life Sciences Education* 6, no. 2 (2007): 132–139.

Chapter 9

1. As noted in chapter 2, each virtue also has a judgment dimension; however, that dimension is less germane to the present chapter.

2. Clark A. Chinn, Ronald W. Rinehart, and Luke A. Buckland, "Epistemic Cognition and Evaluating Information: Applying the AIR Model of Epistemic Cognition," in *Processing Inaccurate Information: Theoretical and Applied Perspectives from Cognitive Science and the Educational Sciences*, ed. David N. Rapp and Jason L. G. Braasch (Cambridge, MA: MIT Press, 2014), 446 (emphasis added).

3. For an illuminating critique of this idea, see Paulo Friere, *The Pedagogy of the Oppressed* (New York: Bloomsbury, 2012), chap. 2.

4. Parker Palmer, *The Courage to Teach: Exploring the Inner Landscape of a Teacher's Life* (San Francisco: Jossey-Bass, 1998), 5.

5. Peter-Hans Kolvenbach, "The Characteristics of Jesuit Education," December 8, 1986, https://www.seattleu.edu/media/university-core/files/CharacteristicsJesuitEducation .pdf.

6. See, for example, Robert Saxe and Gary Stallok, "Curiosity and the Parent-Child Relationship," *Child Development* 42 (1971): 373–384; Barry Zimmerman and Earl Pike, "Effects of Modeling and Reinforcement on the Acquisition and Generalization of Question-Asking Behavior," *Child Development* 43 (1972): 892–907; Susan Engel, "Children's Need to Know: Curiosity in Schools," *Harvard Educational Review* 81 (2011): 625–645; Jamie Jirout, Virginia Vitiello, and Sharon Zumbrunn, "Curiosity in Schools," in *The New Science of Curiosity*, ed. Goren Gordon (Hauppauge, NY: Nova Science Publishers, 2018), 243–266; and Yehudi Judy Dori and Orit Herscovitz, "Question Posing Capability as an Alternative Evaluation Method: Analysis of an Environmental Case Study," *Journal of Research in Science Teaching*, 36 (1999), 411–430. Most of this research focuses explicitly on curiosity. However, the researchers in question often combine elements of curiosity, open-mindedness, and intellectual humility. As a result, their findings may have implications for the cultivation of these other virtues as well.

7. Wendy Ostroff, *Cultivating Curiosity in K–12 Classrooms* (Alexandria, VA: Association for Supervision and Curriculum Development, 2016), 6.

8. Ron Ritchhart, *Intellectual Character: What It Is, Why It Matters, and How to Get It* (San Francisco: Jossey-Bass, 2002), 46.

9. John Dewey, *How We Think* (Boston: D.C. Heath & Co. Publishers, 1910), 47.

10. As discussed, virtues and vices are not binary qualities; rather, they are possessed to a greater or lesser *degree*. Nor is any person strictly virtuous or strictly vicious. Our respective characters are a combination of virtues and vices, each possessed to a greater or lesser degree. For more on this point, see chapter 2.

11. Dewey, *How We Think*, 47.

12. Cari Noble, email correspondence with author, September 6, 2020.

13. This friend explained the experience to me in an email message on July 18, 2018.

14. On the effectiveness of this practice, see Molly Ness, "Learning from K–5 Teachers Who Think Aloud," *Journal of Research in Childhood Education* 20 (2016): 282–292.

15. Michael Lynch, *The Internet of Us: Knowing More and Understanding Less in the Age of Big Data* (New York: Liveright Publishing), chap. 2.

16. Jean M. Twenge, Gabrielle N. Martin, and Brian H. Spitzberg, "Trends in U.S. Adolescents' Media Use, 1976–2016: The Rise of Digital Media, the Decline of TV, and the (Near) Demise of Print," *Psychology of Popular Media Culture*, 8, no. 4 (2019), https://www.apa.org/pubs/journals/releases/ppm-ppm0000203.pdf.

17. Nicholas Carr, *The Shallows: What the Internet Is Doing to Our Brains* (New York: W. W. Norton & Company, 2011), 8–9.

18. Rainer Maria Rilke, *Letters to a Young Poet* (Gearhart, OR: Merchant Books, 2012), 30–31.

19. Aristotle, *Metaphysics*, trans. C. D. C. Reeve (Indianapolis, IN: Hackett Publishing, 2016), 2.

20. Ritchhart, *Intellectual Character*, 162. See also Ron Ritchhart *Creating Cultures of Thinking* (San Francisco: Jossey-Bass, 2015), chap. 5.

21. For more on deliberately modeling intellectual virtues, see Shari Tishman, Eileen Jay, and David Perkins, *The Thinking Classroom: Learning and Teaching in a Culture of Thinking* (Boston: Allyn and Bacon, 1995), 56–59.

22. Thanks to Cari Noble for this suggestion.

23. Parker Palmer, *To Know as We Are Known: Education as a Spiritual Journey* (San Francisco: HarperCollins, 1993), xvii.

Chapter 10

1. Ron Ritchhart, *Intellectual Character: What It Is, Why It Matters, and How to Get It* (San Francisco: Jossey-Bass, 2002), 164–165.

2. As we will see later, we can also use measurement tools developed by trained researchers. However, even these tools have their limitations. For some of the challenges associated with measuring character, see Angela Duckworth and David Yeager, "Measurement Matters: Assessing Personal Qualities Other Than Cognitive Ability for Educational Purposes," *Education Researcher* 44 (2015): 237–251. For useful discussions of some of the pros, cons, and complexities involved with measuring character virtues, including intellectual virtues, see Randall Curren and Ben Kotzee, "Can Virtue Be Measured?," *Theory and Research in Education* 12 (2014): 266–282; Ben Kotzee, "Problems of Assessment in Educating for Intellectual Virtue," in *Intellectual Virtues and Education: New Essays in Applied Virtue Epistemology*, ed. Jason Baehr (New York: Routledge, 2016), 142–160; and Kristján Kristjánsson, *Aristotelian Character Education* (London: Routledge, 2015), chap. 3.

3. See chapter 2 for more on this point. See also Richard Ryan and Edward Deci, *Self-Determination Theory: Basic Psychological Needs in Motivation, Wellness, and Development* (New York: Guilford Press, 2018).

4. See David Dunning, Chip Heath, and Jerry Suls, "Flawed Self-Assessment: Implications for Health, Education, and the Workplace," *Psychological Science in the Public Interest* 5 (2004): 69–106.

5. For some partly overlapping ideas about assessing habits of mind, see Arthur L. Costa and Bena Kallick, *Learning and Leading with Habits of Mind: 16 Essential Characteristics for Success* (Alexandria, VA: Association for Supervision and Curriculum Development, 2008), chap. 11.

6. As this description suggests, these assessments also involve the kind of self-reflection described at length in chapter 6.

7. For assessments of intellectual humility available online, see Shane Snow, "Intellectual Humility Quiz: Take the Official Assessment," https://www.shanesnow.com/articles /intellectual-humility/#take-the-intellectual-humility-assessment; and E. J. Krumrei-Mancuso and S. V. Rouse, "The Development and Validation of the Comprehensive Intellectual Humility Scale," *Journal of Personality Assessment* 98 (2016): 209221. doi:1 0.1080/00223891.2015.1068174, https://seaver.pepperdine.edu/social-science/content /comprehensive-intellectual-humility.pdf. For a curiosity assessment, see Todd B. Kashdan, Melissa C. Stiksma, David J. Disabato, Patrick E. McKnight, John Bekier, Joel Kaji, and Rachel Lazarus, "The Five-Dimensional Curiosity Scale: Capturing the Bandwidth of Curiosity and Identifying Four Unique Subgroups of Curious People," *Journal of Research in Personality* 73 (2018): 130–149, https://www.researchgate.net /publication/321471978_The_Five-Dimensional_Curiosity_Scale_Capturing _the_bandwidth_of_curiosity_and_identifying_four_unique_subgroups_of_curious _people/link/5ae34644aca272fdaf904f6f/download. And for an assessment of active open-minded thinking, see Annika M. Svedholm-Häkkinen and Marjaana Lindeman, "Actively Open-Minded Thinking: Development of a Shortened Scale and Disentangling Attitudes Towards Knowledge and People," *Thinking and Reasoning* (2017), https://www.researchgate.net/publication/319989521_Actively_open-minded _thinking_development_of_a_shortened_scale_and_disentangling_attitudes _towards_knowledge_and_people/link/5bc8433f299bf17a1c5b4712/download. For an eight-item grit scale, see http://www.sjdm.org/dmidi/files/Grit-8-item.pdf. For additional assessments in scholarly journals, see Mark Leary, Kate J. Diebels, Erin K. Davisson, Katrina P. Jongman-Sereno, Jennifer C. Isherwood, Kaitlin T. Raimi, Samantha A. Deffler, and Rick H. Hoyle, "Cognitive and Interpersonal Features of Intellectual Humility," *Personality and Social Psychology Bulletin* 43, no. 6 (2017): 793–813; Megan Haggard, Wade C. Rowatt, Joseph C. Leman, Benjamin Meagher, Courtney Moore, Thomas Fergus, Dennis Whitcomb, Heather Battaly, Jason Baehr, and Dan Howard-Snyder, "Finding the Middle Ground Between Intellectual Arrogance and Intellectual Servility: Development and Assessment of the Limitations-Owning Intellectual Humility Scale," *Personality and Individual Differences* 124 (April 2018): 184–193; Jessica Taylor Piotrowski, Jordan Litman, and Patti Valkenburg, "Measuring Epistemic Curiosity in Young Children," *Infant and Child Development* 23 (2014): 542–553; and Keith Stanovich and Richard West, "Reasoning Independently of Prior Belief and Individual Differences in Actively Open-Minded Thinking," *Journal of Educational Psychology* 89 (1997): 342–357.

8. These reports do not include letter grades or any comparable assigned value.

9. The original version of this exercise was formulated by high school science teacher Appie van der Fluit during a two-year series of meetings with a cohort of teachers interested in teaching for intellectual virtues. These meetings were part of the

Intellectual Virtues and Education Project (https://intellectualvirtues.org/intellectual -virtues-and-education-project).

10. As explained in chapter 5, these readings are often drawn from Philip Dow, *Virtuous Minds: Intellectual Character Development* (Downers Grove, IL: IVP Academic, 2003); or Nathan L. King, *The Excellent Mind* (New York: Oxford University Press, 2021). Two additional readings available online are Carol Dweck, "Even Geniuses Work Hard," *Educational Leadership* 68, no. 1 (2010), http://www.ascd.org/publications/educational -leadership/sept10/vol68/num01/Even-Geniuses-Work-Hard.aspx; and David Brooks, "The Mental Virtues," *New York Times*, August 28, 2014, https://www.nytimes .com/2014/08/29/opinion/david-brooks-the-mental-virtues.html. For a series of short, readable blog posts on IVA's nine virtues, see various authors, "Posts on Master Virtues," Intellectual Virtues Academy, http://www.ivalongbeach.org/library/blog/posts -on-master-virtues.

11. This suggestion is inspired by a practice of IVA math teacher Cari Noble.

12. A further illustration of how teachers might share their character-based observations with their students comes from IVA English teacher Ian McCurry. Once every school year, Ian sends each of his students a postcard in which he highlights their practice of one or more virtues. Not only are these postcards encouraging to students, but they also highlight the fact McCurry is paying attention to and cares about their intellectual character development.

13. Assessments like these could be sent home with students or incorporated into an on-campus event, such as parent-teacher conferences or a back-to-school night.

14. These surveys can be similarly adapted for use by teachers as well.

15. You might also keep an eye on the websites or get on email lists of organizations such as the Character Lab (https://characterlab.org/research-network/); the Collaborative for Academic, Social, and Emotional Learning (https://casel.org/partner-district/); the Jubilee Centre for Character and Virtues (https://www.jubileecentre.ac.uk); and Character.org. These organizations occasionally publicize opportunities for collaborations between researchers and practitioners in the area of character education. Likewise for foundations such as the John Templeton Foundation (https://www.templeton.org /funding-areas/character-virtue-development); the Kern Family Foundation (https:// www.kffdn.org); and the Wallace Foundation (https://www.wallacefoundation.org /how-we-work/our-work/pages/social-emotional-learning.aspx).

Chapter 11

1. While it is best to begin with only a few virtues, as you get comfortable thinking about these virtues and incorporating a focus on them into your teaching, you can expand your list. The benefit of a larger list is that your target virtues will cover a wider range of intellectual activities and skills.

2. See, for example, the virtues discussed in chapter 2 or those explored in Nathan L.

King, *The Excellent Mind: Intellectual Virtues for Everyday Life* (New York: Oxford University Press, 2021); or Philip Dow, *Virtuous Minds: Intellectual Character Development* (Downers Grove, IL: IVP Academic, 2013). For more on what to think about when selecting your target virtues, see chapter 5.

3. Again, for extended characterizations of several intellectual virtues, see King, *Excellent Mind*, or Dow, *Virtuous Minds*. As mentioned in earlier notes, Dow's book has a religious dimension that makes it more appropriate for some audiences than others. For blog posts on each of the virtues discussed in chapter 2, see various authors, "Posts on Master Virtues," Intellectual Virtues Academy, http://www.ivalongbeach.org/library/blog/posts-on-master-virtues.

4. Each of these additional practices is discussed at some length in previous chapters. For an excellent and complementary account of how to "lay the foundation for enculturating" intellectual virtues in the first days of a school year or semester, see Ron Ritchhart, *Intellectual Character: What It Is, How It Works, and How to Get It* (San Francisco: Jossey-Bass, 2002), chap. 4.

5. Plato, *Republic*, Book VII (518b-d), in *Complete Works*, ed. John M. Cooper, trans. G. M. A. Grube, rev. C. D. C. Reeve (Indianapolis, IN: Hackett Publishing, 1997), 1136.

Acknowledgments

This book has emerged from of a unique combination of experiences and opportunities, each of which is tied to a particular person or group of people.

At its core, the book is an expression of my own love of teaching, which I owe in large part to Mr. Harry Hude. It was in his presence, and on account of his extraordinary example, that I first received the call to teach. I'm grateful for his influence, and I continue to carry him with me in my life as a teacher.

I believe that one of the greatest goods life can offer is an opportunity to create something meaningful and impactful with people one loves and respects. Such has been my experience as a cofounder and supporter of the Intellectual Virtues Academy of Long Beach, which opened its doors in 2013. I want to acknowledge just a few of the many people who have contributed to this experience. First, I thank Steve Porter for proposing the outrageous idea of starting a charter school together and for his wise and steady input at every point along the way. Steve's contributions to IVA are countless and ongoing. His thoughtful and psychologically oriented perspective on intellectual character formation has had a deep and lasting impact on my own understanding of the topic.

When IVA was little more than an idea cooked up by two philosophers, the interest and enthusiasm of Jesse and Rebecca Irwin buoyed our efforts. At critical junctures, Danielle Montiel and Eric Churchill stepped up to keep the process alive and moving forward. It is difficult to overstate the magnitude and quality of their contributions. Together they created a solid and lasting organizational infrastructure that continues to reflect IVA's unique educational vision. Although she passed away in 2018 and is sorely missed by everyone who knew her, Danielle's influence at IVA remains tangible and life-giving. IVA founding principal, Jacquie Bryant, and founding teachers, Cari Noble and Ian McCurry, also poured themselves into the development of the school and have done as much as anyone to establish and sustain its vibrant culture. Jacquie's visionary leadership and Ian and Cari's pedagogical thoughtfulness are the inspiration for many of the ideas in this book. I am grateful for who they are and for their outstanding work as educators.

IVA would not have seen the light of day but for the generous support of the John Templeton Foundation, which began with a major grant in 2012 and continues to this day. Craig Joseph and Michael Murray shepherded our initial grant proposal. Subsequent and ongoing support from Richard Bollinger and Sarah Clement has been abundant and invaluable. I am also grateful to the previous and current presidents of the foundation, the late Jack Templeton and Heather Templeton Dill, for their support. The foundation also provided me with generous funding to complete this book. For this as well I am very grateful.

When setting out, over a decade ago, to begin applying virtue epistemology to educational theory and practice, I quickly realized that I was in over my head. Two wise and generous education experts helped me get my bearings. One of them was Marvin Berkowitz, the Sanford N. McDonnell Endowed Professor of Character Education at the University of Missouri–St. Louis. Shortly after IVA received its first major grant, Marvin was kind enough to have a long phone conversation with me, during which he delivered a primer on character education, pointed me to a host of useful resources, and gently corrected some of my mistaken assumptions. His work in character education has been a formative influence on my own work in this area. And he has continued to be generous with his time and expertise.

The work of Ron Ritchhart, senior research associate at Harvard's Project Zero, also has had a profound influence on my understanding of how to educate for intellectual virtues. Again, at a time when I had only a rough idea of what it might look like to apply virtue epistemology in an educational setting, Ron's book *Intellectual Character: What It Is, Why It Matters, and How to Get It* (2002) was a godsend. It reassured me that many of the questions I was grappling with had already been addressed competently and at some length. Ron's work on thinking dispositions, thinking routines, cultures of thinking, and related topics has had a pervasive influence on the educational program at IVA. In addition to his written work, Ron has provided ongoing personal support to the school, leading several professional development seminars over the past several years. Talking with Ron and seeing him interact with other educators is inspiring and has enriched my understanding of the practices described in these pages.

Some of the earliest seeds for the book were planted during conversations with Phil Dow some twenty years ago. At that time, I was completing a dissertation in theoretical virtue epistemology. When Phil learned of what I was writing about, he immediately saw its relevance to classroom teaching and learning, and single-handedly began implementing a focus on intellectual character development into his own work as an educator. In the many years since, I have continued to learn from Phil and his colleagues at the Rosslyn Academy in Nairobi, Kenya, about the substance and value of teaching for intellectual virtues.

Through their words and actions, several other people have helped me better understand the subject matter of this book. This includes James McGrath, Summer Sanders, and Dustin Schmidt, of the IVA high school. The work they're doing is critical and inspiring. They have taught me, among other things, how one's approach to teaching for intellectual virtues must be guided by the unique identity or identities of one's students. I have also benefited considerably from conversations and other interactions with Heather Battaly, Kendall Cotton Bronk, William Hare, Nathan King, Katherine Lo, Sarah Marsh, Tenelle Porter, Nancy Snow, Dan Speak, Agustin Vierya, and Lani Watson.

My home institution, Loyola Marymount University, has also been a source of support as I've worked on the book. This support includes funding provided by the Robert H. Taylor, S. J. Chair in Philosophy for a project titled "Virtue Epistemology and Ignatian Pedagogy and Spirituality," which I directed from 2016 to 2018. I'm also grateful for ongoing assistance and encouragement from Dean Robbin Crabtree and Associate Dean Jon Rothchild.

Research assistance was provided by Stephanie Coyne and Katie Peters. I'm especially grateful to Katie for tracking down and organizing pertinent research from a diverse cross-section of subfields in education, psychology, and related disciplines.

Jacquie Bryant, Cari Noble, and Ian McCurry provided feedback on several draft chapters. This feedback was characteristically generous and penetrating. The book is better off for it.

I also thank Caroline Chauncey of the Harvard Education Publishing Group for reaching out to me many years ago about the possibility of writing a book like this and to my editor, Nancy Walser, for her ongoing conversation, support, and encouragement of the project.

Finally, I am most grateful to my family, Erinn, Brendan, Lily, and Oliver, for filling my days with substance, honesty, humor, and joy.

About the Author

Jason Baehr is Professor of Philosophy at Loyola Marymount University in Los Angeles (LMU), where he has been teaching since 2003. From 2012 to 2015, he directed the Intellectual Virtues and Education Project at LMU, which was sponsored by a grant of more than $1 million from the John Templeton Foundation. This project involved, among other activities, the founding of the Intellectual Virtues Academy of Long Beach, a charter middle school in Long Beach, California, designed to help students make progress in intellectual virtues like curiosity, open-mindedness, and intellectual courage in the context of academic teaching and learning. Baehr continues to work at the intersection of philosophy and education, writing about intellectual virtues, speaking at conferences, and doing professional development work with secondary and postsecondary educators. His other books include *The Inquiring Mind: On Intellectual Virtues and Virtue Epistemology* (2012) and *Intellectual Virtues and Education: Essays in Applied Virtue Epistemology* (editor) (2016). He lives with his family in Long Beach.

Index

A

academic ideals. *see also* relational versus transactional principle
    definition of, 13–14
    relationship to intellectual virtues, 22–23
active versus passive principle, 56–57
ADHD (attention deficit hyperactivity disorder), 31, 41, 142
Adler, Mortimer, 14
Agree-Disagree-Question routine, 152
Aristotle
    on acquiring skills, 56, 137
    doctrine of the mean, 33, 187
    on highest good, 29, 92
    on humans' desire to know, 35, 166
assessment
    feedback regarding, 103–104, 174, 181–182
    limitations of, 173–174, 183
    motivation affected by, 173
    multiple sources for, 175
    parent or peer assessments, 182–183
    reasons for, 171–173
    self-assessment, 116–118, 176–179, 197–200
    target virtues, focusing on, 174–175
    teacher assessments, 179–182
atomistic orientation. *see* holistic versus atomistic principle
attention deficit hyperactivity disorder (ADHD), 31, 41, 142
attentiveness virtue
    ADHD and, 31, 41, 142
    definition of, 39–41, 195
    practices supporting, 147, 151

    self-assessment for, 198–199
autonomy virtue
    control posture prohibiting, 75
    definition of, 36–38, 195
    focusing on, 62, 141
    humility virtue and, 39, 162
    practices supporting, 148, 151, 152
    reflection regarding, 109–110, 143
    self-assessment for, 198
    supporting deep understanding, 134
    thoroughness virtue and, 43

B

Baldwin, James, 155
Ban Ki-moon, 16
behavior, responsible. *see* political and social ideals
Blythe, Tina, 124
Bock, Laszlo, 25–26
bottom-up versus top-down principle, 61–63
Boyle, Gregory, 86
breadth orientation. *see* depth versus breadth principle
Buckland, Luke, 156

C

career preparation. *see* professional and economic ideals
carefulness virtue
    definition of, 41–43, 195
    practices supporting, 148, 151
    self-assessment for, 199
    with thoroughness, 43–44, 144, 180

ideals, educational *(Cont.)*
    economic and professional, 16–17,
        25–26
    social and political, 14–16, 23–25
    definition of, 1, 3, 11–12
    implementing, challenges of, 12–13
    intellectual virtues as, 17–26
    Plato's cave allegory regarding, 26–27
    as vehicle for hope, 12
imagination
    active engagement supporting, 56
    control as detrimental to, 77–78
    Step Inside routine supporting, 147
imperfection. *see also* perfectionism
    carefulness virtue and, 42
    presence and, 86
    in teachers, 160
impression management, 75–76
The Inquiring Mind (Baehr), 5
inquiry-based learning, 134–135
intellectual character, 18–21, 23–24,
        30–32, 138
intellectual conformity, 37
intellectual conscience, 42
intellectual skills, attaining. *see* academic
        ideals
intellectual vices, 31
intellectual virtues
    assessment of. *see* assessment
    compared to moral virtues, 31–32
    compared to postures, 72–73
    content areas requiring, 186
    definition of, 3, 31–32
    dimensions of
        assessment based on, 174–175
        judgment, 33–34, 110–111
        motivation, 32–35, 155–156, 158–
            159, 173
        skills, 32
    as educational ideal, 17–22
    educational significance of, 19–21
    excesses and deficiencies of, 33, 39, 42,
        43, 187
    expectations for achieving, 31, 100,
        160–161

expectations for teaching, 12, 21–22,
    106, 153
framework for teaching
    deep understanding as goal of. *see*
        deep understanding
    initial steps for, 186–194
    language for. *see* language of
        intellectual virtues
    modeling for. *see* modeling
    overview of, 3–4, 8
    postures for. *see* postures
    practices for. *see* practicing
        intellectual virtues
    principles for. *see* principles
    self-reflection, encouraging. *see*
        self-reflection
    introducing students to, 94–99, 118,
        188
    list of, 34–50, 195–196. *see also specific
        virtues*
    manifestations of, 141–143,
        187–188
    relationship to other ideals, 22–26
    skepticism regarding, 12, 55, 65
    sources and research regarding,
        4–6
    target virtues, focusing on, 140–141,
        174–175, 186–188
Intellectual Virtues Academy (IVA),
        5–6, 34, 153
Intellectual Virtues and Education
        (Baehr), 5
interpersonal dimension of teaching
    definition of, 18
    ethos of trust and acceptance with,
        169–170
    modeling supporting, 156–158
    postures supporting, 79–80, 82–83,
        87
    principles supporting, 53–54, 59–61
    spontaneous encouragement with,
        115–116
intrinsic motivation, 34–35, 173
IVA (Intellectual Virtues Academy), 5–6,
        34, 153